SHAMANIC GRAFFITI

100,000 YEARS OF DRUGS,
100 YEARS OF PROHIBITION

Marcus Rummery & Frank Ogden

Published by:
Trine Day LLC
PO Box 577
Walterville, OR 97489
1-800-556-2012
www.TrineDay.com
publisher@TrineDay.net

Library of Congress Control Number: 2016955906

Rummery, Marcus.
—1st ed.
p. cm.

Epud (ISBN-13) 978-1-63424-100-7
Mobi (ISBN-13) 978-1-63424-101-4
Print (ISBN-13) 978-1-63424-099-4
1. Hallucinogenic drugs. 2. Lysergic Acid Diethylamide -- history. 3. Lysergic
Acid Diethylamide -- therapeutic use. 4. LSD (Drug) -- Social aspects -- Cana-
da -- History. I. Rummery, Marcus. II. Title

First Edition
10 9 8 7 6 5 4 3 2 1

Printed in the USA
Distribution to the Trade by:
Independent Publishers Group (IPG)
814 North Franklin Street
Chicago, Illinois 60610
312.337.0747
www.ipgbook.com

For the late Captain (RCAF) Frank Ogden aka Dr. Tomorrow mentor,
and Dianne Rummery – editor and mom

Knowledge Reigns Supreme"
> – KRS-One

"It's not what we don't know; it's what we do know that ain't so."
> – Mark Twain

"If we take in our hand any volume of divinity or school metaphysics, for instance, let us ask, does it contain any abstract reasoning concerning quantity and number? No. Does it contain any experimental reasoning concerning matter of fact and existence? No. Commit it then to the flames: for it can contain nothing but sophistry and illusion."
> – David Hume

"If you find yourself going through hell, keep going."
> – Winston Churchill

Acknowledgements

The first person that turned me on to multiple realities was Peter Kramer with his masterpiece *Listening To Prozac.* The gatekeeper to altered consciousness for me was Lee Bain and Mike Leonard stood at my side during the most transformational moment in my life. John Robert Columbo, Tanya Kaps, Christina Walkinshaw, Katie Cooke, Ben Miner, Rhoddy Lising, Leigh Austin, Andrew Buttle, Shannon Watts (now Buttle), Steve Bentley, Deborah Power, Tony Bailey, OJ, Ben, Sonny Dean, Douglas Hanna, Kevin Timms, Kim Aureli, Yonta Taiwo, Chris Leduc, Collen Lornie, Olive Leung and Jeff Scharf were all instrumental in creating a tribal culture where ideas could flourish. Dave Tarc and George Baker Jr. are fellow neuronauts of the first class – without whom this book wouldn't exist. Lillian Tseng, Herminder Ghossal and Bikram Choudhury have all contributed vitally to my Yoga and my livelihood. The late Frank Ogden and his late Wife Carol's kindness and inspiration were indispensible.

Preface

In the Greek myth of Prometheus, the rebellious half--man/half--God stole fire from the heavens and gave it to humanity. He was tortured for eternity for his offense and much of humankind, though blessed with the boon of fire, cursed the new and many dangers it brought and longed for the innocence of the past.

This is a book about change. Dr. Tomorrow (Frank Ogden) had one quote posted at his computer desk which read "Charles Darwin didn't say only the strongest or the smartest shall survive but only those adaptive to change." One way of changing is by taking psychedelic drugs, in fact in the late sixties many scientists were convinced LSD was capable of changing people at a geneticlevel and damaging their chromosomes, referring to them as "radiomimetic" or mimicking the effects of radiation – in other words users had not only changed themselves they had changed the next generations. They also referred to these agents as psychotomimetic, meaning mimicking psychosis or madness. One thing is for certain, whether you love, hate or are indifferent to them, taking radioactive crazy-pills will obviously change you.

Although this book does attempt to build some brand new bridges I am mostly striving to reveal the ones already there. One bridge hinted at by the hysterical sixties scientists with their theory of "radiomimetic" drugs is the link between atomic and psychedelic science, *the controlled reaction of the atom versus the controlled reaction of the mind.* After all the first and most efficient of LSD apostles was Uranium and shipping tycoon Al Hubbard, who built a radioactive battery in 1919. LSD guru Dr. Timothy Leary used to compare psychedelics with "fissionable material" and argued comparable care and control should be exercised with both. LSD inventor Dr. Albert Hofmann discovered the psychoactive properties of the compound at the same time the United States began testing its new atomic bomb.

Another thing the "radioactive crazy pills" can change is the social games we play and the rules, roles, rituals, goals, values and language we play them with. Early shamanism scholar Mircea Eliade described a higher caste of priest in religious societies called *hierophants* from the Greek for hiero – sacred and phaney – bring to light. Only they communicated directly with the highest Gods and determined what would be considered sacred and how Divinity would be worshipped. Putting your brain under a psychedelic microscope or entheogenic telescope sends you directly into the mystery of the Unconscious – each of us his or her own hierophant.

I believe that in ten to twenty years all around the world in Universities, hospitals and specialized clinics, neuronauts will take a range of psychedelic medicines about one to ten times over about six months with a male and female therapist. Over the next 200+ pages I will make my case and hopefully build a bridge from my vision of the future to the reader.

Introduction

"A couple breaths of winter air and every cell in my body seemed to let go, leaving a feeling of total visceral relaxation and a kind of perfectly grounded selfdom."

From 1957 to 1975 in New Westminster British Columbia near Vancouver Canada Hollywood Sanitarium offered LSD, mescaline psychotherapy for five hundred dollars. About a thousand customers signed up and for a period spanning from Elvis to the Sex Pistols the "single overwhelming dose" model was put to work.

From 1961-1968 the therapist or sitter was Frank Ogden.

I met Frank in May of 2007 when I was taking a documentary film-making course and needed a subject for my final project. Too nervous to call him myself and after procrastinating a dangerously long time I had a friend call him. "When are you coming over?"

Frank was ready – over the next three months we made *Big Medicine*, a film about his career as a psychedelic therapist and his work in Haiti where he was initiated into voodoo – two of many swashbuckling adventures. I graduated from my film course and tried to get *Big Medicine* into film-festivals while I worked on getting funding for another documentary. This lasted about a year.

Then I got a second round of bed-bugs – apparently my apartment building had been infested for years – my hard-drive crashed taking everything with it and the economy tanked, heading into the Great Recession. I was sitting at Frank's electronic cottage/houseboat in Coal Harbour Vancouver, lamenting my predicament. Frank had talked briefly about his notes from his eight years as a psychedelic therapist.

"Why don't we write a book based on your work at Hollywood Hospital?" "Okay – just get out of here. I get itchy every time I look at you."

The fear of contaminating the boat and becoming a social pariah couldn't overcome my euphoria at having finally figured out a way to look at those notes and see for myself what happened at the world's longest enduring psychedelic clinic. Having a psychology degree already I enrolled in an on-line abnormal psychology class to understand better the contemporary meaning of psychedelic drugs. But I am no rookie when it comes to brain chemistry – after seventeen years of "gonzo psychopharmacology" beginning with *Listening to Prozac*.

The most important event of my life occurred fifteen years ago to the day on February 19, 1995 when I personally experienced a transformational death-rebirth experience after taking psilocybin mushrooms. A year earlier, I had smoked a joint and had a full-blown panic attack; I fell into a deep depression, lost thirty pounds, quit University, and became covered in psoriasis. A few weeks before that infamous day in February, my Mushroom Armageddon, I had begun taking desipramine, one of the first modern anti- depressants marketed after imipramine emerged in the early 1960s.

Just after ingesting the psychoactive fungi I happened upon an *Omni* magazine with an article by LSD discoverer Albert Hofmann. In it he laments his problem child's descent into the unsupervised and unscientific underground, but the last paragraph puzzled me; it said LSD showed promise in the treatment of alcoholism and depression. Hallucinations and uncontrollable laughter as psychotherapy?

This question was interrupted by the specter of an old high-school friend comforting his terrified girlfriend. "I'm going to take her home," he said sheepishly, "it's her first time." My attention was diverted by a strong taste of pepper, apparently due to a conversation happening beside me. This gustatory hallucination continued as we headed in a cab to a party called "Who's Your Daddy." Anxiety was mounting, tracing it to thoughts was impossible. I thought I saw an old woman at a bus stop draw her finger across her throat.

When we arrived at the party I was in full-blown panic/insane/suicide mode. My skin was white and the cupboards were a melting nauseous green. I begged my friend for the keys to his apartment where I had some valium, wondering if I could resist the temptation to hurl myself off a bridge on the way. He pleaded with me to stay and suggested we leave the party and get a breath of fresh air. We went outside, I sat on an electrical box and the next one or two minutes of clock time would confound every assumption my mind possessed.

A couple breaths of winter air and every cell in my body seemed to let go, leaving a feeling of total visceral relaxation and a kind of perfectly grounded selfdom.

Psychologists use the term depersonalization to describe feeling alienated from one's self; this was an experience of repersonalization.

Everyone agrees that a drug can make someone feel really good or really bad – but going from bad to worse to utter transformation was an astonishing surprise. The following six months I was a changed man – spiritual (thinking and feeling beyond my "skin-encapsulated ego"), pragmatic and happy.

The second most important event was being sexually abused as a child. Trauma primed me for an explosive reaction to psychedelics that reverberates to this day. Depression and alcoholism are over-represented on my family tree and when a sensitive nervous system meets a vicious and uncompromising world an angry ruthless suffering is the result. Not that my life has been a miserable one, for as I would ultimately learn, it was in the misery itself where the mystery of transformation lay.

Needless to say the "afterglow" waned in about six months but I had learned that the worse I felt the closer I was to getting better. Being an optimistic greenhorn of 21 I figured it was only a matter of time before psychedelic therapy would be widely available. I had failed to appreciate the controversy that surrounds this enterprise. Whether communist or capitalist, Christian or Muslim no power structure embraces psychedelics – possibly because their use seems to dissolve structure.

The first scientist to resume American psychedelic research after the moral panic finally receded in the 1990s was psychiatrist Dr. Rick Strassman. In addition to his scientific work Strassman spent over two decades training in Zen Buddhism. Over the years he had spoken with many Zen monks and "most of them had gained their first view of the spiritual path while on psychedelic drugs." Furthermore throughout his research he discussed his work with a "chief assistant to the abbot" at the monastery in New Mexico where he practiced his religion.

Buddhism is extremely sophisticated in the categorization of states of consciousness and Dr. Strassman used his training to create questionnaires and guide his approach to "sitting" for subjects who were receiving massive doses of DMT, considered the most potent hallucinogen. This symbiotic relationship between psychedelic science and Buddhism would be disrupted however when the abbot died and the monks began competing for the title of most orthodox in the power vacuum left behind. This was followed by the publication in the Buddhist magazine *Tricycle* of an article Rick had written advocating the synthesis of psychedelics with the 2500 year old religion.

Not only was his affiliation with the order terminated this would prove the last straw for his psychedelic research. "I resigned from the University and returned the drugs and the last years worth of grant money to the National Institute on Drug Abuse." If a professor of psychiatry at a prestigious medical school can't escape the controversy surrounding psychedelic drugs what chance does that give the rest of us?

I regularly see a therapist and needless to say my opinions on psychedelics are intimately woven into my own experience of trauma. She is an excellent, experienced therapist trained in a variety of techniques and currently studying Self-Regulation Therapy (SRT), a system designed by California Psychologist Dr. Peter Levine for the treatment of trauma. She asked her mentor in British Columbia about the combination of psychedelics with SRT and he was categorical in his opposition.

Sometimes people can agree to disagree and I have become accustomed to the condemnation of the helping professions, but what it is about psychedelics that provoke such hysteria? In addition to defensiveness about their own traumas, birth and otherwise, one possibility is what the late philosopher Alan Watts called "the taboo against knowing who you are." In my opinion psychedelics extinguish the illusion that as Watts described we "are a separate ego walking around in a bag of skin" and this fundamental realization is a one-way ticket.

Bringing it all back to earth, there is the more obvious taboo against "knowing what actually happened." Some childhood traumas are criminal but all are a disgrace to the family and denial, repression and projection can usually defend against the truth – that is until the big medicine comes out.

Leary believed most of the world's problems could be boiled down to "armed men abusing women and children." This happens on a micro family level and macro societal level with the ultimate cultural trauma of genocide and just like the mystification that occurs on a small-scale genocide denial is considered an inevitable phase after such an atrocity occurs.

George Orwell: "A known fact may be so unbearable that it is habitually pushed aside and not allowed to enter into logical processes, or on the other hand it may be entered into every calculation and yet never admitted as fact, even in one's own mind."

Assuming the memories elicited on psychedelics, whether recovered or just intensified are truthful to the experiencer, this type of therapy delivers the best means of processing trauma and the condemnation of the competing helping professionals is just bigoted jealousy.

Opinions aside, the recent publication in the *Journal of Psychopharmacology* of a study evaluating the psychedelic amphetamine MDMA in the treatment of Post Traumatic Stress Disorder (PTSD) may prove the fatal blow to the prohibition of psychedelic psychotherapy (at least officially-underground therapists like Leo Zeff never stopped). Using the most rigorous of scientific methodology (randomized controlled trials, double-blind, active placebo, independent raters) and published by a peer-reviewed journal, this could signify a new dawn for the hundreds of millions of people who survive trauma. Before 18 about 15% of us survive sexual abuse, and 25% of us survive physical abuse or vital neglect (averaging data). In a little over half the results are devastating.

One of the truly puzzling aspects of human behaviour is the compulsion on the part of survivors of trauma to get themselves into similar situations again and again. Everyone knows someone with an alcoholic parent married to an alcoholic. Originally Sigmund Freud proposed this "traumatic reenactment" represented an attempt at mastery; seeking a different non-traumatic outcome. But the outcome was almost always the same or worse and this need for many of his patients to be re-victimized combined with the mindless carnage of World War I may have prompted Freud in 1920 to propose "Thanatos" or the death instinct. This proposed dynamic opposite to "Eros" or the life instinct drew a parallel to biology where anabolic (growing) and catabolic (shrinking) processes regulate cellular behaviour.

Another explanation for this epic of self-destruction is the opponent process theory, which states that trauma is re-enforcing because extreme negative affect will be followed by the opposite – euphoria – as though unconsciously traumatic stress survivors are trauma junkies engineering life for the next fix of disaster.

But the theoreticians behind "attempts at mastery," "the death instinct" or "opponent-process" did not have LSD and their own nervous system as well as thousands of subjects to draw data from like Czech psychiatrist Stanislav Grof. The transpersonal psychology pioneer-engineer proposes unconscious dynamics can operate as "governing systems" influencing us to manifest our outer world to resonate with the inner world.

When Grof would administer LSD repeatedly to the same subject their sessions tended to begin with traumatic events from the past, often abuse or surgery, and proceed to experiences of such elemental intensity that he grouped them according to the distinct clinical phases of birth. Most importantly, working through these death-rebirth sequences yielded therapeutic breakthroughs even more dramatic than "abreacting" or reliving traumas from post-natal life. This is what I believe I experienced in Ottawa in February of 1995.

Traumatic reenactment can then be understood as acting out elements of the birth trauma. Grof divides birth into four "Basic Perinatal Matrices" or BPMs. In the first the fetus is in symbiotic union with the Mother and although negative elements are reported in this BPM, it is often characterized as "oceanic ecstasy." Next in the second BPM the womb collapses and the helpless fetus is trapped in a hopeless "no exit" nightmare, activating this governing system is the opposite of fun. In the third BPM the cervix opens and the fetus engages in an active survival struggle of biological frenzy down the birth canal. Finally in the fourth BPM the child is born.

Unresolved unconscious dynamics must either be worked through or fiercely repressed, often leaving a joyless dissociated zombie. As filmmaker Paul Thomas Anderson observed in his film *Magnolia*, "you may be through with the past, but the past isn't necessarily through with you."

Put another way, you can burn your karma or you can live it. With psychedelics we have a way to burn it. Grof tells the story of a man working through the third perinatal matrix, who got a job testing parachutes! Each time he jumped out of the plane he would experience the sheer terror he unconsciously craved. Once he had worked through the perinatal material he quit his parachute job immediately.

When the unconscious sees an opportunity to work through a conflict – it seizes it – because, to use Freud's term, the opportunity is "over-determined." For example someone with repressed deep rage turns the trivial traffic accident into Armageddon. This may be due to an energy blockage in BPM III caused by unmetabolized trauma and given the violent nature of BPM III civilization relies on the control of such volcanic emotions, whereas the helpless depression of the trapped fetus is far less threatening.

From conception to about three years old the electric cables or axons that carry electricity through the brain are slowly coated in a fat called myelin, therefore mainstream science has rejected birth memory as even a possibility – never mind being instrumental in the "architecture of emotional disorders" as Grof advocates. But whether the birth experiences are historically accurate or not is secondary to the unparalleled therapeutic breakthroughs they provide.

When the subjects at Hollywood Hospital took their psychedelic medicine what emerged was not how they projected themselves to the world or even how they projected themselves to themselves. Unless the process was undermined by the defenses of a fevered ego, what emerged was the real psyche. Psychedelic drugs are to the mind what the telescope is to astronomy and the microscope is to biology. Studying consciousness without psychedelics is like studying electricity by standing on a hilltop and waiting for lightning.

If psychedelic experiences ended with achieving a "death-rebirth" transformation, science and medicine could have accommodated them. But it gets much, much weirder than that. The sequences tended towards biographical (surgeries, accidents, abuse) traumas first, perinatal traumas second and then the elemental affective charge of the psychodrama diminishes and here lies Grof's third level of the unconscious – the transpersonal – archetypes, past-lives, "becoming animals or plants," telepathy, the "clear-white light" of the meta-cosmic void, experiences difficult to integrate into consensus reality.

Right at the time of psychedelic therapy's brief heyday in the early sixties, a pharmacological revolution of another kind was taking the less mystical factions of psychiatry by storm. Anti-psychotic drugs like chlorpromazine (thorazine), anti- depressant drugs like imipramine (tofranil) and anti-anxiety drugs like chloradiapoxide (Librium) were introduced. Although similar drugs already existed these new drugs were clearly safer and more effective and most importantly they didn't require a quantum paradigm shift to integrate transformations or "religio-mystical" challenges.

After seventeen years in the field Grof left psychedelic research and therapy in 1973 and created a system of altered breathing, evocative music, bodywork and art therapy designed to facilitate similar non-ordinary states of consciousness without drugs, called Holotropic Breathwork. Holo meaning wholeness and tropic meaning growing towards, whereas the more neutral term psychedelic simply means "mind-manifesting"; holotropic experiences are considered positive. Drug guru Timothy Leary used to call psychedelics "brain-change" drugs.

In other words the changes in brain activity remain indefinitely, non-holotropic drugs could instead be considered hydraulic, moving brain chemistry mechanically in a linear direction followed by return to baseline or if enough of the wrong hydraulic drug is taken, a severe depression of whatever system(s) the compound affects may follow. The above-mentioned psychiatric medicines that emerged alongside LSD are hydraulic. Holotropic drugs are taken a few times, hydraulic drugs may be taken daily for a lifetime and are consequently far more lucrative.

Humanity always favours the latest technology as a metaphor for the brain/mind and the most far-out technological metaphor now is the hologram – a three dimensional image that can be derived from any part of a recording because the information stored is not the image itself but the interference pattern between two recordings of the image. Psychedelic stand-up philosopher Terrence McKenna even suggested the super-hallucinogen DMT bonded to DNA, causing the two strands to vibrate, creating signal interference that illuminated the whole – the ultimate holotropic experience.

Beyond the DNA lay the nucleus of each atom, perhaps another holographic system. Drug guru Timothy Leary believed the experience of the "clear white light" where the moment of ego death manifested in the final ecstasy was the "ghost in the shell" (ego) communicating with the intelligence in the nucleus.

In Dr. Leary's worldview consciousness occurs when energy is received by an organized structure and when processed and transmitted as information intelligence is also present. Leary proposed eight structures or circuits starting with the unicellular amoeba's single brain. From there the mammalian second brain emerged followed by the symbolic-tool simian third brain, then the tribal civilized fourth brain. At Hiroshima Leary demarcates the crescendo of these first four "earth" levels and at this auspicious midpoint of human evolution he celebrated the emergence of the second four circuits. In the brain's "better half" consciousness can tune into the body itself (5), then the brain (6), the DNA (7) and finally the nucleus of the atom (8). The manipulation of chemistry, gasses and electricity allow us to pilot these worlds.

All of this is a long way from a converted old house in a Canadian suburb, but the story of psychedelic drugs isn't limited to Hollywood Hospital. Indeed, from 1947 to 1966 all over the world there were 40,000 subjects treated, 2,000 papers published and 100 medical textbooks written on this kind of therapy. What's different about Hollywood Hospital was its unique blend of science, medicine and business – they published papers in journals and textbooks, treated about a thousand clients and made lots of money.

Frank's notes describe people experiencing themselves in a totally new way. Not the self they were accustomed to but all of the unprocessed selves that had been banished from consciousness and that surged forth when the banishing ego was chemically undermined. Among this unprocessed stuff is the universal birth trauma or perinatal unconscious, and trying to escape this ego-death is reasonable. Grof would eventually warn patients that ego-death might be associated with the fear of physical death, permanent insanity and homosexuality. But when it is surpassed the numinous dimensions of the transpersonal unconscious become more accessible.

To understand how psychedelics affected the clients at Hollywood Hospital we need to go back to the question of how these drugs affected our ancestors when they were first introduced to their diet.

According to the late philosopher Terrence McKenna, some time after the last ice age receded from Africa one million years ago, Homo erectus began consuming the psilocybin mushrooms newly growing there and the story of modern humanity and psychedelic drugs begins.

Table of Contents

Dedication iii

Epigraphs v

Acknowledgements vi

Preface vii

Introduction ix

PART ONE: THE STORY BEHIND THE FIRST STORY

Chapter One – First Wave – Pre-History 3

Chapter Two – Second Wave – Indigenous Use 13

Chapter Three – Third Wave – Classical Use 21

Chapter Four – Fourth Wave – Chemists Turn the Key 28

Chapter Five – Brainwashing 101 33

Chapter Six – A Brief History of Trauma 39

Chapter Seven – Continuity and Theoretical Convergence ... 43

Chapter Eight – Fifth Wave – Dr. Stan Grof 47

Chapter Nine – Fifth Wave – Dr. Timothy Leary 59

PART TWO: HOLLYWOOD HOSPITAL

Chapter Ten – Canadian Medicine and Mysterium Tremendum 81

Chapter Eleven – Ross MacLean meets Johnny Acidseed 90

Chapter Twelve – Frank Ogden – Psychedelic Flight Engineer 95

Chapter Thirteen – Preparation 109

Chapter Fourteen – Listening to Acid 120

Chapter Fifteen – Character Building – Incomplete Reactions........... 123

Chapter Sixteen – Abnormal Suffering – Liberation Reactions I - 141

Chapter Seventeen –- Normal Suffering – Liberation Reactions II -.. 177

PART THREE: TOWARDS AN INTEGRAL PSYCHEDELIC THEORY

Chapter Eighteen – The Eight-Brained Biped Migrates to the Stars... 199

Chapter Nineteen – Addiction 225

Chapter Twenty – Drug War 233

Chapter Twenty-One – Risks, Applications/Current Research 241

Chapter Twenty-Two – The Future 252

Biographies 255

Index 261

Part I

The Story Behind the First Story

Chapter One

Pre-History: Between 100,000 and 7,000 Years Ago Psilocybin Entered the Human Diet

In Dr. Leary's worldview consciousness occurs when energy is received by structure and when processed and transmitted as information intelligence is also present.

Once when psychedelic icons Timothy Leary and Terrence McKenna were both speaking in Germany, they were sitting down together before the show backstage.
"You know why I really like you Terrence?" "Why?"
"For keeping it with the Irish."
Leary often waxed romantically about the wild, intuitive, creative God-intoxicated Irish Celts as the dynamic opposite to the rigid, linear authoritarian English.

The "it" Dr. Leary was referring to was being the world's leading advocate for psychedelic drugs. And advocate he did – while Hollywood Hospital and to a lesser extent Timothy Leary advocated extensive preparation and support, McKenna advised his audiences to take five dried grams of psilocybin and sit alone in the dark.

"Similar to Jesus or Buddha in terms of input."

McKenna died at age 53 from brain cancer, but in those years he pushed his grey matter as far anyone can and still come back to talk about it. The record he left, mostly in his lectures, with the elfin lilt of Joycean scientific prose he used, is extensive. One of his books *True Hallucinations* explores a very pressing philosophical problem – are all human experiences generated from within each brain?

In a survey study inspired by McKenna's work 36% of 118 psilocybin users reported hearing a voice that seemed external; materialists would describe this as a projected rather than an introjected hallucination. (If the subject believes the voice is coming from outside his or her mind the hallucination is projected – from within it is introjected.) McKenna personally claimed he heard a voice on high doses of psilocybin that raved instructions such as "create a plan before you become trapped in someone else's" and generally provided fairly valuable advice.

Dynamic opposite to the materialist philosophy, what might be called the shamanic perspective implies that the world experienced in non-ordinary states of consciousness is not only real but is in fact even realer than the everyday world. Conversely materialists believe all the phenomena of consciousness are attributable to the physiological structures of the brain – an auditory hallucination caused by drugs is the way the "voice" would likely be interpreted by this most popular philosophy.

Easy as it is I am now going to erect a straw man that I will then proceed to deftly destroy–

What might be called the atheistic-materialist worldview proposes that the big- bang occurred 14 billion years ago and then 10 billion years later electricity somehow triggered the elements to produce life on earth. Then, according to the process of random mutation and natural selection, a species evolved with adequate brainpower to become as fully conscious as we are today.

DNA co-discoverer Francis Crick believed the chances of random mutation and natural selection producing the complexity of DNA to be "just one chance in ten followed by 260 zeroes." (There are only one times ten with 80 zeroes beside it atoms in the universe.) Timothy Leary and Francis Crick both believed panspermia was a better explanation. This theory proposes that DNA in the form of simple bacteria were seeded on either meteors or spaceships and either randomly or intentionally landed on earth about 4 billion years ago. With much of DNA already constructed random mutation and natural selection combined with (in Leary's view) consciousness-intelligence (contelligence) could begin their work and create the "self-conscious" human brain of Homo sapiens sapiens at least 100,000 years ago.

Another organism besides bacteria capable of withstanding the rigours of space flight is a mushroom spore. Psychedelic researcher Terrence McKenna suggested that psilocybin mushroom spores may have also been seeded on either meteors or spaceships and either randomly or intentionally landed on earth. Once here they waited for the bacteria, and through "infinite creative intelligence" combined with natural selection and random mutation to evolve a smart enough hunter-gatherer monkey to eat the mushrooms and keep eating them.

Animals eat everything once but to keep eating something there must be a reason (even just intoxication) – but psilocybin may have carved a niche in the early human diet for the drug's enhancement of visual acuity improving hunting success. But then in higher doses they may have begun communicating with a "higher intelligence" or projected hallucination depending on your perspective. Regardless, it could be this symbiotic relationship between, as Leary described, the "animal kingdom and the plant queendom" that is the true origin of human consciousness as we understand it – psilocybin as the first exopheromone.

The basic brain hardware for Homo sapiens had already existed for a while but McKenna argued psilocybin was needed essentially to turn the circuits on.

Similarly in the 1960s the computer hardware had basically been ready since World War II but (often) psychedelic-using youth were required to turn on the circuits and give it meaning – a transformation every bit as dramatic as the emergence of Homo sapiens. Not only have Apple founder, the late Steve Jobs, and Microsoft founder Bill Gates admitted LSD use, but psychedelic pioneer Al Hubbard gave the drug to anyone willing in the burgeoning high-tech scene of what would become silicon valley in the late fifties and early sixties. When psychedelics met the computer hardware the results have been encouraging but what would have been the result of psychedelics meeting the brain hardware for the first time?

McKenna's psilocybin initiation hypothesis posits many generations of low dose mushroom use for enhanced visual acuity and hunting success building to the time as recently as 7,000 years ago when this therianthrope (part animal part human) mushroom God appeared on a cave in Algiers Africa.

Others suggest psilocybin use must have emerged by 40,000 years ago inspiring the shamanic themed cave art in Europe. Whatever the timing (100,000 to 7,000 years ago) and whatever the dose the effect on early Homo sapiens or Homo sapiens sapiens if they had already crossed that threshold must have been profound. Two published studies prove that psilocybin, when given to well adjusted, spiritually ambitious people with a supportive set and setting, will facilitate a peak spiritual experience considered either the most or among the most important of their lives in two of three subjects.

It has been speculated that Homo erectus and antecedents transitioned from foraging to hunting between 2.5 and 2,000,000 years ago and 500,000 years ago fire was tamed and by 200,000 years ago anatomically modern humans or Homo sapiens roamed the earth.

Whether Homo sapiens started using psilocybin 100,000 years ago or much more recently, could the visionary state produced by the drug be related to the "shamanic graffiti" created all over the prehistoric world? Could the drug be what facilitated the move from Homo sapiens 200,000 years ago to Homo sapiens sapiens by 40,000 years ago?

And although it was thought that only humans had a descended larynx making speech possible the discovery of many animals like deer and others with this feature suggest humanity isn't as much a matter of hardware but software and operating system as well. Perhaps psilocybin did more than improve eyesight but introduced new ideas into the minds of our ancestors and beginning with these practical survival strategies a more mystical experience evolved.

Anthropologists Drs. David Lewis-Williams and Jean Clotte wrote a book called *The Shamans of Prehistory: Trance and Magic in the Painted Caves* in 1998 in which they develop the theory that trance states inspired the ancient cave art. The painted images tend to range from geometrical designs, handprints, people alive, injured and killed, animals and finally human-animal hybrids known as therianthropes. Using interviews with elders of the Sans, a South African tribe, Lewis-Williams and his colleagues have worked out a system of shamanism where tribe specialists go into trance states to enter the spirit world, which they have learned over many generations to navigate skillfully. This mythology and the art the San created are similar to the cave art throughout the world according to this theory.

Juxtaposing this with laboratory research on the "closed-eyed visuals" produced by mescaline, LSD and psilocybin further supports the critical significance of Paleolithic drug use, although many non-pharmacological technologies were subsequently developed. Using marathon dancing to induce trances and other meditation techniques were likely developed only after consuming the psychoactive foods in the early human diet.

One explanation for the rapid development of non-drug shamanic technologies is biologist Dr. Rupert Sheldrake's *morphic fields*, which proposes that when each member of a species learns something a change occurs in the morphic fields allowing all the other members access to the same new information. In this hypothesis the brain isn't the generator of consciousness but an instrument for accessing another dimension made of consciousness. Experiments where subsequent generations of animals learn skills faster than their ancestors were the data that helped Sheldrake form the theory – he was practically burned at the stake by the scientific community.

After enhanced visual acuity McKenna proposed human psilocybin use served the hunt by anticipating the movements of the prey, for instance by becoming or "shape-shifting" into the wooly mammoth – and it this Paleolithic shape-shifter that is the progenitor of the shaman. McKenna also claims the sense-blending (synesthesia) effects of psilocybin helped the shamans produce pictures from sounds, improving language. Higher psilocybin doses he claims are aphrodisiac which led to an orgiastic society where men never knew the paternity of their children – leaving the women in charge because only they could produce life.

This Goddess worshiping utopia would eventually be crushed by the ego based world that emerged with agriculture, writing and civilization about 8,500 BCE.

It is possible, however, that other non-drug techniques were developed first and psilocybin simply re-inforced a prehistoric reverence for trance states. In fact the first scholar of shamanism Mircea Eliade believed only "degenerate" shamanism resorts to drugs; however at the end of his life he is reported to have recanted and psilocybin and other psychoactives remain the most parsimonious explanation for the prehistoric fascination with non-ordinary states.

It seems humanity has had our narcissism and egocentrism crushed repeatedly over the centuries, from our position as the center of a divine universe through sciences such as astronomy, biology and psychology we have learned that humans are not even the only sources of consciousness intelligence (contelligence). Once we became intelligent enough we began seeking intelligence elsewhere.

The role of psilocybin in prehistoric spirituality ignores the question of whether experience is generated exclusively in the brain or if the brain receives as well as generates contelligence. On high doses of psilocybin McKenna heard a voice that he compared to the Greek Logos – an all-knowing intelligence he believed external to his own brain. On high doses of the super-hallucinogen DMT McKenna saw "self-transforming machine tyke elves made of language" which again he believed didn't come from within.

1,000 000 - 200,000 years ago	100,000 - 7,000 years ago	35,000 - 5 000 years ago	10,000 years ago - Now
Many hominids compete – Homo sapiens emerges with our current brain size but less physically robust than it's ancestors.	Humans first encounter psilocybin and perhaps begin using it first to enhance visual acuity for hunting, then specialists begin using higher doses and "shapeshifting" into the prey, and at still higher doses they experienced synesthesia (sense-blending) in this case turning pictures into words.	Specialists at higher doses become shamans – healers 40,000 BCE oldest cave painting (shamanic graffiti) religious and sexual ecstasies at the top doses – a utopic matriarchy emerges where paternity is uncertain and the ego marginal.	Agriculture and writing emerge with humans settling along the Nile, Tigris, Euphrates rivers and the Yellow Valley in China – civilization as we know it starts – the ego begins its fevered ascent until the 1990s when the next evolutionary leap the internet, a global electronic brain emerges.

The Late Psychologist Dr. Julian Jaynes in *The Origin of Consciousness in the Breakdown of the Bicameral Mind* forged an argument even stranger than McKenna's. He claimed that until about the time of the Greek bard Homer around 850 B.C.E. no self-consciousness, as we understand it, existed, people could not lie or deceive, as they had no "theory of mind." Under extreme stress individuals would hear "God" and would do whatever was commanded. For instance in a fire one would hear a voice command them to "GET OUT!"

Jaynes further suggested kings were mummified and the subjects would look at the statue and hallucinate the dead king's orders. When civilizations started to overlap each other these hallucinations became impractical because the voice usually commanded the death of a stranger. Jaynes suggested schizophrenia is a holdover from this ancient legacy but only mentions hallucinogens in passing in regard to religio-mystical spiritual experiences.

Two experiments have confirmed that psilocybin facilitates subjectively meaningful spiritual experiences if set (past experiences, temperament, personality and expectations) and setting (the environment) are taken into account. One study was conducted by the infamous Dr. Leary who we will discuss at length later, the other was done by Dr. Roland Griffiths from Johns Hopkins Medical School in 2006 and found 22 of 36 subjects had "complete mystical experiences" while only 4 of the 36 in the control group did. The experimental group scored 5 times higher than placebo, where as even the most positive prozac study doesn't double placebo.

Producing spiritual experiences alone doesn't prove psilocybin as the catalyst for meta-consciousness, language, religion and art – but something had to trigger the revolution in humanity that led to the cave art of 40,000 BCE. Romantic speculations about a lost psychedelic Atlantis aside, before we can assess how drugs affect the brain we need to have some idea of how our grey matter actually works.

The famous Montreal brain surgeon Dr. Wilder Penfield would stimulate a specific neuron and the patient would encounter a specific memory, which he called an engram, the term later used by Dianetics creator L. Ron Hubbard to describe an unprocessed trauma. According to Penfield's theory, each of these brain cells had a memory (engram). But we are born with most of the neurons we will ever possess, so how can we keep encoding new memories – shouldn't they be filled up by age five? Researchers have since learned that although nerve cells can't divide like other cells do, they can forge new links and thus new memories, without new cells being necessary.

However, a memory being stored not in a neuron, but in a web of interconnected neurons, still doesn't explain how difficult it is for researchers to eliminate a memory in animals. Even taking out a piece of the cerebrum (which is a part of the brain involved with memory) can't destroy recall, only removing the whole cerebrum totally kills a learned pattern in rats. In other words the memory is somehow distributed across many cells and structures.

Neuroscientist Dr. Karl Lashley proposed that although the intensity of recall was related to the mass of the brain, the essence of the memory was recorded throughout the cerebrum. One scientist scrambled salamander brains 700 times but could not scramble the programs; he even used a tadpole brain in a salamander cranium and the salamander acted like a tadpole!

If information was stored on several hundred photocopies and we were to remove half – the basic information would remain intact. But if we were to remove, cut, paste and rotate half and the message still remained intact this is a different kind of system – a "holotropic" complex system such as the brain, the DNA and the nucleus of the atom. Stanislav Grof derived his concept of holotropic experiences from holographic photography.

From Wikipedia: "Holography is a technique for making lensless, three- dimensional photographs – where a low intensity laser beam is passed through a semi-opaque mirror, causing part of the beam to pass through the mirror onto the object that is being photographed. This light is then reflected from the object onto a photographic plate. Simultaneously the other beam is reflected off a series of mirrors and lands on the holographic plate as well but at an angle to the other beam. The interference pattern between the two signals is recorded onto the photographic plate. This interference pattern looks nothing like the object photographed but when it is re-illuminated by another beam – floating in empty space just above the plate lies a perfect 3-D replica of the object that can only be differentiated from the original by passing a material object through it! It is a standing waveform – an apparently motionless arrangement of photons."

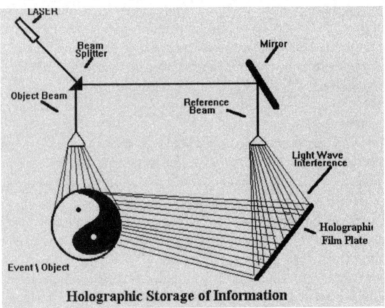

Holographic Storage of Information

If the plate is placed at a slight angle from where the first image was recorded, another image can then be stored and re-illuminated by using the appropriate position. Furthermore, because the recording is of signal interference patterns and these patterns are equal throughout, any piece of the hologram can be re- illuminated to create the original image.

Holographic networks are therefore qualitatively superior to their linear counterparts because you can store more information, and no matter how much the system deteriorates – unless totally destroyed – the essence remains. So if brains and minds may work through holographic principles – where else in nature are these principles apparent?

Terrence and his brother Dennis McKenna in their 1975 classic *The Invisible Landscape* claim DNA is also holographic-holotropic – the DNA in one cell has the information necessary to create any cell in the body. The McKennas went on to argue that the atom and the quantum levels operate on holographic principles as well. Recall that a hologram requires three beams, one aimed directly at the object with the reflection recorded on a holographic plate, one aimed through mirrors and then onto the same holographic plate on an angle from the original beam, and a third "reconstructing" beam to re-illuminate that pattern and produce the hologram.

McKenna presented the hypothesis that tryptamine hallucinogens, of which psilocybin is one, bond to RNA, which is the messenger between the DNA and the cell, and cause the DNA to vibrate – the resulting resonance creates the interference signal required to reproduce this holographic representation of the mind, the brain and possibly all consciousness.

One of the remarkable features of psychedelics is the range of experiences they are capable of facilitating. Grof observed that there was not one predictable effect, even pupil dilation was absent in some subjects and the same subjects would have different experiences on different days – sometimes moving into "a completely different diagnosis." A psychedelic holographic and holotropic action would explain this.

In his classic essay "Three Contributions to Psychopharmacological Theory" Timothy Leary popularized the phrase set and setting, which is used to this day. Leary proposed that the effects of a drug were over-determined (more than one cause) by extra-pharmacological factors. To review, set means the personality and experiences of the subject and his or her expectations and setting is the environment, particularly the people in it. In the case of the placebo effect set and setting are all that happens. If the brain works on holographic and/or morphic field principles, when the mind is opened to infinity by psychedelics, set and setting determine where it goes.

However it works and however it happened the first time humans "tripped" must have been remarkable to say the least. A golden age before history full of magic and angelic languages where each word means exactly what it sounds like are common themes in mythology and McKenna surfed the lucrative New Age seminar market skillfully. The Greeks had Atlantis, and Islam, Christianity and Judaism share a common Eden.

But prehistory is by definition speculation and whatever it's noble synergy with early humanity may have been, the story of psychedelics now moves out of the mists of archaic speculation and into the light of today.

Chapter Two

The Second Wave:
Indigenous psychedelic drug use

The shaman can travel between the worlds

Our culture is often criticized for being pragmacentric – for favoring or even only tolerating rational consciousness. This is unique to the modern West, the Indigenous people of the world on the other hand, tend to revere non-ordinary states of consciousness and the plants and other means that facilitate them.

According to McKenna's pre-history the psychedelic drugs had to be virtually eliminated by climate change or made occult (hidden) in order to allow for the conquest by the "male-ego" and the facilitation of technological civilization. The notion that rational "left-brain" consciousness is not only superior but also the only acceptable mode of experience is symptomatic of moving from an I-Thou way of being in the world to the I-it attitude that still dominates.

For example, my "Myth and Symbol" professor, Tom Henighan, began his course with this story:

> An anthropologist was in Africa studying a tribe one night when he came upon a native dancing by himself without music.
> "Who are you dancing with?" The anthropologist asked. The native looked at his white friend like he was insane.
> "The stars, the trees, the sky."

The word shaman comes from the Siberian Tengus tribe's own word "saman" meaning "to ride" and has become "an anthropological term referencing a range of beliefs and practices regarding communication with the spiritual world." To this day these Siberian healers/entertainers/priests use Amanita Muscaria mushrooms. The earliest evidence of A. Muscaria use as an intoxicant is based on linguistic analysis from northern Asia.

Around 4,000 BCE, the Uralic language split into two branches, both of which contain similar root words for inebriation. These linguistic similarities suggest (but do not prove) that A. muscaria was known to be intoxicating before the languages split around 4,000 BCE. Dating from as early as 2,000 BCE petroglyphs along the Pegtymel River, which drains into the Arctic Ocean in northeastern Siberia, "depict anthropomorphic figures with mushrooms appended to their heads." The Pegtymel river area is currently inhabited by the modern Chukchi culture that is known to use A. muscaria as a traditional inebriant.

According to psychedelic researcher Jonathan Ott the shaman would enter the house via a hole in the roof, carrying a sack of mushrooms, wearing a red and white outfit and some suggest Santa Claus may draw some inspiration from these traditions. Apparently Joseph Stalin used to persecute Siberian shaman by throwing them out of airplanes and taunting them, "You said you could fly!"

Originally shamans in Siberia were family shamans who would have been otherwise ordinary members of communal society. Professional shamans emerged later and although persecuted by Buddhists, Christians and Communists are still practicing today.

In Siberian shamanic cosmology, there is an under-world, an over-world and the ordinary middle world all connected by a "tree of life" or "axis mundi" whose roots reach down and branches reaches up, while the trunk exists here on earth. The shaman is able to travel the worlds.

In some cultures the shaman eats the mushroom and the other revelers drink his urine, which is still hallucinogenic but less toxic. In other cultures only the shaman receives the hallucinogen and in eastern Siberia the drug is used in both religious ritual and recreationally.

shamanic societies were communal rather than hierarchal and accepted some degree of mutual responsibility for all members. In the western world, we have taken a long time to recognize the debilitating effects of trauma – whereas resolving trauma specifically is central to the shaman's role. Fortune telling, finding lost objects, healing other illnesses and it seems to me show business are all part of the job description as well.

Dr. Peter Levine, a California psychologist specializing in trauma who created the system of Self-Regulation Therapy (SRT), discusses shamanism in his book *Waking The Tiger*:

> Since pre-civilization, shamanistic healers from many cultures have been able to successfully orchestrate the conditions that encourage

the "lost soul" to return to the body. Through colorful rituals, these so-called "primitive" healers catalyze powerful innate healing forces in their patients. Often the proceedings continue for days and may involve the use of plant substances and other pharmacological catalysts. Significantly … the subject would always shake and tremble as the event nears its conclusion."

The shamans believe the ill member's soul has left the body and must be brought back. Mircea Eliade was one of the original scholars of shamanism. He wrote of a Toleut (a tribe in Siberia) shaman calling the soul of a sick child home to his body,

> Come back to your country; to your people … to the Yurt, by the bright fire! … Come back to your Father … to your Mother..."

On the other side of the earth the oldest sample of peyote yet discovered dates back to 3,700 BCE, it was found as part of what appeared to be a religious altar in a cave in Texas. But possibly even earlier the use of mescal emerged, which is a kind of deliriant and stimulant used to produced altered states that may have been usurped by the more palatable peyote. Confusion between these two totally different plants (mescal and peyote) is responsible for the naming of mescaline, which is the most active chemical in peyote.

Psychedelic authority Jonathon Ott wrote,

> "*Mezcalin* (or mescaline, as this is now rendered) derives its name from *mezcal*, owing to confusion on the part of European scientists as to the nomenclature of *peyotl*. Dried *peyotl* "buttons" had been erroneously known as *mescal buttons* in Europe. "*Mezcal*" originally comes from the Nahuatl *mexcalli*, the Aztec name for a whole species of plant, the *Agave* species, from which *octli* or *pulque*, a fermented beer, is still made. After the conquest, the Spaniards began to distill *pulque*, and the resulting liquor came to be known as *mezcal*. As for the active principle of *peyotl*, *Mezcalin* or *mescaline* is a misnomer."

The Native American Church, which is licensed to use the drug legally, doesn't refer to peyote or mescaline very often but instead simply speaks of medicine.

At the time of the Spanish conquest and the first historical reference to peyote, its use had spread far beyond the limited area it grows in. So from at least 3,700 BCE, and probably much earlier, until the European conquest in the fifteenth century all the tribes of Mexico and Southern Texas were familiar with the cactus and it was a staple of Mexican markets. Although given the possible significance of Paleolithic psychedelic drug use 3,700 BCE isn't very long ago, researchers believe humanity only first entered the more remote parts of South and Central America around 8,500 BCE. Which may indicate the Peruvian shamans of Machu Picchu represent our closest link to our hunter-gatherer past.

It is difficult to know the extent of peyote use when the Spanish arrived. Different cultures have different attitudes to drugs and there is some evidence the Mayans were a hippie-astrology tribe while the Aztecs were Spartan prohibitionists. The conquistadors viciously suppressed both the religious and even medical use, which, for the natives, was the same thing.

When other Europeans arrived to colonize North America one hundred years later there was no peyote use to prohibit. Nonetheless by the time the American government began to ghettoize natives into reservations in 1868 peyote had become a major religious and medical force in Oklahoma, far north of where it had ever been used in the past. Kiowa-Apache medicine men were among the first tribes to integrate the cactus into a religious ceremony, derivatives of which are still practiced today. Before long peyotism had been integrated with Christianity by some groups although many peyote leaders condemned this syncretic or "fusing opposites" practice.

The roadmen or peyote meeting leaders were usually political as well as religious figures and tended to be co-operative towards white Americans. Peyote was never used by more than 90% of any reservation and most likely had less than half practicing. In 1919, 60% of adult Kiowa Indians were disciples of the cactus and 4% of American Indians total. It was popular with the recently displaced, the young and newly educated that craved a uniquely Indian Christianity, and of course with those it cured of disease. Native Americans who had been Christian for generations reacted as their white counterparts did – condemning peyote and its newly re-invented culture as barbaric. However, many roadmen were also active in Christian churches and even served as ministers.

A Midwestern Native recalls: "Father was a Baptist minister and peyote roadman at the same time. Many times I attended peyote meetings with Dad on Saturday night; then left with him Sunday morning and helped sing in the Baptist church service, and then returned and ate the noon peyote feast with the Indians."

At the turn of the 20th century fierce resistance emerged from medical and religious puritans and what will become a familiar narrative unfolded. In 1918 hearings were held about a federal prohibition of peyote and Utah, Nevada and Colorado outlawed the practice, meanwhile cannabis, heroin, cocaine and everything else were legal and readily available. For instance many middle-aged, middle-class women were opiate addicts.

In response to this persecution the Native American Church was formed in 1918 and by the election of Roosevelt in 1932 dozens of chapters had been established across the country. Although there were many local skirmishes with fines imposed and religious paraphernalia stolen for lack of payment and many politicians tried to enact a federal ban, the American tradition of religious freedom was not undermined.

In 1954 The Native American Church was established in Saskatchewan Canada and a quarterly bulletin began publication. Today there are more than 250,000 adherents.

The western hemisphere has many more psychedelic plants than its eastern counterpart. The shamans of Europe were burned as witches and to this day the major defining element of counterculture is illegal psychoactive drug use. Two exceptions are the Siberians from which the word shaman is derived and the African religion Bwiti, who use a plant called Iboga. In the West African nation of Gabon a tribe called the Fang practice this religion that they believe originated with the neighbouring Pygmies millennia ago.

Similar to peyote, ibogaine is used in varying doses as a recreational stimulant, medicine and pathway to spiritual experience. In 1864 a French doctor named Griffon du Bellay identified Tabernathe (named after the church Tabernacle) Iboga root. In the late nineteenth century at roughly the same time as the rediscovery of peyote on the other side of the world, the Fang people of Gabon, West Africa established Bwiti, another psychedelic syncretic (merging opposites) church.

Reminiscent of the peyote eaters many combine two religions, although some sects of Bwiti reject Christianity, many attend Sunday mass after having participated in the Bwiti mass Saturday night. Each sect has 10-50 members usually living in the same village who worship at a temple resembling the structure of the human body surrounded by Iboga bushes.

Bwiti is open and the Gabon relish contact with the West and proselytize or seek converts freely. Like most psychedelic religions ceremonies are held at night on Saturday, and on Christmas and Easter in the syncretic Christian sects, and Iboga is eaten. The revelers dance all night, with some sects allowing the use of alcohol, and at dawn everyone shares a feast.

During one's initiation a much larger dose of Iboga is given after a full confession and bath. According to Bwiti psychology should a sin be omitted in the confession, permanent insanity may result – should that sin be murder the initiate will die. (Ibogaine proves fatal about 1 in 300 times.) The Iboga is eaten over 7- 12 hours and the effects last for three days, during which a male and female couple serves as the "Father" and "Mother." Usually on the third night the initiate is poked with a thorn and if he or she doesn't react it is assumed they are undergoing the climax of the experience where a new name will be heard and added.

Some children 8 to 10 are initiated but often the experience is repeated in adulthood. Although their temples were burned and their leaders slaughtered at the behest of the Catholic missionaries, Bwiti grew and contributed to the 1960 formation of the new Gabon Republic, whose first president was a member of the church.

In Slovenia a religion called Sacrament of the Transition based on Iboga has been established and recognized by that country's government.

An active ingredient in Iboga called ibogaine is the most promising treatment for addiction the world has ever known. This drug reduces addictive behaviour in opiate- and stimulant-dependent rats – to be discussed later.

Central America has more hallucinogens than any other part of the world, with mescaline-containing plants, psilocybin-containing mushrooms, compounds similar to LSD like morning glory seeds and many plants that contain the super- hallucinogen DMT and other alkaloids that render it orally active.

Not only is DMT the most common psychedelic throughout nature it naturally appears in the human body. DMT is also the most potent psychoactive drug available – its effects are described as a full-blown acid trip condensed into five minutes, when smoked or injected its effects are compared to being blasted out of a canon.

A burial site was found in Northern Chile dating from 800 CE, which contained DMT in addition to other similar compounds, although its use likely goes back much further. Once again the Christian missionaries were horrified and repressed it viciously, but given the ubiquity of plant sources could not extinguish it completely.

In the 1920s, about thirty years after peyote and Iboga inspired new religions elsewhere, a rubber-tree planter named Raimundo Irineu Serra of Brazil started the religion Santo Daime, based on a drink called Daime, which uses plants with DMT combined with ones containing a mono-amine oxidase inhibitor which prevents the DMT from being destroyed in the stomach and allows its psychoactive effects to emerge.

What this means is that perhaps thousands of years ago Amazonian shamans figured out that combining these two totally different compounds found in totally different parts of the jungle, rendered the first one (DMT) orally active. When asked how his ancestors came to this realization one shaman replied, "the plants told them."

> "All who drink this holy beverage must not only try to see beautiful things while correcting their faults, but give shape to perfection of their own personality to take their place in this battalion and follow this line. If they would act this way, they could say, I am a brother."
> – Daime founder Raimundo Irineu.

Syncretic religion means an attempt to "reconcile disparate or contrary beliefs, often while melding practices of various schools of thought" merging opposites is one definition of Yoga – to yolk, unite or bridge. Syncretic Santo Daime incorporates folk Catholicism, African Animism and Amazonian shamanism.

There are branches in Europe as well as New Mexico and Oregon and the United States Supreme Court has confirmed their right to use the drug. In 1992 after an extensive study that demonstrated the religion's contribution to the community, the Brazilian government legalized DMT containing tea.

Another Brazilian DMT-based religion originated in 1961 by Jose Gabriel de Costa called Uniao Do Vegetal or UDV just won in the U.S. Supreme Court its right to import and use DMT containing tea.

Interestingly, in modern day Brazil ayahuasca is illegal except for religious use, which means that the less than 90-year-old DMT religions are protected but the shamanic use perhaps thousands of years older is forbidden. This is in sharp contrast to Peru where shamanic use is endorsed by the government and is the driving force behind the lucrative ayahuasca tourism industry.

Amanita Muscaria	peyote	Ibogaine	DMT
Origin of the word shaman meaning to ride is from Siberia where A. muscaria has likely been used since at least 4,000 BCE.	Oldest sample is from 3,700 BCE in Texas –almost totally exterminated but re-emerged in 1880s in Oklahoma Native American church which now has 250,000 members.	Rumored to have been used by the pygmies in Gabon millennia ago but emerges in the 1880s as the central focus of the Bwiti Religion.	Oldest sample from Chile 800 CE but use likely dates back much further – reemerges in 20th century South America w/ Santo Daime and UDV – religions centered around DMT.

There are two trends in this new world revival of indigenous psychedelic culture; one is the re-emergence of psychedelics in response to colonialism that often progressed to outright genocide and the second is the capacity of the "psychedelic priest" to thrive in mainstream Western society.

The shaman can travel between the worlds.

Chapter Three

The Third Wave: *The longest enduring, the second written and one of the first monotheistic religions likely utilized psychedelic drugs*

"Fathers that which our hearts have drunken, Immortal in himself, hath entered mortals. So let us serve this Soma with oblation, and rest securely in grace and favour." – Rig Veda

Although some scholars disagree, Amanita Muscaria, psilocybin, opium, cannabis and Ephedra may have been at least active ingredients in the ancient Iranian Haoma and the Indian Soma as early as 2,000 BCE. In 1,600 B.C.E., four hundred years later, the Eleusinian mysteries began in Greece, the heart of which was the libation Kykeon. The exact nature of Soma, Haoma and Kykeon were protected secrets and so the specific ingredients are not confirmed, but given the properties of psychedelics these types of compounds were likely present.

McKenna argues that humans began using psilocybin as long as 100,000 years ago when the glaciers receded from North Africa leaving stropharia cubensis psilocybin containing mushrooms. This lasted until about 6,000 BCE when the town of Catal Huyuk in modern day Turkey was taken and the matriarchal partnership mushroom religion began fleeing around the world into present day Iran and Minoan Crete near Greece. Some of these Indo-Europeans (Aryans) moved from the middle east to India about 1,500 BCE taking their psychedelic religion with them. Eventually though the ideal compounds became unavailable and substitutions were made which ultimately too succumbed to scarcity and we are left with the purely symbolic rituals of modern religions until peyote, ibogaine and ayahuasca returned religion to chemistry.

The *Rig Veda,* the first part of the Hindu bible, is the world's second oldest religious text, next to Egypt's *Book of the Dead,* consisting of just over one thousand hymns, containing over ten thousand verses divided into ten books written about 1,000 BCE. Although three other later Vedas complete the text the original *Rig Veda* is the foundation of Indian religion and philosophy.

In almost every one of the thousand hymns reference is made to the Divine Plant "Soma" and one hundred and fourteen are devoted exclusively to it. Soma was a sacred plant that was *itself* considered a deity. It is conceivable that Soma contained many plants and other ingredients because the medicinal properties it is praised as possessing transcend the facilitation of spiritual experience.

The sacred hymns were the collected work of intoxicated seers and sages and are filled with ecstatic praise of the God/drink referring to its mountainous natural habitat, brilliant red or gold appearance, the processing sequence used to make the drink and extolling it's healing and life-extending virtues;

> 3. We have drunk Soma and become immortal; we have attained the light, the Gods discovered. Now what can a foeman's malice do to harm us? What, O Immortal, a mortal man's deception?

> 4. Absorbed into the heart, be sweet, O drop, as a kind Father to his son, O Soma, As a wise Friend to a friend: do thou, wide-ruler, O Soma, lengthen our days for living.

> 5. These glorious drops that give me freedom have I drunk. Closely they knit my joints as straps secure a chariot. Let them protect my foot from slipping on the way: yea let the drops I drink preserve me from disease.

> 11. Our maladies have lost their strength and vanished; they feared, and passed away into the darkness. Soma hath risen in us, exceedingly mighty, and we have come to where men prolong existence.

> 12. Fathers that which our hearts have drunken, Immortal in himself, hath entered mortals. So let us serve this Soma with oblation, and rest securely in grace and favour.

The fact that Soma was taken not just by priests, pursuing religious ecstasy in the context of ritual, but was apparently taken by others daily, for a long period of time, indicates the drink may have been prepared differently for different purposes. Some have suggested the Hindu worship of the sacred cow is related to the production of mushrooms on cow dung harkening back to the hypothesized cow goddess cults of Ancient Africa. Whatever Soma was or represented it appears cannabis remained and Yoga entered to fill the pharmacological vacuum in India as the mysterious entity faded from memory.

Yoga is first recorded around 3,000 BCE with stone figures in asanas or postures and codified in 200 BCE – 200 CE with the sage Patanjali's *Yoga Sutras* – part of the same spiritual milieu that produced Soma and the *Rig Veda* about a millennium before.

By 10,000 BCE cannabis was being cultivated as hemp in present day Taiwan and was being burned and inhaled as incense in braziers by 2000 BCE in present day Romania and in 800 – 500 BCE a satchel of cannabis seeds was found with a mummified shaman in China. Although a hollow bone with what may be burnt plant matter inside dating back 1, 000 years has been discovered in present day Thailand it is believed smoking in pipes, cigarettes and cigars only arrived from the New World in the 15th century although Africa had been indulging for centuries prior.

At the beginning of the fourth of the Yoga Sutras Patanjali describes the means to attain siddhis or psychic powers – "Siddhis are born of practices performed in previous births, or by herbs, mantra repetition, asceticism or by Samadhi (meditation)." The attainment of siddhis was considered an essential step on the path to enlightenment. Virtually every other Yogi after Patanjali however condemns drug use as a dangerous and ineffective means of finding God.

Some have suggested Tantra Yoga, developed in India from 200 – 600 CE has integrated disciplined drug use into their religious systems. Tantra is divided into the right- and left- handed path; the right-handed path is a conventional Yoga life of austerity, meditation, Yoga postures (asana) and breathing exercises (pranayama) while the left-handed path involves the use of sex and drugs as means to higher experience. Most believe the purpose of the left-hand path is to prepare the aspirant to clean up their act and travel the correct path. As St. Augustine said, "Purify me oh Lord, but not yet."

In present-day India Sadhus or Hindu monks practice a life of total renunciation and austere Yoga, breathing and fasting regimens, they also often smoke copious amounts of cannabis to connect them to the God Shiva who, with the Goddess Shakti, are two of the primary divinities.

In 2,000 BCE the Aryans split into three tribes, one settled in India drinking Soma and another settled in Persia drinking Haoma in a remarkably similar religious system.

Zoroastrianism is one of the first monotheistic religions in recorded history, beginning around the 8th to 6th century BCE and based on the teachings and philosophies of Zoroaster, the religion's prophet and founder. Central to the myth of Zoroaster's conception is the brew Haoma. In this story, Pouroshaspa, his Father, took a piece of the Haoma plant and mixed it with milk. He gave his Wife Dugdhova half of the mixture and he consumed the other. They then conceived Zoroaster who was instilled with the spirit of the plant. The word Haoma is probably linked to the Indian Soma, both words apparently taken from the proto- Indo-Iranian sauma that means, to press or to pound.

Although banned shortly after the religion's founding and composed of unknown ingredients Haoma played a significant symbolic role in Zoroastrianism and in later Persian culture and mythology. In the *Avesta*, the Zoroastrian Holy Book, three chapters deal with Haoma.

> It furthers healing (Yasna 9.16-17, 9.19, 10.8, 10.9) It furthers sexual arousal (Yasna 9.13-15, 9.22)
>
> It is physically strengthening (Yasna 9.17, 9.22, 9.27)
>
> It stimulates alertness and awareness (Yasna 9.17, 9.22 10.13) The mildly intoxicating extract can be consumed without negative side effects (Yasna 10.8).
>
> It is nourishing (Yasna 9.4, 10.20) and 'most nutritious for the soul' (Yasna 9.16).

In those hymns, Haoma is said to appear before Zoroaster in the form of a "beautiful man" (this is the only anthropomorphic reference), who prompts him to gather and press Haoma for the purification of the waters. Haoma is 'righteous' and 'furthers righteousness', is 'wise' and 'gives insight' (Yasna 9.22). Haoma was also the name of the first priest.

Although the worship of Haoma continued Zoroaster condemned actually drinking the intoxicating beverage; however to this day a symbolic version is sipped on New Year's but only by the officiating priest and newborn babies have their lips steeped in the brew. Frankly the absence of the Haoma seems to have had a devastating effect on the poetry. Compare Soma's verse – "Fathers, that which our hearts have drunken, Immortal in himself, hath entered mortals. So let us serve this Soma with oblation, and rest securely in grace and favour." To the clinical Haoma's – "the mildly intoxicating extract can be consumed without negative side effects."

Again the drink seems to have such a range of effects that its formula likely varied. Given the holographic properties of mind, holotropic (transcendence of the "skin-encapsulated ego") experiences tend to convince the experiencer that consciousness transcends death. The theme of eternal life as represented by the perennial regeneration of plants is a central theme with Soma, Haoma, and the Greek brew called Kykeon.

Kykeon was crucial to the Greek Eleusinian Mysteries, which began in 1600 BCE and continued until the Roman emperor Theodosius I officially closed them down in 392 CE. But for the 2000 years before that they were a hit all across the classical world.

> "For among the many excellent and indeed divine institutions which your Athens has brought forth and contributed to human life, none, in my opinion, is better than those mysteries. For by their means we have been brought out of our barbarous and savage mode of life and educated and refined to a state of civilization; and as the rites are called 'initiations', so in very truth we have learned from them the beginnings of life, and have gained the power not only to live happily, but also to die with a better hope."
>
> –Cicero, Laws II, xiv, 36

The mysteries were divided into the greater and the lesser. The lesser mysteries were held in the winter and the greater in the summer. This cycle continued for almost two millennia and Kykeon was central to what was then the world's longest enduring religion before a gang of Christians and Visigoths burned the temple and slaughtered the priests and priestesses in 392.

But 800 years earlier under Pisistratus of Athens, the Eleusinian Mysteries became pan-Hellenic and pilgrims flocked from Greece and beyond to participate. Around 300 BCE the state took over the Mysteries with two families officially allowed control – this led to a vast increase in the number of initiates. The only requirements for membership were a lack of "blood guilt," meaning having never committed murder, and not being a "barbarian" (unable to speak Greek). Women and even slaves were allowed initiation.

There were four categories of people who participated in the Eleusinian Mysteries:

1. Hierophants (highest priest/priestesses).

2. priests, priestesses.

3. Initiates undergoing the ceremony for the first time.

4. Those who had attained epopteia or who had learned the Secrets of the greater mysteries.

The Rites at Eleusis were based on the myth of Demeter, the Goddess of agriculture and fertility; much of the story is described in one of the Homeric hymns dating back before 800 BCE. According to the myth Demeter's daughter Persephone was gathering flowers with her friends one day when her Uncle Hades, the God of Death and the Underworld, kidnapped her with the consent of her father Zeus. Hades (Zeus' brother) took her to the Underworld and Demeter, being upset and trying to put pressure on Zeus caused a long drought and many people starved. Since the drought would deprive the Gods of sacrifice Zeus relented and offered to return Persephone to her Mother. However Hades, before releasing her, held a great feast where Persephone ate six pomegranate seeds and because she had eaten the fruit of the underworld she had to remain there one month per seed. Demeter's compromise was to deprive the world during winter of fertility, but relent in the spring when Persephone is returned.

According to Classicist Dr. Thomas Taylor,

> "the dramatic shows of the Lesser Mysteries occultly signified the miseries of the soul while in subjection to the body, so those of the Greater obscurely intimated, by mystic and splendid visions, the felicity of the soul both here and hereafter, when purified from the defilements of a material nature and constantly elevated to the realities of intellectual [spiritual] vision." And that according to Plato, "the ultimate design of the Mysteries was to lead us back to the principles from which we descended & a perfect enjoyment of intellectual [spiritual] good."

In late February the lesser mysteries occurred; to qualify for initiation a piglet was sacrificed and the initiates were ritually purified in the River Illisos.

Then every year in late summer the ten-day Greater Mysteries began with sacred objects being brought from Eleusis to the Eleusinian temple. On the third day the celebrants washed themselves in the sea at Phaleron. On the fifth day they walked from the Athenian cemetery to Eleusis. Upon arrival they would fast for a day to replicate Demeter's fasting while searching for Persephone – a mysterious drink called Kykeon broke the fast. They then entered a great hall called the Telesterion at the center of which stood the Anaktoron or palace that only the hierophants or highest priests/priestesses were allowed to enter. Before entering the temple, the mystai or initiates would recite, "I have fasted, I have drunk the Kykeon,

I have taken from the box, and after working it have put it back in the basket." Since revealing any of the details was punished by death little is known of the exact nature of the ritual or the symbols they used, but presumably they were related to the myth of Demeter, the themes of rebirth, regeneration and eternal life. At the climax of the mystery fire was presented as a symbol of life after death and a single ear of corn rose at the top of the stage as a metaphor for regeneration, a symbol that endures in the Christian Eucharist.

In another example of classical psychedelia, the ancient Romans had a proverb that if someone appeared mad, "he ought to visit Anticyra." This ancient clinic is much more reminiscent of the project at Hollywood Hospital than any of the examples so far. For here, primarily mental illness was treated with black and white hellebore, which the famous Roman historian Pliny said "inspired vast religious awe."

Writer and poet Robert Graves speculated that "...both hellebores are narcotic. The treatment evidently included a form of drug-abreaction combined with strong suggestion." The procedure was apparently so intense women, children and the frail were considered inadmissible.

Soma	Haoma	Kykeon	Hellebore
2,000 – 1,500 BCE a Middle East Aryan tribe splits into three – one in India another in Iran – Aryans in India write the first book of the Hindu "bible" the Rig Veda with 114 of its 1 000 hymns devoted exclusively to the magical God/plant.	800 BCE-600 BCE Zoroastrianism begins in modern day Iran – with a similar worship of a plant/ God – the words Soma and Haoma apparently both derive from the common proto-Indian word sauma to pound.	1,600 BCE – 392 CE in Greece at the mysteries of Eleusis initiates at the end of an elaborate cleansing ritual drink a brew called Kykeon and experienced death/ rebirth and regeneration.	100 BCE – 215 CE in Anticyra in ancient Rome a medical clinic used black and white hellebore to "induce a form of drug abreaction" possibly similar to Hollywood Hospital.

Chapter Four

The Fourth Wave: 1790s-1930s:
Chemists turn the key by producing a number of psychoactive liquid and gaseous chemicals inspiring artists and scientists

"The keynote of the experience is the tremendously exciting sense of an intense metaphysical illumination. Truth lies open to view in depth beneath depth of almost blinding evidence." – William James

The brain is the most complex system in the known universe; it is made of matter but uses electricity, magnetism, liquids and gasses as messengers in its infinite information networks. Consciousness can of course be changed at the electrical level as in Electro-Convulsive Therapy, where electric current is applied to the brain to induce seizure. The brain can also be altered with gases such as the anesthetics nitrous oxide and ether.

In 1798 Humphrey Davy was appointed chemical superintendent of the Pneumatic Institution to investigate the medical potential of various gases. One of which was nitrous oxide, which had been invented a few years earlier. A "scene" developed that included the Romantic poet and author of *Kubla Khan*, Samuel Taylor Coleridge.

It wasn't until the 1840s however that nitrous oxide, at roughly the same time as ether, began its still ongoing career as a surgical anesthetic. Both gasses were popular at parties in Europe and the United States from the 1850s on. Ether, nitrous oxide and their chemical cousins have been staples of anesthesia ever since.

William James who is described by Timothy Leary as the "Father of American psychology" tried nitrous oxide in 1882.

Although a champion of his own "pragmatism" philosophy James believed the religious experience was valid and that until these alternative states of consciousness were understood no system of thought was ready to "close its account with reality." He also tried chloral hydrate, amyl nitrate and in 1896 James tried peyote, then already popular among American Natives.

After the desecration of Eleusis psychedelics became the property of the occult, which literally means hidden, although there is evidence presented by Classicist Dr. Carl Ruck and others of psychedelic mushroom use by monks throughout the Christian era. However the official Church doctrine regarded the very notion of inducing visions as evil and consciousness generally as a dragon-infested inferno – best kept narrowly focused on "God."

But in 1897 Arthur Heffter, a German chemist, using both animal and self- experiments showed that mescaline was the alkaloid responsible for the profound psychoactive properties of peyote. At the same time as peyote religions emerged in North America and ibogaine religions in Africa the western scientific and cultural worlds would turn on as well.

One of the ways the brain communicates with itself is by chemical messengers called neurotransmitters. Psychoactive drugs are usually structurally similar to these naturally occurring compounds found in the brain.

There are classic indole psychedelic psychoactives that operate primarily on the neurotransmitter serotonin like LSD and psilocybin. Then there are those that operate primarily on noradrenalin like mescaline and MDMA. Then there are the dissociative psychedelics like ketamine, which operate mainly on glutamate, and finally there are the cholinergic psychedelics that operate on the neurotransmitter acetylcholine – an example being Amanita Muscaria, which are the mushrooms used by the Siberian shamans.

Serotonin based (indole)	Noradrenalin based	Glutamate based	Acetylcholine based
LSD, DMT, psilocybin, ibogaine.	mescaline, MDMA (ecstasy) MDA.	Ketamine.	Amanita Muscaria Belladonna Scopolamine.

The acetylcholine-based psychedelics are generally considered the most unpleasant, tending to produce symptoms of confusion reaching delirium, amnesia and physical debilitation. Interestingly there is ample evidence that the witches, for ritual and possibly medicinal purposes, used preparations of these substances as salves. It has even been suggested they may have used an ergot dildo – ergot being the basis for many psychedelic compounds. If the witches were really just European shamans they certainly needed a better publicist; the church's fear of witches and possibly women in general have left them demonized.

There are 138 species of mushrooms that contain psilocybin and they are distributed generously throughout the world, so it seems like poor form to use atropine and scopolamine, which are usually thought of as deliriants, when psilocybin is available. The secrets of these wizards were burned at the stake with them so we can only speculate.

One of the most common crimes during the Spanish Inquisition was possession of controlled substances, and just like today they could seize your property.

Certainly when they discovered peyote and other psychedelic drug use in Central America in the 1500s the Catholic Church's missionaries were appalled.

> "The use of the Herb or Root called peyote … is a superstitious action and reproved as opposed to the purity and sincerity of our Holy Catholic Faith, being so that this said herb, nor any other cannot possess the virtue and natural efficacy attributed to it for said effects nor to cause the images, phantasms and representations on which are founded said divinations, and that in these one sees notoriously the suggestion and assistance of the devil, author of this abuse."
> –Inquisitors against heresy, depravity and apostasy, Mexico City, 1620

For the Inquisitor it was easier to believe the devil was causing the effects rather than the plant itself.

Given the occult nature of psychedelic drug use throughout Europe it is difficult to assess its effect on culture. English Romantic poets like Shelley, Coleridge and Lord Byron were known to use opium-based libations like laudanum liberally but, before mescaline emerged, it is not clear what else, other than nitrous oxide and ether would have been available.

Although recent evidence shows Shakespeare's pipe contained cannabis the drug didn't reach mainstream European consciousness until 1798 when Napoleon invaded Egypt, where many members of the lower classes smoked hashish, which is a concentrated preparation of cannabis. While Napoleon forbade the practice many soldiers brought some back with them anyway. In 1840 Psychiatrist Dr. Jacques-Joseph Moreau began a study of the drug as a "model psychosis" and started the Hashish club, which included many of France's leading writers, poets and artists. Many books were published about the club and many of the writers used hashish as a plot device.

By the turn of the century the whole bohemian world of Europe knew of opium, cannabis, mescaline and cocaine (all legal) and of course artists have always sought their muse without deference to convention.

In 1919 chemist Ernst Spath created the first synthetic version of mescaline and the first wave of "laboratory" psychedelic research began with the first purified version of such a drug available.

Also in 1919 a new German Republic was born, known as the Weimar Republic because the constitution was written in that city. The following years would prove to be a renaissance comparable to the 1960s in California. German Kurt Beringer was the first scientist to systematically explore the mescaline state – in 1927 he published *Der Meskalin-Rausch* (The mescaline Inebriation) detailing 60 experiments among doctors, medical students, natural scientists and philosophers.

His group published hundreds more papers on peyote, cannabis, opiates, ayahuasca and cocaine. Beringer believed that mescaline produced a psychotic state and was primarily interested in the drug's ability to facilitate closed-eyed imagery – integrating such an experience with psychotherapy seems to have never occurred to him. Despite not promoting the drug or even exploring its healing potential at all psychedelic researcher Dr. Charles Grob observed:

> A dispute anticipating the virulent controversies of the 1960s ensued, however, pitting proponents of this new model of consciousness exploration against those who questioned the propriety of their colleagues enthusiasm for self – experimentation and penchant for sweeping proclamations. The history of hallucinogen research in the 20th century has revoled around this regrettable polarization, and as such has impeded the evolution of the field.

In the same year that *The Mescaline Inebriation* was published, Nobel Laureate Herman Hesse released his novel *Steppenwolf,* considered a classic of psychedelic literature. Timothy Leary developed the novel into a "psychedelic celebration" theater performance, feature film and accompanying record.

Although some scholars disagree it seems highly probable that Hesse would have tried mescaline.

In the novel the main character Harry Haller is going through a mid-life crisis and is on the brink of suicide. He meets Hermine who leads him through the jazz-filled nightlife and eventually meets him at the "Magic Theater – price of admission – your mind."

Haller is blasted through a psychedelic experience and realizes the simple inner duality of a feral (wild) Steppenwolf and a civilized man that had obsessed him, is merely an illusion and he gains access to the multiplicity of possible selves within.

The Nazis and the Americans continued to experiment with mescaline during World War II apparently without much to report. It was immediately after the war had ended however when the Central Intelligence Agency (CIA) was formed that the newly minted organization began investigating any and all psychoactive drugs. In fact the CIA provided the majority of funding for the early psychedelic research in the United States in the 1950s.

Some American jazz musicians including Louis Armstrong and later the beat poets used marijuana and at least in the case of the beats every other drug available. In the mid 1940s American comedian Lord Buckley started the Church of the Living Swing, which celebrated mescaline as its sacrament. By the mid- sixties the issue was ready to leave the circle of scientists and artists and emerge into mainstream consciousness to become the primary issue of the culture wars to follow.

Chapter Five

Brainwashing 101

"The terror exhibited...is electrifying to watch. The body becomes increasingly tense and rigid; the eyes widen and the pupils dilate, while the skin becomes covered with a fine perspiration. The intensity of the emotion becomes more than they can bear; and frequently at the height of the reaction, there is a collapse and the patient falls back in the bed and remains quiet for a few minutes..."

In the preceding examples of psychedelic religion and indigenous shamanic rituals what takes place could be considered brainwashing. That is the identities, beliefs and realities are to an extent removed and replaced with new ones. If the hardware is the brain and the software the mind, brainwashing could be considered a change in operating system.

Even if one grows up in a psychedelic culture like Amazonian Indians or classical Greeks, when the initiation happens no mere words can prepare the psyche for what it faces.

In 1957 British psychiatrist William Sargant published *Battle for the Mind* concerning religious and political conversions and his work using drugs to facilitate the abreaction or re-living of battle trauma and thus heal, cure or treat the symptoms of what would now be considered Post-Traumatic Stress Disorder (PTSD).

Using the work of Nobel Prize winner Ivan Pavlov (1849-1936) as his starting point Sargant created a mechanistic system to explain brainwashing whereby old patterns are replaced with new ones and stress is the secret ingredient. Pavlov was a very diligent scientist and although his explanations for his findings were criticized as reductionist and simplistic, the findings themselves were replicated and are considered bona fide to this day.

To discover the principles of classical conditioning Pavlov rang a bell before feeding the dogs each time until the sound of the bell alone caused the dog to salivate in anticipation of food. He would then measure the salivation and see if and how he could change the dog's conditioning. The best method he discovered for reversing the conditioning was stress. During a flood in Leningrad many of the dogs were killed, which may have lead him to this method – after the flood the conditioning that had been created over the preceding months was virtually extinguished.

Pavlov categorized the dogs according to four inborn temperaments based on the 5th Century BCE physician Hippocrates' choleric, sanguine, phlegmatic and melancholic typology. Similarly, in traditional Indian medicine or Ayurveda there are three doshas or constitutional types – Vatha(air), Pitta(fire), Kapha(earth) and medical science proposes ectomorph, endomorph and mesomorph as basic metabolic types. In other words different animals have different temperaments and respond to stressors differently.

Pavlov differentiated the strong excitatory or choleric type from the more stable weak excitatory (lively) or sanguine type. These dogs responded to stress with increased arousal (anabolic), the choleric reacting more strongly than the sanguine. Conversely some dogs he categorized as weak inhibitory or melancholic or strong inhibitory or phlegmatic. These animals would respond to stressors in the opposite way with decreased arousal (catabolic). Pavlov found the sanguine or weak excitatory and melancholic or weak inhibitory subjects could sustain more stress before having a "breakdown" and losing their conditioning than their more temperamental counterparts. Although all dogs would massively inhibit brain activity, eventually under enough stress the strong inhibitory or phlegmatic dogs would reach a state of total paralysis the quickest. The strong excitatory (choleric) dogs would require five to eight times as much sedative (lithium bromide) to calm them down compared to the strong inhibitory or phlegmatic dogs.

Pavlov	Strong Excitatory	Weak Excitatory (lively)	Weak Inhibitory	Strong Inhibitory
Hippocrates	Choleric	Sanguine	Melancholic	Phlegmatic
Response to Stress	highest increased arousal	increased arousal	reduced arousal	highest reduced arousal

As the stressors were increased Pavlov documented three distinct phases of "trans-marginal inhibition" or brain protecting activity. The first is the equivalent phase where all stimuli whether important or trivial evoke similar responses, this first stage is familiar to many people who have experienced extreme stress and fatigue. As stress continues the paradoxical phase occurs next when strong stimuli evoke weak responses and weak stimuli evoke strong responses, this is because the strong stimuli are protectively inhibited while the weak ones are not. Finally an ultra-paradoxical phase emerges where conditioning is often totally reversed – a dog may attack its beloved owner or become attached to a laboratory attendant it had previously hated. Finally if the stress continues "terminal exhaustion supervenes."

Long before the stress reaches the levels required to induce "trans-marginal inhibition" as the hysteria increases so does the suggestibility. For instance in *Battle for the Mind* Sargant describes how during WWI in Britain people believed Russian soldiers were marching through England with snow still on there boots – a geographic impossibility. Preachers, salesmen, politicians and rock stars have known for a long time that as affective (adrenalin – noradrenalin) arousal goes up so does their chance of reaching people. This kind of hyper-suggestability may be part of the reason for the brain's self-inhibition systems.

TRANSMARGINAL INHIBITION

Stress Level	High	Higher	Higher	Higher	Highest
Response	hysteria and hyper-suggestibility	both strong and weak stimuli evoke the same response "Equivalent phase"	paradoxical reaction – strong responses inhibited but weak stimuli evoke strong responses	ultra- paradoxical Conditioning often reversed	"transmarginal inhibition and terminal exhaustion supervenes" brain ready for reprogramming

Drugs, electric shock and insulin coma were all used to induce sufficient stress on the brains of psychiatric patients that a terminal state of stupor supervened and the old neurotic mind could be erased and a new healthier one either emerged organically or was "implanted" by the therapists.

William Sargant and others working with the CIA applied these techniques to psychiatric patients, without their consent, with disastrous consequences. While psychedelic therapy seeks to strengthen the ghost in the shell or ego and help the master meta-programmer integrate as much as possible, these Eisenhower-era brainwashers wanted to capture spies, effectively erase their minds and then replace them with ones designed by the CIA. The poor souls suffering from anxiety and depression that wandered into the clinics were the guinea pigs.

First they were to be "de-patterned," which would involve a drug-induced sleep coma that would go on for months interrupted by Electric Convulsive Therapy (ECT) which they would often not even remember receiving. With Montreal's Dr. Ewan Cameron's treatment this was then followed by "psychic driving" where new patterns were implanted with the use of LSD, methamphetamine and tape- recorded messages that would loop for days. Similar projects occurred in Australia and England but only the Montreal program was the subject of a massive lawsuit that resulted in the CIA paying out millions to the victims.

Dr. Sargant never tried on himself any of the techniques he describes in *Battle for the Mind*, including voodoo and other religious ceremonies, ECT, or any of the drugs he gives to other people. Perhaps if he had he would have had more insight.

It should be noted here that in 1966 virtually all LSD research was terminated in the U.S. *except* the military mind control experiments. In other words it was only legal to use LSD as a weapon while LSD for spiritual, medical or other scientific purposes was forbidden except for a handful of projects that survived the pogrom.

Despite Sargant's later work with military intelligence his work on WWII battle trauma was much more humane and is closely linked to the contemporary work involving MDMA and PTSD. By 1940 barbiturates were being used in low doses chronically to dampen anxiety and high doses to facilitate abreaction, or the reliving of traumatic episodes.

Freud said that "affectless memories, memories without any release of emotion" had little or no therapeutic value. Even if recalled episodically, a traumatic memory without the terror and rage that accompanied it would not produce a cure. Thus Freud believed that even well-remembered trauma could be responsible for neurosis.

The objective according to Sargant was to excite/stress the brain through the protective phases of trans-marginal inhibition until "terminal exhaustion supervened" and they were cured.

As long ago as WWI, hypnosis and barbiturates were being used to relive combat trauma, a departure from the standard use, which was simply inducing a state of suggestibility and then implanting the desired suggestions. At the recommendation of a colleague Sargant started using ether as a superior abreactive alternative to barbiturates.

> In most cases, ether released a far greater degree of explosive excitement … sudden states of collapse, after emotional outburst induced by ether, were far more frequent than those induced by hypnosis or barbiturate. Often they would wake up and report themselves cured, the images no longer provoked the terror and they would be discharged from hospital.
>
> A soldier in his twenties had been admitted to an aid post on the Normandy beachhead, weeping, speechless, and paralyzed. Proving unresponsive to a fortnight's sedation treatment he was evacuated to England. At this stage an intravenous barbiturate was administered and he was asked to describe what happened…. He described being under mortar fire for eight days when he was ordered to attack. He then became increasingly nervous, and began to tremble and shake. Several men were killed around him whereupon he lost his voice, burst into tears and became partially paralyzed. But the barbiturates induced very little emotion as he gave his recital, and no change was observed…
>
> That afternoon, however, he was given another abreaction, and this time ether was used instead of a barbiturate. He told the story this time with far greater emotion, and at last became confused and exhausted…. When he came to and rose from the couch, he smiled for the first time and looked relieved. A few minutes later he said most of his troubles had gone away with the ether."

The most important feature of a successful abreaction was not the *accuracy* of the reliving but the emotional intensity evoked – therefore the heightened suggestibility could be exploited and events described that never even happened. As long as the subject was sufficiently excited to the point of exhaustion the abreaction was considered successful.

Two American psychiatrists, Drs. Grinker and Spiegel, described abreaction even more provocatively.

> The terror exhibited … is electrifying to watch. The body becomes increasingly tense and rigid; the eyes widen and the pupils dilate, while the skin becomes covered with a fine perspiration. The intensity of the emotion becomes more than they can bear; and frequently at the height of the reaction, there is a collapse and the patient falls back in the bed and remains quiet for a few minutes…

Sargant goes on to describe the exploitation of these techniques to produce religious and political brainwashing conversions by groups such as 18th Century English Methodists and cold war Chinese Communists. Curiously given that LSD research had been ongoing for almost ten years when *Battle for the Mind* was published Sargant only mentions the psychedelic drugs in passing regarding their capacity to encourage mystic states as reported by Aldous Huxley.

Dr. Carl Anderson at Harvard looked at the brain's electrical activity during rapid eye movement (R.E.M.) dream-states, under the influence of the psychedelic drug ibogaine, and in sufferers of trauma. The hemispheres of the brain in trauma survivors show greater difference in electrical activity between them compared to normal control subjects. During REM sleep and ibogaine use, the relationship with the old "feeling" brain and the newer "thinking" hemispheres enters a state of dynamic functional plasticity where, "re-wiring" may be possible. *Dreaming* and not just sleeping have been found to be important in learning, memory consolidation and emotional health. Trauma survivors show less R.E.M. sleep limiting their access to this unconscious resource. Anderson also compared the hemispheric asymmetries of trauma survivors before and after ibogaine psychedelic therapy and reported encouraging results; ibogaine and other psychedelics are sometimes referred to as *oneiric* or dream inducing drugs.

Terrence McKenna offers the analogy of the hydrofoil, a tiny metal plate placed at the end of boats and planes to improve aerodynamics that vibrates at an ever- increasing rate the faster the craft accelerates, up to a threshold or self-organizing critical state (SOC), after which the vibration nearly stops. Psychedelics may induce such a chaotic state of acceleration and intensification, similar to dreaming, but awake and ideally at the side of a shaman.

Whether it's the battle-scarred WWII soldiers or the trauma survivors in Dr. Anderson's research, opening up the relationship between the old and new brains and between the left and right hemispheres isn't enough – it seems the whole network has to be driven harder through the chaos. The subject's neurons must be stimulated to a critical threshold of stress and activation where the brain self-organizes (self-organizing critical state) and the ego can be "reborn."

When seeking the Holy Grail the Knights of the Round Table were instructed by King Arthur to go to the darkest part of the forest.

Chapter Six

A Brief History of Trauma

"Insufficient emotional and motor reaction by a patient to an original traumatic event results in "jamming" of the effect: the strangulated emotions later provide energy for neurotic symptoms." – Freud

Three kinds of developmental trauma are known to be pathogenic (causing illness) sexual abuse, physical abuse and vital neglect. In 1896 Freud published a paper entitled *The Aetiogoly of Hysteria*, which documented 12 patients who had repressed trauma of sexual abuse occurring before age ten. Their hysteria emerged often in puberty when a relatively minor experience would trigger symptoms. He helped them to abreact (re-live) their trauma and reported cures.

He later recanted and speculated these traumas were in fact fantasies confabulated (invented) through wish fulfillment during the difficult periods of childhood psychosexual development. Carl Jung also believed that many of the traumas reported by his patients were merely symbolic. Conversely, contemporary Pierre Janet agreed with Freud's initial thesis and carried on abreacting trauma in his neurotic patients until the end of his career.

The modern bible of trauma is *Trauma and Recovery* by Dr. Judith Herman – her treatment employs alternating individual and group psychotherapy with an objective of metabolizing the trauma through "remembrance and mourning."

The traumatic material must be worked through in all of the following examples, however some modern clinicians reject this notion as barbaric and cruelly forcing a victim into being constantly re-traumatized, pharmacological management of symptoms, usually considered necessary for life, is considered the best course.

While almost everyone else agrees on the need to metabolize the trauma heated debates rage over how this should be done. Many other theoretically linked types of psychotherapy for trauma have evolved – holotropic breathwork, rebirthing and primal scream are other examples of non-drug experiential psychotherapies. In Self Regulation Therapy ab-reaction and catharsis are considered dangerous and counterproductive. Instead the goal of therapy is a gradual process of activation and release while maintaining a grounded sense of self and not "over-doing it."

Stages of Recovery

Syndrome	Stage 1	Stage 2	Stage 3
Hysteria (Janet 1889)	Stabilization, symptom-oriented treatment	Exploration of traumatic memories	Personality reintegration, rehabilitation
Combat trauma (Scurfield 1985)	Trust, stressman-agement, education	Re-experiencing trauma	Integration of trauma
Complicated post-traumatic stress disorder (Brown & Fromm 1986)	Stabilization	Integration of memories	Development of self, drive integration
Multiple personality disorder (Putnam 1989)	Diagnosis, stabilization, communication, co-operation	Metabolism of trauma	Resolution, integration
Traumatic disorders (Herman 1992)	Safety	Remembrance and mourning	Reconnection

It is estimated that 5%-15% of boys and 15%-25% of girls experience some form of sexual abuse before they reach 18, and one American study places physical abuse of boys at 30% and girls at 20%. Child abuse in the form of neglect occurs in 20%-30%. Many suffer all three forms of abuse but sufferers of at least one make up at least a third of the population. Of these it is estimated that 50%-60% will suffer some form of psychopathology (over one billion worldwide). Similar to Pavlov's estimate of half the population of dogs being more vulnerable than the other half.

> "I had given them the solution to a more than 1,000 year-old neuro-logical problem – a cuput nili." [the source of the Nile. (i.e.; the true origin of a thing)]
>
> –Sigmund Freud

There is a great difference between trauma occurring in adulthood ver-sus childhood or developmental trauma. Researchers have even proved surviving abuse changes the body at the level of DNA. To use the tortured computer analogy for the human brain, developmental trauma represents dysfunction in the operating system. On January 1, 1966 there were as many as 210 independent investigative teams working with LSD in the United States alone, by the end of that year there were six remaining. If you are unlucky enough to be in the roughly one-third of the populace subjected to developmental trauma (particularly the half of whom suffer psychopathology as a result) this fact represents a catastrophe.

When traumatized, animals react in one of three ways or in combination, fight, flight and freeze. Dr. Peter Levine, who created Self Regulation Therapy, quotes emergency room medics as saying, "as they go in, so they go out." If a patient enters surgery panicked and, in Levine's terminology "activated" then when the anesthetic wears off, they will revert to a similar state. Freezing is the brain's own version of anesthetic – Pavlov called it trans-marginal inhibition – it is adaptive in the short term, but prevents the fight or flight from working through the body and being integrated into the brain.

Going back a hundred years from Levine, Freud and his less famous colleague Breuer proposed a similar phenomenon. "Insufficient emotional and motor reaction by a patient to an original traumatic event results in "jamming" of the effect: the strangulated emotions later provide energy for neurotic symptoms."

One complex issue with trauma is recovered memories – this is where a survivor dissociates enough to repress the traumatic memory completely but recalls it later. Even well-adjusted adults exposed to natural disasters like earthquakes can have total amnesia of the event for a few weeks after, so the general legitimacy of recovered memories is not in question. Some experts estimate about 10% of trauma survivors demonstrate total amnesia and one study looked at documented cases of child abuse and noted a third of subjects had repressed the memory completely for long periods. However, fierce controversy arose when Freud published his 1896 paper discussing the abreaction of traumatic childhood sexual memories and then again, almost a hundred years later in the 1980s, when therapists began capitalizing on public hysteria.

Often patients would come in with vague complaints like depression and therapists would hypnotize them, regress them to an earlier age when they would discover a buried memory that they could relate to their adult symptoms. Some of these memories were apparently false and many accusers later became retractors and a few therapists were successfully sued for large settlements.

It's not just physical/sexual abuse and neglect that traumatize us; emotional abuse, accidents, surgeries and the death of a loved one during development can all leave a deep emotional and physical wound in need of healing. But there is one trauma that is universal and metabolizing this trauma will take some stronger medicine than sedatives or suggestion.

During WWII barbiturates and ether were used to un-jam or unfreeze the nervous energy jammed from trauma, but in 1947 work would begin on a substance whose cathartic or abreactive properties were perhaps its least astonishing.

Chapter Seven

Continuity and Theoretical Convergence

Just as psychopathology can be related to unresolved experiences after birth, re-experiencing birth itself produced therapeutic breakthroughs like nothing he had ever witnessed after the more superficial biographical sequences.

B
ut before we start tripping we have to lay a bit more foundation. In addition to formulating and testing hypotheses scientists also must consider how new ideas relate to the old ones (continuity) and the other new ones (theoretical convergence) in theirs and related fields. Psychedelics entered at a time of Freudian dominance where most of the problems of the mind were understood as being symbolic in nature and related to childhood trauma and fantasy. From this extreme the pendulum has swung back to the dynamic opposite where the problems of the mind are reduced to abnormal stress responses with linear chemical aberrations as though sufferers had underactive prozac glands.

The early importance Freud applied to the emotionally charged abreaction (re- living) of trauma was replaced by a detached intellectual analysis of dreams and free association, but when LSD emerged its stunning efficiency revived the early psychoanalytic foundation. Another idea from psychoanalysis that was much less controversial than abreaction was the value of transference or analyzing what the client transfers from their feelings towards others, usually parents, and projects onto the therapist. Freudian trained LSD therapists tended towards *psycholytic therapy* where small doses are administered more frequently, this mode fit the psychoanalyst's expectations much better than the massive dose sessions at Hollywood Hospital.

The bridge between the psychodynamic perspective, which by the early sixties was receding quickly, and the biochemical perspective, seemed to be psychedelic drugs until about 1964. After that much of the mainstream psychiatric enthusiasm for the strange visionary adventures and ordeals that characterize this kind of therapy waned.

In the late nineteenth century barbiturate tranquilizers (downers) and amphetamine stimulants (uppers) were introduced that allowed crude manipulation of the brain. However, when LSD was at its peak of credibility new tranquilizers called benzodiazepines (valium), the tricyclic (referring to chemical structure) antidepressants (imipramine) and antipsychotics called phenothiazines (thorazine) all emerged and a new age of psychiatric treatment began. Instead of trying to shock the system into a spontaneous healing the focus became modifying the brain with drugs to alleviate specific symptoms. After all, if they already had these effective drugs currently, why bother with "religio-mystico" nonsense when the pharmaceutical future seemed so bright. Unfortunately, other than prozac, progress has been limited in the hunt for better drugs, with an increasing proportion of pharmaceutical profits invested in lobbying and marketing instead of research.

Psychedelic researcher Dr. Stan Grof invented *Holotropic Breathwork* in the seventies. In this treatment clients are divided into pairs – one sitter and one "breather" who is encouraged to "over-breathe" as much as possible while provocative music plays and, if appropriate, bodywork employed. Not surprisingly coming from the Godfather of LSD this system converges perfectly with the principles applied at Hollywood Hospital. Techniques of rebirthing, primal scream and other experiential psychotherapies overlap as well. While all non-drug these methods do use non-ordinary states of consciousness for healing.

Conversely however, Heilkunst homeopathy, Self Regulation Therapy (SRT) and the Scientology precursor Dianetics do not emphasize non-ordinary states of consciousness and are generally opposed to any drug use; yet they all seem to overlap with the adventures at Hollywood Sanitarium as well.

In *Heilkunst Homeopathy* the body, each with its own constitution or type, is seen as a repository of trauma. Therapy involves identifying each trauma and preparing a remedy to create an "identical energetic vibrational frequency." The principle is that if the vibration of the remedy is identical to the vibration of the body because like cures like, healing occurs, but the process can be very difficult to work through. One client related a story of taking a remedy for his LSD use from twenty years prior and tripping again. The Heilkunst process is easier in the case of vaccines or other chemical assaults (LSD included) but the theory is also applied to disease, surgery, accidents or abuse, and remedies are prepared to match these as well. Obviously suggestion could play a huge role in this process but the results achieved are encouraging.

Before creating the religion of Scientology in 1952, founder L. Ron Hubbard created a system of psychology called Dianetics in 1950 that also resonates with psychedelic therapy. *Dianetics: The Science of Mental Health* outlined Hubbard's philosophy of two minds – the reactive and the analytical. The analytical mind is perfectly rational while the reactive mind is composed of unprocessed traumas, which Hubbard called *engrams,* a term borrowed from neurosurgeon Dr. Wilder Penfield who used it to refer to a specific memory encoded in a neuron. From conception on any unprocessed traumatic experience resides in the reactive side and environmental triggers can "restimulate" the engram and undermine the analytic mind.

As one website describes it, "The goal of Dianetics is to re-file these memories, called Engrams, into the Analytical mind, where they can be properly indexed and utilized. The Reactive mind is an evolutionary throwback to how animals think, and is therefore a weaker area of the mind in the human."

Hubbard began using the "e-meter" or galvanometer, a device invented in the 1880s and employed similarly by Carl Jung fifty years before, that directs a weak electric current through the body and measures the intensity of the signal after passing through. Basic physiological arousal changes the body's conduction of electricity and Dianetic *auditors* ask subjects questions, recording the e-meter response and seeking engrams in the reactive mind, which they then process until the e-meter response changes. Writer William S. Burroughs said, "A half-hour on the cans (e-meter) was worth a couple of years of psychoanalysis."

Once the reactive mind's engrams have been processed by the analytic mind the subject is declared "clear." Scientology then takes the clear through the next levels of spiritual development. Considered a dangerous cult by many and accused of championing a bizarre mythology quite distinct from the exquisite simplicity of Dianetics, Scientology continues to provoke controversy around the world.

> "Where do you feel that in your body?" My SRT counselor asks.
> "On the right side of my abdomen."
> "How does it feel on the left side?" "Fine."
> "Go into the left side then and feel how good it feels. Notice the support of the chair and then if it's all right go back into the right side and see if it feels hot or cold, if it moves, try to feel the boundary between where it starts and ends, and then go back into the left side and notice the support of the chair."

In Self Regulation Therapy this is the process through which traumatic responses are activated and released through discharge, sometimes tremors or yawns and sometimes through visualizations often suggested by the therapist. Gradually the energy is worked through and the client heals and integrates the entire trauma into a new stable identity.

Similarly in Kundalini Yoga, where an energetic force coiled in the base of the spine is aroused to rise through to the top of the head, a process of "kriyas" sometimes accompanies the serpent coil's ascent. As the Kundalini website adishakti.org describes it,

> Thus as intense energy moves through the body and clears out physiological blocks, a person may experience intense involuntary, jerking movements of the body, including shaking, vibrations, spasm and contraction. As deeply held armoring and blockages to the smooth flow of energy are released, the person may re-access memories and emotions associated with past trauma or injury.

In the effort to stimulate repressed energy and then discharge it to the periphery psychedelic drugs are many orders of magnitude more powerful than all these methods combined. To use the analogy of energy SRT, Heilkunst homeopathy, Dianetics and even Kundalini Yoga are comparable to hydroelectric dams or fossil-fuel burning electrical plants; psychedelics are nuclear fission.

Chapter Eight

The Fifth Wave:
Stan Grof the GodFather of LSD

"Feeling an emotion through to completion is its funeral pyre."
–Stan Grof

LSD's psychoactivity was discovered when Sandoz research chemist Dr. Albert Hofmann accidentally or serendipitously absorbed some into his skin while synthesizing it. The first model of the drug's action was labeled psychotomimetic, meaning it induced a temporary madness (crazy pills). Effective in doses as small as a twentieth of a milligram, it was thought schizophrenics might produce a similar compound that caused their illness. No such compound has yet been discovered but this model encouraged mental health professionals to try LSD so they could better relate to their patients. Phenomenologically, however, the LSD state is quite distinct from organic psychosis, which is actually a rather vague term meaning simply mental disease of unknown origin characterized by hallucinations and delusions. Chemotherapy with LSD where patients received daily increasing doses produced inconclusive or negative results as well.

Schizophrenic psychotic episodes often follow a predictable course with a climax that often involves sequences of total destruction and death and rebirth – after which the prognosis is actually quite good. Mental illness in general is often regarded as episodic with each episode having a beginning, middle and end. Electric Convulsive Therapy (ECT) is believed by some to accelerate the episode through its natural trajectory more quickly. Italian Psychiatrists Drs. Jost and Vicari gave patients LSD and when their symptoms worsened used ECT to accelerate the disease's progress, reporting some success. But it was primarily LSD's capacity to produce abreaction or reliving of trauma that began a scientific renaissance with thousands of papers and a hundred medical textbooks published.

By the 1950s many psychiatrists were using LSD as an aid in psychotherapy. Research projects were established in Australia, Japan, Mexico, Argentina, Chile, Canada, all through Europe and especially Great Britain, The United States and Prague, Czechoslovakia the home of the man who would become in the words of pioneering chemist Albert Hofmann, "the Godfather of LSD."

When Stanislav Grof started working with the research chemical in 1956 he was a classically trained psychoanalyst, raised in a non-religious family living in an atheistic Marxist country. In addition to LSD they were working on brainwave entraining where pulses of sound and light are used to change brain activity. A stroboscope was employed at Hollywood Hospital before drug sessions to prime the brain for visualization.

A few hours into his first trip, his colleague turned on the strobe machine and Stanislav Grof was catapulted out of his body into the realm of what he describes as "cosmic consciousness." The research program called for the serial administration of LSD to patients representing all psychiatric diagnostic categories. By the time he left for the U.S. in 1967 eleven years later, he ran a seventeen-bed locked ward all dedicated to LSD therapy.

After leaving psychedelic research in the early 1970s he analyzed 5,000 records from LSD sessions and couldn't find one symptom common to all of them. His conclusion was that LSD was a "catalyst" or "a non-specific amplifier of psychic dynamics." Using eyeshades and headphones playing carefully selected instrumental music he believes the drug operates as an "inner-radar" freeing the mind to gravitate to its area of "highest emotional charge." It is the role of the therapist to encourage the complete experience, expression and integration of whatever material emerges.

Grof divided the phenomena of LSD experiences into four broad categories. The first was sensory, a period at the beginning of the session where there is some shift in one or another perceptual modality, usually visual. He describes this as the "sensory barrier" and regards it as the gateway to the unconscious.

The next three levels in Grof's map are the biographical, perinatal and transpersonal unconscious. Analysis of transference (the projections from the patient onto the therapists, usually of their parents) and abreaction of trauma were at this time considered valid therapeutic approaches, both of which the biographical level includes. Transference usually takes place at the biographical level and these exchanges can be emotionally corrective if handled properly. If the phenomenology of LSD were limited to the personal history level of abreaction and transference LSD would be an indispensible part of psychiatry today.

However the second two realms of the unconscious he proposed would create a schism in psychology and psychiatry that he compares to the revolution in physics when scientists began to formulate quantum theory.

In Dr. Grof's cartography (map) the biographical level is organized into COEX systems or systems of condensed experience. COEX systems are often organized according to affective or emotional themes like shame, fear or joy. A traumatic COEX system would call for an abreaction where subjects relive the event. What's unique about psychedelic drugs compared to other methods of abreaction is the capacity of the subject to retain their adult consciousness either simultaneously with the relived memory or in an alternating fashion.

Grof did find verification for Freud's notion of blockages at various levels of libidinal or "life-energy" development through the oral, anal, phallic, latency and genital phases. Regarding trauma generally Grof proposes the earlier the abuse and the closer relative the abuser is the worse the psychopathology.

In Europe a method called psycholytic therapy was developed where low doses (25 to 100 mcg) were used often over dozens of administrations and generally by Freudian trained therapists. If experiences beyond the realm of the psychodynamic occurred they were considered defensive against the real pain that was causing their neurosis.

With Dr. Grof's approach he noticed that even after abreacting obviously pathogenic experiences sometimes patients would get even worse and so he continued to administer the drug, assuming there were more traumata to uncover and "discharge the energy to the periphery" or "exteriorize." What he found instead was the simple narrative of life being overwhelmed by experiences so elemental they were clearly not related to developmental phases, transference or even abuse or surgeries.

Grof noted that as he administered the drug to patients over and over again they eventually manifested (although often in a non-linear way) the three clinical phases of birth and the period before in the womb. He labeled this second level of the unconscious *perinatal* or around-birth. Just as psychopathology can be related to unresolved experiences after birth, re-experiencing birth itself produced therapeutic breakthroughs like nothing he had ever witnessed after the more superficial biographical sequences.

Grof labeled these phases the basic perinatal matrices or BPMs. The first or BPM I is before the birth process begins when the fetus is in symbiotic union with the maternal organism. Typical features of Basic Perinatal Matrix I are oceanic ecstasy, cosmic unity and visions of paradise. However there can be negative aspects to this BPM as well if the mother was unsure about the pregnancy, under stress or ingesting noxious chemicals.

In addition to energy blockages in the form of unprocessed traumatic experiences being located in the biographical unconscious the same is true for the perinatal.

The key differences between the biographical and perinatal unconscious are to some extent the content of the subject's experience, but mostly the intensity of the affect associated with it. In Self Regulation Therapy there is a distinction made between sadness and anger versus rage and despair and this could describe the difference between the biographical and perinatal unconscious. When an energy blockage, whether located in the biographical, perinatal or transpersonal unconscious is triggered and activated into consciousness Grof describes it as a *governing system* and what we resist persists.

Due to the greater intensity of the perinatal unconscious, activation of the Basic Perinatal Matrices (BPMs) produces much more severe symptoms. If a subject had a governing system activated during a session but not resolved or integrated they will return to normal consciousness under its influence. Patients would some times move through different diagnostic categories, sometimes getting "better" and sometimes getting "worse."

BPM I, although primarily a positive range of experiences, he links to certain symptoms of schizophrenia, hypochondriasis and an inability to distinguish daydreams from reality. Being a classically trained Freudian psychiatrist he also related the BPMs to the Freudian erotogenic zones or phases of libidinal (life-energy) development. BPM 1 is consistent with feelings of total satisfaction in all zones, ecstasy of rocking and nursing or the experience of oral, anal, phallic and genital satisfaction.

The affective or emotional themes of the basic perinatal matrices are consistent with the biographical unconscious. For example a relived memory of a happy childhood moment with friends and pets could intensify into BPM I. Other memories from "postnatal" life associated with this matrix are "fulfilling love relationships, romances, trips or vacations in nature, exposure to great art and swimming in lakes or oceans."

Basic Perinatal Matrix II (BPM II) is based on the first phase of clinical birth where the oceanic bliss of the womb is destroyed by fierce muscular contractions and noxious chemicals intended to squeeze the baby out. The cervix has not yet opened and the situation to the fetus seems utterly hopeless.

Psychopathology related to BPM II includes other symptoms of schizophrenia, severe inhibited depressions, irrational inferiority and guilt feelings, hypochondriasis, alcohol and other drug addictions. BPM II is similar to oral frustration, retention of feces and/or urine, sexual frustration and experiences of cold and other forms of pain in terms of the Freudian erotogenic zones.

Postnatal experiences of war, accidents, injuries, near-drowning, physical abuse, severe psychological trauma such as emotional isolation, rejection, oppressive family atmosphere with ridicule and humiliation are also thematically related.

LSD subjects may experience immense physical suffering where relief is impossible, Hell, no-exit, agonizing guilt and inferiority, apocalyptic perspective, living in a meaningless cardboard world, oppression, compression, cardiac distress, sweating and difficulty breathing.

Basic Perinatal Matrix III represents the second phase of clinical birth where the pressure of the womb is sustained but the cervix begins to open and the fetus, in a state of biological frenzy, begins their final struggle to be born.

BPM III represents an obvious affective shift (passive to aggressive) from the preceding phase. People with governing systems from this matrix suffer from yet another set of schizophrenic symptoms, agitated depressions, sexual deviations, asthma, tics, stammering, conversion (psychosomatic) disorders and anxiety, frigidity and impotence, migraine headache, psoriasis and ulcers. Related Freudian erotogenic zones feature chewing and swallowing food, defecation and urination, orgasm, phallic aggression and ballistic sports like gymnastics and skydiving.

Evoking this third perinatal matrix in life after birth are struggles, fights and adventures, air, sea and road dangers, orgies, childhood observations of adult sexuality (primal scene), seduction and rape and in females the birth of their children. Subjects may feel their suffering escalate to cosmic dimensions where the borderline between pain and pleasure explodes in volcanic ecstasy, brilliant colours, fireworks, sadomasochistic orgies, murder and human sacrifice, active fighting in wars, intense orgiastic feelings and scenes of harems or carnivals, suffocation, muscular tension and discharge in tremors and twitches (similar to SRT), nausea and vomiting.

Suicide is often divided into types one and two with one being violent like a shotgun wound to the head and two being passive like overdosing on pills or carbon monoxide poisoning. The first active type is associated with governing systems from BPM III and the second passive type from BPM II.

In light of these findings the term "bad trip" has no meaning whatsoever. Even if a subject is well adjusted, eventually these phenomena will occur and they're always bloody awful. As one neuronaut described it "the worst feeling in the world."

Psychopathology may represent the energy blockage and non-integrated material itself or it may represent what Freud might have called a "reaction- formation" in response. For instance, while the third perinatal matrix features tremendous sexual arousal and aggression, people repressing this BPM may suffer from frigidity or impotence.

Finally comes the moment of rebirth. Grof labeled this Basic Perinatal Matrix IV and a well-integrated transmodulation from three to four is perhaps the best possible result in psychedelic therapy. However, another set of schizophrenic symptoms is associated with this matrix, along with mania and exhibitionism.

Satiation of thirst, hunger, libidinal feelings after defecation, urination, orgasm or in females the delivery of their children are other BPM IV manifestations.

Escape from extreme danger, surviving an accident or operation, overcoming obstacles with active effort and spectacular natural scenes are all associated memories from life. Subjects may feel enormous decompression, expansion of space, visions of gigantic halls, radiant light, and beautiful colours, feelings of rebirth and redemption, sensory enhancement, brotherly feelings of charity and humanitarianism, sometimes manic and grandiose, "whistling in the dark" and possibly transitioning into elements of BPM I.

One of the problems in psychedelic therapy is counter-transference where the subject's experiences release similar unresolved dynamics in the therapists. In other words if the client is suffering through something similar to nonintegrated dynamics inside the therapist, the results may be counterproductive to say the least.

Dr. Gary Fisher was a psychologist who used LSD very successfully with mentally ill children who had become wards of the state. He eventually built a psychedelic team and if a client provoked something that needed to be worked through with a therapist, a session was scheduled right away. In the modern PTSD/MDMA model both the male and the female therapist are required to undergo drug sessions before working with clients.

The perinatal level of the unconscious is considered impossible by mainstream science because the brain is assumed not to be developed enough to encode memories. However historically accurate one's rebirth experience is, the fact of these incredibly intense shifts or, in Grof's lexicon *transmodulations*, that occur at many levels of consciousness under the influence of psychedelic drugs is established. In one study with death anxiety in the terminally ill a subject who normally would have been excluded because of her traumatic childhood was accepted due to her quick and uncomplicated birth, allowing easier access to the positive perinatal matrices.

The third and final level of the unconscious is even more controversial than the second. Transpersonal psychology is based on Jung's notion of the collective unconscious and Grof describes the common denominator of these experiences as the subject's intuition that he has left his ego and his body behind. Some subjects like Al Hubbard believe they have experienced their own conception or another life they believe to be a past life or even the consciousness of animals or cells. Sometimes people merge with another person or groups of people and experience reality as they do. They may become the planet or even the entire material universe. Extra sensory perception (ESP) falls into this category along with encounters with the dead and supra-human spiritual entities. Archetypal deities and demons along with the Kundalini rising and the chakras activating are also examples. Supracosmic and metacosmic void is what Grof describes as "the ultimate experience" where the empty fullness of all existence in infinite potential form is experienced, often in the presence of a "clear white light."

The organization of the transpersonal level of the unconscious is much looser than the perinatal and biographical. Fundamental elements of our way of being and knowing are so challenged by these experiences that organization and classification becomes a near impossibility.

The Unconcious

Sensory Barrier	Biographical	Perinatal	Transpersonal
closed eyed visuals or other distortions of the senses.	organized according to affectively charged events – abuse, surgeries, accidents – or affective themes like shame and called systems of condensed experiences (COEX).	Basic Perinatal Matrix BPM I – pre-birth – oceanic bliss BPM II – womb collapses – passive no exit BPM III – active life or death struggle down birth canal BPM IV – re-birth.	past-lives, identifying with animals, plants, archetypes – spiritual experiences, metacosmic void, clear white light, psychic phenomena.

Once a transmodulation in the perinatal realm occurs the relativity of reality itself is obvious. The notion that the different BPMs are all part of the same reality is astounding. Furthermore the fact of their transition from one to the other is even more shattering; as is the possibility of more than one governing system being active at a time.

People will unconsciously engineer their lives to be consistent with their governing system(s). For example, someone governed by the second perinatal matrix may do things to justify the guilt and shame they feel. Again, Dr. Grof describes one man who was struggling with BPM III and took a job testing parachutes. Needless to say once his material had been worked through he quit his job.

By using LSD and holotropic breathwork, a system of altered breathing patterns, evocative music and bodywork designed to induce functionally similar states – Grof has worked for over fifty years in the maelstrom of rapidly shifting realities – the most important thing seems to be the encouragement of whatever his patient experiences, even psychosis.

Sitters and set and setting are key concepts in Grof's model. Although appearing from the beginning in psychiatric research Leary popularized set and setting with *The Psychedelic Experience: A Manual Based on The Tibetan Book of the Dead* written in 1964 with Drs. Ralph Metzner and Richard Alpert. The term sitter is used rather than guide because the objective is the exteriorization and expression of the subject's inner voyage rather than being guided into an experience created by someone else. *Set and setting* were common terms in psychology in the 1950s. *Set* meaning what one brings to a situation – who they are and their frame of mind. Experiments were done on creativity where different sets or frames of mind were experimented with to measure their effects on problem solving. Another experiment measured a subject's attraction to a girl waiting on the other side of a high-altitude suspension bridge or on a street corner – different sets – same girl. (The subjects liked her more after the suspension bridge.)

Setting is the environment the person finds herself in, most importantly the other people present. Grof believes sitters to be an essential element of the setting because "a person taking a psychedelic drug alone cannot fully abandon control at the crucial moment of ego death." Few non-military psychedelic research projects used the uninitiated as sitters.

The model psychosis (crazy-pills) sets common in early experimentation were usually extremely unpleasant and often operated as self-fulfilling prophecy. Slipping acid into the food or punch bowl was another nasty set that Grof condemns, "It is obvious that under these circumstances LSD can have a profoundly disorganizing effect and precipitate acute uncontrollable panic and even psychotic decompensation." Before a CIA Christmas party in the fifties a memo went out addressing a rumor that some agents were planning on "spiking the punch-bowl" – this was strongly discouraged.

In order to improve the set careful preparation of clients was always provided. Assurances of the safety of the therapy were combined with warnings about the intensity of some of the potential experiences. Fear of physical dying and madness, entering a no-exit Hell and fear of becoming homosexual were all possibilities explored with clients. Keeping the eye-shades and headphones on with eyes closed was emphasized to encourage the continued internalization and integration of the process. Clients were further warned that their symptoms might worsen after some sessions. Grof describes a male and female therapeutic dyad as ideal and this seems to be the dominant model in contemporary research.

He distinguishes three phases to the psychedelic experience: preparation, culmination and termination. Therapists interact with the clients more during the preparation and termination portions but during the culmination period subjects are often totally silent and every thirty minutes checked in on. The main reason for this is to ensure the ideal choices with music.

Music was a very important part of the Hollywood Hospital project and psychedelic research generally. The evoking of emotion and the surrender of the ego were all facilitated by music. Instrumental music that didn't have cultural significance like *The Wedding March* was preferred. Grof believes "it is often possible to facilitate the emergence of a certain emotional quality such as aggression, sexual feelings, 'psychedelic breakthrough' or a transcendental experience with a specific choice of music."

As the drug begins to wear off, usually in the sixth-eighth hour, the termination period begins. This is "the most crucial part of the session" – the plasticity of the brain returns to the normal range where the generation of new governing systems is almost impossible. If a negative governing system remains active it will dominate the experiential field for the coming weeks. An especially disturbing example of this is the emergency admission of "psychedelic" drug users suffering psychotic decompensation and who are treated with benzodiazepine (valium) tranquilizers and admitted to psychiatric facilities. The psychotic symptoms are frozen and the necessary libidinal energy to discharge them is chemically suppressed. They could remain in that state until their death.

One technique Grof developed for the termination period is hyperventilation, which he would combine with pressure to any areas of the body where the subject felt "psychosomatic distress." This technique formed the foundation for Holotropic Breathwork, which Dr. Grof went on to develop after leaving the Maryland Psychiatric Research Center in 1973.

Exposure to water, preferably in a natural setting, is considered the ideal conclusion to the termination phase. After which a pre-arranged party takes place with just one lover or a few friends and relatives sharing a "psychedelic dinner."

Subjects would generally sleep overnight and if unresolved material emerged while falling asleep or waking up at least one sitter and a nurse would be prepared to help them work through the experience.

The next day subjects were encouraged to relax and remain meditative, possibly listening to the music played during the session. A long interview with the sitters, the subject writing a full session report and a Mandela painting or drawing was usually completed as well.

Poorly resolved sessions were treated with further hyperventilation and bodywork, dreams and the moments of waking and falling asleep are sometimes opportunities for integration as well. If this didn't result in adequate resolution a new psychedelic session was arranged as quickly as possible.

In Grof's model treatment can be terminated at any point when a positive dynamic governs or a negative one has been *fully* integrated. This is a more cost-effective approach but often leaves the underlying structures of the disorder untouched.

For instance a certain paraphilia or sexual disorder may easily dissipate with the resolution of some perinatal material, but the psyche remains vulnerable to depression because serious blockages exist in other unconscious matrices.

There is a key distinction between activation and blockage of unconscious dynamics. If there is a choice between material in terms of the perception of threat and danger, the ego will activate the less threatening while leaving the more dangerous blocked safely in the unconscious. For instance, recall the second matrix is when the womb collapses and the cervix is not open yet, in associated with depression, hopelessness and despair – not much fun but not as dangerous as the third matrix where the cervix opens and the biological survival fury begins. The ego is governed by BPM II, because the BPM III material is too dangerous to even explore.

The major risks of psychedelic drugs are not directly related to pharmacology but to the intensity of emotions they trigger. People with serious heart problems or pregnant women were excluded as candidates. Although some cases of epilepsy responded well to LSD, in others it precipitated severe seizures.

Dosages of between 25 and 2000 mcg have been used on patients aged up to 83, some with end-stage terminal cancer, without casualties. Grof did occasionally treat severely psychotic individuals in Prague but these required specially trained staff and a locked ward. However, the research protocol at Maryland Psychiatric Research Hospital was limited to three sessions and no long-term beds were available. Despite these limitations only two subjects had prolonged reactions (greater than 48 hours), both easily managed. Even the most emotionally healthy person will eventually have intensely difficult experiences.

Often this provokes the mobilization of defenses and the subject will refuse the eyes-shades and headphones and start talking or pacing. The evasive maneuvers they resorted to were usually reflected in their ego's day-to-day functioning. Sometimes subjects, in the middle of a high-dose session, would suddenly "sober up." Sitters must remain calm no matter how outrageous the client becomes. Grof personally supervised over three thousand sessions and only resorted to tranquilizers three times, all early in his career.

Experiences of death and rebirth represent the most crucial aspect of the culmination period and must be handled appropriately. Since the situation seems like authentic death to the client he or she may react as though facing actual biological termination. The client must be encouraged to let go and internalize and integrate the experience with eyeshades and headphones in place.

Providing that no one was in danger psychotic episodes were *encouraged,* including paranoia, which would almost always manifest eventually. Physical contact was sometimes considered appropriate but adult sexual behaviour always avoided. Sometimes sexual acting-out or aggression during a session may be a reaction to something deeper that the therapist can actively provide insight into. Problems surrounding urination and defecation, physical pain, breathing problems and nausea can be severe, especially during perinatal sequences.

Physical discharge creates potentially dangerous situations as well because subjects may experience violent movements to the point of seizure-like episodes that represent energy being released. Self Regulation

Therapy differentiates between activation and release, activation meaning general arousal and release its discharge, a third possibility – dissociation is considered detrimental. Similarly psychedelic therapy emphasizes the encouragement of all experiences allowing them to naturally crescendo and thereby become integrated.

After a psychedelic treatment a range of problems can arise including, "intensification of the original symptoms, emergence of new forms of psychopathology, prolonged reactions, psychotic breaks or the emergence of LSD-like states at a later date, sometimes called re-emergent phenomena ("flashbacks")." Grof attributes these to incompletely integrated dynamic structures that require immediate working through with or without psychedelics.

Over time the drug experiences tended to lose their affective charge as more and more blockages were resolved. While sometimes symptoms worsen considerably between sessions they were usually within the range of normal functioning. Generally subjects begin with psychological trauma and proceed to serious diseases, physical/sexual abuse, surgeries and accidents. "Survival threats or severe psychological trauma in infancy" often represents a crossroads where the biographical veers into the perinatal, whereas death-rebirth sequences may represent a crossroads between the perinatal and transpersonal unconscious.

As many as one hundred sessions were prescribed and by the end of the series the "world-view and hierarchy of values" was always transformed.

Including Holotropic breathwork Grof has conducted over 7,000 sessions of "non- ordinary states of consciousness" over 53 years. The current renaissance in psychedelic research abides by the principles he outlines in his work.

But four years after Grof began his long strange trip, on the other side of the world in Mexico, another scientist would enter the field of psychedelics – and nothing has really been the same ever since.

Chapter Nine

Fifth Wave: *Dr. Timothy Leary –*
The Most Dangerous Man in America

"Bluebird, Bluebird, sub that spy."

–Tim Leary

While Grof was a Freudian-trained psychiatrist he ultimately became interested in psychedelics from a classical shamanic perspective, however Dr. Timothy Leary's field was *social* psychology. Not only were their scientific fields worlds apart but they seemed like cultural and temperamental opposites as well.

In western Siberia only the shamans eat the Amanita Muscaria mushrooms but in the eastern part of the region, in addition to its traditional healing uses, everyone takes it together – what the Irish might call a party. The difference in approach between one or more therapists sitting *with* someone and Leary's group trip philosophy couldn't be wider.

Historians tasked with explaining the transformation that occurred during the 1960s will find one man at the center of it all. Timothy Leary presented his work in more forms or media than anyone before or since, from scientific papers and books, to pamphlets, autobiography, fiction, "spoken word" records, music, theater, lectures, documentary, fictional film/television and finally, as early as 1986, computer software. If the media is the message it may be the incredible range of media that so outraged the "establishment." Or was it the ideas themselves?

Whether he is remembered as merely a charismatic gadabout or a great philosopher will depend largely on the fate of his theory of the serial imprinting of the eight-circuit brain. Combined with my own seventeen years of psychopharmacological (gonzo) research and the eighteen years at Hollywood Hospital, we will examine the fruits of Leary's restless mind at the end of the book.

Harvard psychologist Dr. Richard Alpert was Timothy Leary's "lieutenant," from the beginning of the drug work until 1965 when the two split. In the 70s Alpert travelled to India where he found a new guru in Neem Karoli Baba. One of the first things the venerable Indian asked about was LSD. Alpert gave him two massive doses on two separate occasions, which both times produced no effect whatsoever. To Alpert this indicated that his new guru was "high all the time." Neem Karoli Baba also noted that drugs had been around for thousands of years but they only allowed one to "sit with the Christ, not become the Christ." Even so, because the purification rituals that had accompanied the drugs in antiquity had vanished, Baba claimed this method had fallen into disrepute. Whatever his opinion on psychedelics, anyone that can take a thousand mikes of Sandoz and not flinch has definitely got his neurological shit together.

Similarly Art Kleps who lived at the Millbrook New York "psychedelic" compound with Leary noticed that while when most people took large doses of acid they could barely function, Leary became "cold, calculating and brilliant." Perhaps this ability to withstand large acid doses is where the similarities between the Harvard lecturer and Karoli Baba end, but both men were apparently wired very differently from the rest of us.

In 1955, on his thirty-fifth birthday, his wife and the mother of his two children committed suicide in their home in Berkley, California – Leary had been unfaithful to her and both were drinking heavily.

After a checkered academic career marred with booze and womanizing Tim had settled into The University of California at Berkley where he earned a PhD in psychology and in 1957 published a book called *The Interpersonal Diagnosis of Personality*. In it Leary described the ego's mission as "to ward off anxiety and increase self-esteem." He categorized behaviour into eight dimensions, each with a corresponding opposite, for instance docile-dependent versus competitive-narcissistic. This way one's personality can be "measured" as can personal growth and change. Leary likened this to a proton accelerator where a single particle is isolated for analysis – in this analogy the behaviour is the particle. The Leary circle made a huge impact and is still used today -

Interpersonal Diagnosis of Personality was called the "most important book on psychology written this year" by the *Annual Review of Psychology*. Many of Leary's colleagues accused him of taking credit for others work and it is obvious a huge team of researchers contributed to the book, but Leary got out in front and became the "heir apparent to Maslow," whose introduction of the "hierarchy of needs" in 1954 had made him the

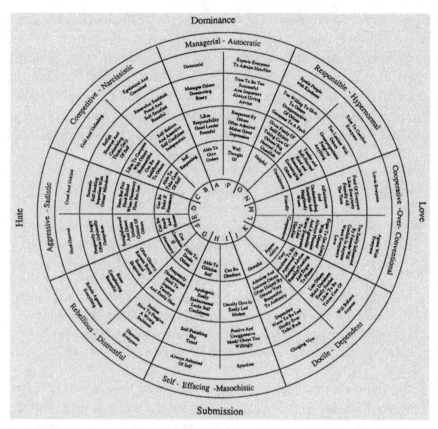

founder of humanistic psychology – a new sub- discipline that shifted the focus from curing illness to realizing one's inner – potential. Psychotherapy split at this point with one camp focused on adjusting to conventional societal norms and the other on the actualizing of the self.

In 1959, while writing his next book *The Existential Transaction,* Dr. Leary accepted a job at Harvard. Then in January of 1960 he began his new life in Cambridge, Massachusetts, only to see it utterly transformed that same summer in Mexico. Living the comfortable life of an academic Leary had rented a villa where he and some colleagues had heard about "magic mushrooms" and decided to try them.

"Do you see it Dick? Our little minds." Leary whispered to his tripping friend. The most fundamental insight and consequently the theme of Leary's life and work might be "every reality is an opinion." Every perspective is an arbitrary structure of mind frozen from the limitless possibilities of consciousness.

Having the "veil drawn" Leary initiated the Harvard Psilocybin Project in the fall of 1960. On the project's board of directors was world-re-

nowned intellectual and the first to bring psychedelics to mass consciousness – Aldous Huxley.

Dr. Leary's plan was to use the concepts in his latest book, *The Existential Transaction,* to inform his research model. Therapists would sometimes take very small doses of psychedelics while sitting for patients, but
generally this would be considered unprofessional and even malpractice;
however in Leary's version of humanistic psychology the "therapist" giving "drugs" to the "patient" was old- fashioned.

In his 1982 autobiography *Flashbacks*, Leary explains his second book
like this,

> ...By existential I meant that the psychologist should work with
> people in real-life situations, like a naturalist in the field, observing
> behaviour in the trenches. "We should treat people as they actually
> are and not impose the medical model or any model on them."
>
> By transaction I mean that psychologists shouldn't remain de-
> tached from their subjects. They should get involved, engaged in
> the events they're studying. They should enter each experiment pre-
> pared to change as much or more than the subjects being studied."

The populations chosen by The Harvard Psilocybin Project (HPP) for
study were intellectuals, artists, religious seekers and graduate students.
Psychologists taking the drug with the experimental subjects, where at
least one sober professional was there as "ground control," was totally revolutionary. Leary described his research contract in a 1961 paper this way:

> 1. Participants alternated roles of observer and subject, i.e., the re-
> searchers took the drug with the subject. The humanizing effect of
> this procedure cannot be overestimated. Among other things, the
> subject-object issue is clearly settled.

> 2. Participants were given all available information about the drug.
> An atmosphere of mystery and secret experimentation was avoid-
> ed.

> 3. Participants were given control of their own dosage. The research
> team determined a maximum dosage, and this maximum number
> of tablets was given to the subject, and he was free to dose himself
> at the rate and amount desired.

> 4.A comfortable, homelike environment was employed. The sterile
> impersonality of the laboratory was avoided.

5.Subjects were allowed to bring a relative or friend. No subject took the drug in a group where he was a stranger.

From the fall of 1960 until 1967 when anything close to formal research seems to have pretty much stopped, Leary or someone from the Harvard Psychedelic Project (HPP) or one of its many reincarnations sat for over two thousand psychedelic trips. About two-thirds reported "peak mystical experiences that brought genuine religious feeling and love for humanity."

Rebellious in spirit, Leary ignored the pleas of his more conservative colleagues primarily in psychiatry to keep it within the system. He also ignored the occasional research subject who attempted suicide or was committed while he and his team were taking psilocybin, sometimes several times a week.

In March of 1961 Leary initiated a second psychedelic program – The Concord Prison Project. Dozens of prisoners were involved, some having "peak mystical experiences" and Leary claimed that only 10% of his subjects returned to jail – seven times less than would be expected. While the short-term results were impressive, after a while prison return rates went back to normal and Dr. Leary was ultimately busted for "suspect data" when a follow-up study was conducted.

Later that year in the summer of 1961 the Harvard Psilocybin Project's directors flew to Copenhagen to address the World Psychological Association. This was probably a turning point in the scientific community's relationship to psychedelic drugs. Frank Barron, another psychologist in the project who had introduced Leary to mushrooms, presented with Leary and colleague Dr. Richard Alpert.

Effusive praise of the drug experience and little information of substance caused a few psychiatrists in the audience to rise and loudly denounce them for the non- medical use of drugs. The tabloid press got hold of the story and printed a lurid account by a reporter who had taken psilocybin with Alpert adding to the scandal. Harvard was not amused.

That autumn for his PhD in Divinity Dr. Walter Pahnke (MD) began a project to study psilocybin and religious experience with Dr. Leary advising. The "Marsh Chapel Experiment" would use an active-placebo, double blind (where neither experimenter nor subject knew who had the experimental drug) and independent data raters – all the features of modern experimental methodology. On Good Friday 1962 two-thirds of the psilocybin group had the full-blown "religious experience" compared to only a couple in the control group. One subject however wandered into traffic in a "psychotic" state and was given the anti-psychotic drug thorazine, a fact Leary never mentioned. Psilocybin's capacity to facilitate religious experience was confirmed again by Dr. Roland Griffiths of Johns Hopkins in 2006.

Psychedelic Peak Experiences include the following from Walter N. Pahnke in *LSD, Man and Society:*

> 1. *Unity* is a sense of cosmic oneness achieved through positive ego- transcendence. Although the usual sense of identity or ego fades away, consciousness and memory are not lost; instead, the person becomes very much aware of being part of a dimension much vaster and greater than himself. In addition to the route of the "inner world" where all external sense impressions are left behind, unity can also be experienced through the external world, so that a person reports that he feels a part of everything that is (e.g. objects, other people, nature or the universe), or, more simply, that "all is one."

> 2. *Transcendence of time and space* means the subject feels beyond past, present and future and beyond ordinary three-dimensional space in a realm of eternity or infinity.

> 3. *Deeply felt positive mood* contains the elements of joy, blessedness, peace and love to an overwhelming degree of intensity, often accompanied by tears.

> 4. *Sense of sacredness* is a non-rational, intuitive, hushed, palpitant (throbbing) response of awe and wonder in the presence of inspiring realities. The main elements are awe, humility and reverence, but the terms traditional theology or religion need not necessarily be used in the description.

> 5. *The noetic quality* as named by William James, is a feeling of insight or illumination that is felt on an intuitive, non-rational level and has a tremendous force of certainty and reality. This knowledge is not an increase in facts, but is a gain of insight about such things as philosophy of life or sense of values.

> 6. *Paradoxicality* refers to the logical contradictions that become apparent if descriptions are strictly analyzed. A person may realize that he is experiencing, for example, an "identity of opposites," yet it seems to make sense at the time, and even afterwards.

> 7. *Alleged ineffability* means that the experience is felt to be beyond words, non-verbal, impossible to describe, yet most persons who

insist on the ineffability do in fact make elaborate attempts to communicate the experience.

8. *Transiency* means that the psychedelic peak does not last in its full intensity, but instead passes into an afterglow and remains as a memory.

9. *Persisting* positive changes in attitudes and behaviour toward self, others, life and the experience itself.

Later that spring of 1962, less than two years after his initiation to psychedelics Leary tried LSD for the first time. He described it as "the most shattering experience of my life." By now substantial resistance had grown to his projects with professors, jealous of losing precious graduate students to Leary's glamorous drug work (twelve out of fifteen according to Leary) holding hearings and narcotics police paying him their first visit. At that time he met Peggy Hitchcock, an attractive billionaire heiress who began providing independent financial support. During the summer months they ran a very successful "psychedelic summer camp" in Mexico that they planned on making permanent.

The late psychedelic researcher Dr. Gary Fisher maintained he sat for a 400-mcg trip with Leary long before Tim claims to have been initiated into LSD. According to Fisher, "He had a hard time." This illustrates well the opposing perspectives of Leary and Grof – for Grof the focus is internal and therapeutic but for Leary the objective is a *social*, religious experience. As his psychedelic sidekick from '60- '65 Dr. Richard Alpert observed forty years later, "I was taking psychedelics to clean myself out. Timothy was taking psychedelics to clean the society out."

Film icon Cary Grant took LSD nearly a hundred times and was a very public advocate. In the late fifties and early sixties psychedelic science was the most prestigious field in psychology and psychiatry and the drug remains the most studied psychoactive in history. Leary claims to have slept with Marilyn Monroe and "turned on" President Kennedy's girlfriend Mary Pinchot Meyer during this period, training her to turn on the commander in chief. She was murdered shortly after JFK's assassination under similarly dubious circumstances. Of course the seduction of Marilyn and turning on the president may have been "Irish facts," which Leary describes as "just like regular facts only better." According to the late writer Robert Anton Wilson, "even near his death, he was always the funniest guy in the room."

In the fall of 1962 he and his two closest associates Richard Alpert and Ralph Metzner, along with their families, moved into a house in Newton

Center near Boston; neighbours tried to have them evicted, even though Alpert had bought the house. Alpert's father personally litigated and the team of academics had what would turn out to be their last legal victory for a long time.

One of the defining elements of the sixties was tribal living and Leary's pagan compound drew the top philosophers, artists and scientists of the time. This lifestyle seems to revert to an archaic form of communal living and working that is much more conducive to shamanism and psychedelics than our current "nuclear, cubicle" families. Excluding his time in prison, Leary would live this way for the rest of his life – surrounded by the smartest people and the best drugs.

Tim Leary loved parties. One of his early ideas was the value of hybrids, the idea that if you could merge two very different entities, even opposites, you would end up with stronger and stronger results. This was true in plants and people but also in groups or scenes. In the sixties Leary assembled the best and brightest, sexiest and richest people he could find and mixed them with prostitutes, heroin addicts, religious fanatics and seekers – the catalyst for the reaction was LSD and the results are still with us today.

By early 1963 Leary was using LSD one to three times a week in place of the tamer psilocybin. Notorious artists like William S. Burroughs, Indian Yogis and paranormal researchers were visiting Harvard and the more conservative professors were appalled. Dr. Leary was dating models and socialites, supervising and publishing with two research projects, and writing and lecturing prolifically.

They turned the house into a tripper's paradise, decorated the walls with Arab rugs and built a "time chamber" in the attic with no furniture only art. They also developed the "experiential typewriter" that allowed trippers to communicate their inner world. The machine identified "eight levels of consciousness: stuporous, emotional, symbolic, somatic, sensory, cellular, molecular and out of body." A tripper would report their experience and it would be recorded for later examination. Auditory loops of heartbeats and other sounds were combined with slides and films of cellular processes and other visuals so that the experimental subject, for the non-verbal levels, could summon them. Much of this technology would be featured at nightclubs in a few unusually eventful years.

The International Foundation for Internal Freedom (IFIF) was founded as a first step to move the research away from Harvard and liberate the team from the restrictions of University life. Thousands of membership applications and fees immediately arrived. In a flippant article in the Harvard newspaper Leary wrote, "It is as unfair to expect a university to do research in Visionary states as it is for the Vatican to subsidize research in aphrodisiacs."

By now in the third year of the drug project many students were experimenting with the still legal psychedelics and University officials were worried. Clearly the entire research team was taking drugs regularly and the work they were doing was not being well received by academia. When Richard Alpert gave LSD to an undergraduate, forbidden even for scientific purposes, he was fired.

When Dr. Leary arrived in Mexico in May of '63 to prepare for the next psychedelic summer camp he heard that he had been dismissed as well for failing to finish his academic requirements. Leary claims he had already quit at this point but it is difficult to determine. More than any other single event the firing of Richard Alpert and Timothy Leary, the first firing of professors at Harvard since Ralph Waldo Emerson, was the tinderbox that caused the explosion of psychedelic drugs into mainstream consciousness. IFIF, 76 million baby boomers and most of all Timothy Leary were ready.

• • •

The summer camp was as brilliant as ever; filled to capacity, subjects would trip one day, integrate one day and guide one day. One tripper always sat on the twenty-foot guard tower watching the ocean and occasionally reporting to "ground control" below. All the major networks, magazines and newspapers sent down crews and the story of the two defrocked Harvard professors and their psychedelic drug resort was the headline in Kennedy's America for a few weeks. CIA described their operation as a "happiness hotel."

When Mexican police ordered them out of the country that summer it is assumed that CIA was involved in the deportation. The reason given was their visas were only for tourists and they were running a business. Like dissidents from centuries past they roamed the Caribbean islands looking for a new homeland. After being exiled a few times, in early fall 1963 they landed in Millbrook, an upper-state New York castle and the greatest house party in the history of civilization officially began.

Tim professed that his regime at the time featured only one acid trip a week. "Each trip was programmed by a guide who would use whatever media, religious system or philosophy he was interested in at the time and create an ecstatic experience for the rest of the group. The estate was an ideal location for such experiments and more dignitaries from the new world of 'consciousness expansion' stopped by to pay tribute."

At one point Tim's colleague Dr. Richard Alpert was suffering from a cold. The Millbrook crew wheeled in two giant speakers and placed them beside the ailing psychologist's bed. Beethoven was ready for one speaker and Wagner the other. A massive dose of the super-hallucinogen DMT was injected into his thigh and the music cranked – he awoke in total shock but when the drug wore off his cold was gone.

In 1964 the group published *The Psychedelic Experience,* based on *The Tibetan book of the Dead* and designed to guide trippers through a "peaceful dying of the ego." One eager consumer was John Lennon, who later befriended Tim and financially and creatively supported Leary's 1968 California gubernatorial campaign with the song *Come Together.*

That same year Timothy Leary married model Nena von Schlebrugge, who would later marry Buddhist scholar Robert Thurman and give birth to Uma Thurman, and for their honeymoon they travelled through the east to India. Unfortunately the newlyweds were already drifting apart. On their travels Leary noticed the sacred use of marijuana, an illegal drug that he had little experience with but which would ultimately cost him his freedom for almost a decade. When they returned in June of '65 Millbrook had degenerated into a wild scene populated by "rowdy omnisexuals."

Some of the wilder Millbrook guests used to play what Tim called "neurological demolition derby." At one point there were a dozen of them in the living room tripping and playing a game where they would speak into a microphone and describe what they would take with them to another planet. When the microphone came to Tim the power suddenly went out and all that could be seen was a strobe light in the backyard illuminating a man wearing only a kilt doing flips on a trampoline.

Tim's two closest colleagues Richard Alpert and Ralph Metzner both eventually left a year later. Alpert went to India and found a new guru and went on to become Baba Ram Das and remains a world-renowned authority on meditation and spirituality, while Ralph Metzner continues his research on shamanism and pharmacology 48 years later.

Later on in 1965, when the nearby Ananda Yoga Ashram kicked out eighteen people for using psychedelics, Tim invited them to live at Millbrook, almost doubling the group's size. Many of the children who lived there were very unhappy with their childhoods, as Kim Ferguson Exon who grew up at Millbrook remembered in Robert Greenfield's biography *Leary*:

> In the beginning, it was a really beautiful clean place. In the beginning. There was a lot of meditating. Take a group of people who have come together with a shared goal of changing the world. In this ideal environment, this fantasy setting, bring in the drugs. Start stepping those up. And then put in the pressure of the cops and the politics, and all of a sudden, those people are fighting amongst themselves. And then all these beautiful women and attractive men come in to stir the soup and then put in the rule that everybody should be fucking everybody and you tell me how it goes downhill.

Gradually Millbrook returned to a slightly more monastic atmosphere but nonetheless Timothy and Nannette were divorced. Throughout these years the public were invited on weekends for psychedelic workshops that provided a "non- drug" multimedia acid trip. Added to these revenues were Leary's prolific publications and lectures. Using the top light-sound wizards in the industry, Leary's group, now known as the Castilia Foundation after a group of mystic scientists in the Herman Hesse novel *The Glass Bead Game,* took their show on the road.

Tim's divorce with Nena paved the way for Rosemary Woodruffe to enter his life – the couple became an icon of the counterculture, famously singing along with John Lennon at his Montreal "bed-in" in 1968. As Leary remembers in *Flashbacks,* shortly after they had fallen in love and Rosemary moved into Millbrook they painted the "oriental symbol for sexual union, interlocking triangles, on the red brick chimney. Drawn eight feet tall the Maha Yantra of fusion dominated the approach to our castle."

Even in a psychedelic paradise after over two years at Millbrook the harassment from law enforcement had become unbearable, despite the fact that almost all the drugs being used were still legal. The beleaguered acid guru, his soon-to-be wife Rosemary and Leary's two kids Jack and Susan headed to Mexico where Tim was planning to write his autobiography. The group was arrested with $10 worth of marijuana in Texas and Dr. Leary was later sentenced to thirty years.

Leary was out on bail and back at Millbrook with a bustling psychedelic workshop schedule well underway in the summer of '66, when future Watergate burglar G. Gordon Liddy led a midnight invasion of twelve "armed and booted" sheriffs and more arrests were made. During this time the "League for Spiritual Discovery" (LSD) was formed replacing the Castilia Foundation. Also in 1966 the number of American LSD research teams dropped from as many as 210 to six as a full-throttle moral panic swept the nation.

Leary launched a "scientific defense" claiming special rights as a researcher – a strategy that had gotten him nowhere in Texas. Pivoting from this dead end, from this point forward the focus of his work would be religious and, whether out of legal necessity or genuine religious feeling, this began a very romantic period in his life that was ultimately terminated by prison. When they first began using psychedelics they assumed graduate students, artists and scientists would open their minds at Universities, but in the end it was mostly young spiritual seekers that would provide the audience for their crusade and they loved some good old religious ecstasy.

The League for Spiritual Discovery produced psychedelic multimedia shows based on classic "death-rebirth" or "mystical" stories such as Herman Hesse's *Steppenwolf, The Resurrection of Jesus Christ* and *The Assassination of Socrates.* Receiving little success in New York they headed west to California where audiences seemed "light-years ahead."

Psychedelic Prayers was released in 1966 as the second "psychedelic manual." The new book, based on ancient Chinese Taoist philosophy, continues to function as a guide for trippers. "Turn on, tune in and drop out" became his catch phrase based on the advice of Canadian media scholar Marshall McLuhan, who had advised him to create an "advertising slogan" for LSD.

In *Flashbacks* Leary wrote:

> "*Turn On* meant to go within to activate your neural and genetic equipment.
>   *Tune In* meant to interact harmoniously with the world around you–
>   *Drop Out* suggested an active, selective, graceful process of detachment from involuntary or unconscious commitments."

The number of people experienced with LSD, mescaline, psilocybin and a growing number of other drugs described as psychedelic, had grown from the hundreds of thousands to the tens of millions in the four years since the Leary group had left Harvard. When The Beatles released *Sergeant Pepper's Lonely Hearts Club Band* in the summer of '67, complete with a picture of Aldous Huxley on the cover and the lyrics "I'd love to turn you on," in one ultimately banned song, the golden age of psychedelics was officially over.

The John Birch society, an extreme right-wing organization accused the band of using "advanced brain-washing techniques" on the record and as the baby- boomers began turning twenty-one that summer it appeared they might have been right.

Had such a popular psychedelic crusade not swept the world Hollywood Hospital, Maryland Psychiatric Research Center, Saskatchewan, California's International Federation for Advanced Studies and other leading teams would certainly have continued to thrive but the numbers of turned on human beings would only be tens of thousands vs. tens of millions – Leary was almost universally despised for his effect on this field.

His psychedelic circus moved on again when too much heat led them out of Millbrook and they moved to a California ranch where he was a sort of scholar in residence with the Brotherhood of Eternal Love a gang of "God-intoxicated" drug dealers who worked primarily with acid and cannabis, both regarded as sacred. He became an advisor to leftist political radicals like Abbie Hoffman who had become a major force in American politics when the whole society seemed to be falling apart.

Speaking of the anti-war movement in San Francisco in the middle-sixties Hunter S. Thompson observed that it seemed "our energy would simply prevail." A few years later it was obvious that that wasn't going to happen without a fight and plenty of people were ready to go on all sides. On April 4, 1968 Martin Luther King was killed and on June 5, a second Kennedy brother, Bobby, was assassinated. That summer during the Democratic Convention in Chicago, the pugilistic mayor whipped his police forces into a frenzy that resulted in a police riot with many unarmed protesters injured, even though as many as one-third were probably undercover government agents.

By now Dr. Leary had dozens of charges filed against him, one of which was violation of the tax stamp law. In the thirties, when cannabis was outlawed, instead of changing the constitution, which they had done and then undone regarding alcohol, they created the tax stamp law. Anyone in possession of cannabis without a stamp issued by the Treasury Department was guilty. Leary and his legal team ultimately won in the Supreme Court because the law violated the right to avoid self- incrimination. When a dozen media crews approached the desert ranch with the news of his victory he announced he would run for governor against incumbent Ronald Reagan. However, gubernatorial candidate Leary was quickly eliminated when the culture wars hit home again in December of that year and he claimed a policeman planted some weed on him and his rap sheet grew even longer. Having a pending felony charge in California eliminated Timothy Leary from the election.

Later in the decade the Woodstock success was cancelled out by the Charles Manson murders and the public opinion of LSD was hysterically negative. Despite his victory two years earlier in the U.S. Supreme Court, in January of 1970 Timothy Leary was finally incarcerated. During his hearing the judge held up a copy of a *Playboy* interview the defrocked professor had done about LSD and sentenced him to ten years for two roaches and a few flakes of grass.

When it was time to determine which prison the doctor should serve his time in the tests administered were based on his own work. Early in his career with personality diagnosis he had designed questionnaires for classifying people. He answered to "appear normal, non-impulsive, docile, conforming."

A few years after Leary went to prison, Stan Grof left Spring Grove, the Maryland research project he had run and became scholar in residence in Big Sur California – the home of Esalen – a world-famous resort-retreat for spiritual seekers. With Leary in jail and the Godfather of LSD retired the sixties were really over.

On September 12, 1970, nine months after arriving, the fifty year-old professor climbed a telephone pole, shimmied across two hundred feet of cable and escaped into the protection of the Weather Underground, a violent, radical leftist organization. After receiving amnesty from Black Panther Eldridge Cleaver's "American government in exile" in Algiers Africa, Leary fled again to Europe where his adventures as a fugitive continued.

Unfortunately during his exile his epic romance with Rosemary ended but still a ladies-man, soon he met a twenty-seven year old aristocrat named Joanna Harcourt-Smith. She was very keen to meet the "pope of LSD" and the two became inseparable.

After a few acid trips together they had yet to consummate their relationship. Tim picked her up in the brand new Porsche he bought with the advance on one of his books and took her to a four-star hotel in the Swiss countryside. "He was dressed like a professor with glasses and he was carrying a briefcase. He sat down and opened it and took out a *Time* magazine with some of the first brain-scans featured in it. He showed me the parts of my brain he was going to make love to."

Incredibly it took them over two years to capture him, during which time he wrote three more books. Eventually the U.S. Government abducted him in Afghanistan and he was returned to his native country. His bail was set at $10,000,000, then the highest in American history and he was sentenced to five more years for the escape. Joanna describes watching him being taken away.

"I saw his eyes becoming more and more empty. As though he was retreating deeper and deeper inside of himself. As if he was erasing the world from his reality. So that all that counted now was his inner-life." Dr. Leary was placed in the hole in Folsom prison next to another acid apostle name Charlie Manson.

Leary recounts their conversation in his 1982 autobiography *Flashbacks*:

> "I've been watching you fall for years, man. I knew you'd end up here. I've wanted to talk to you for a long time. I wanted to ask you how come you blew it."
> "Blew it?"
> "You had everyone looking up to you. You could have led the people anywhere you wanted."
> "What I had in mind was to teach people to avoid teachers and direct their own lives," I said wearily. '

Later according to Leary biographer Robert Greenfield:

> "When they talked again the next morning after breakfast, Manson had more questions. He wanted to know what Tim called the moment of truth when you took acid and your entire body dissolved into nothing but vibrations, space and time fused, and it all became just pure energy. Bouncing the question right back at him, Tim asked Manson what he had found there. "Nothing," Manson said. "Like death must be. Isn't that what you've found?" Having fielded this question many times before, Tim told Manson this was a trip someone else had laid on him. "It's the moment when you are free from biochemical imprints," he said. "You can take off from there and go anywhere you want. You should have looked for the energy fusion called love." "It's all death," Manson insisted. "It's all love," Tim responded. "I hang on to death," Manson said. "I live by life," Tim replied."

It would seem from this conversation at least that the moral sanity of humanity hangs from a thread of paradox.

In his books Tim describes Folsom Prison as a trip to camp but he was drugged heavily with the anti-psychotic Thorazine, even though his prison psychologist described him as, "not at all psychotic." Joanna recalls that before an anticipated visit from her and poet Allen Ginsberg, "they had yanked him out of his cell in the early morning and insisted on shaving his head. They shaved it in an extremely clumsy way and he got cut. It was only later that I realized they did it on purpose. They wanted him to look awful in front of his visitors. To show their supremacy over Tim to Ginsberg."

Sadly Leary informed on his prison-escape collaborators, not to mention other comrades that had committed crimes to earn release in 1976, but whatever his testimony it caused no arrests. Why not? Because Rosemary stayed in hiding until the 90s to protect the people he had informed on. To the criminal underworld this a cardinal sin, but to a middle-aged academic facing the rest of his life in prison who can alter his identity, beliefs and reality almost at will, this is the next reasonable move. This changed his relationship with the counterculture considerably and allowed him to repackage himself yet again as futurist and high- tech guru.

He moved as effortlessly from leftist revolutionary to pragmatic aging convict turned snitch as any other of his identity transformations. What kind of a person was Timothy Leary?

Evidently the genius of his mind cast a spell, which beguiled those around him from the beginning, but when psychedelic drugs were added to the mix even the ghost in the shell inside the man seems to have been seduced. This kind of facile or flexible identity, manipulated to suit the immediate needs is typical of a psychopath, and Leary was certainly impulsive and a world-class confabulator.

Taken as a whole the identity of Timothy Leary is impossible to determine but at any one point, whoever he was from professor to scientist to mystic to pied piper to fugitive to snitch to cyberpunk, he inhabited new identities totally like a Faustian chameleon. He used to joke that, "everybody gets the Timothy Leary they deserve."

He pioneered technologies for reality and identity change – and they worked. Whatever the shortcomings of his character his genius as a thinker and writer are beyond question. Leary's 1964 paper "Three Contributions to Psychopharmacological Theory" began with the slogan "you've got to go out of your mind to use your head." There are trillions of actions going on in the brain and the "ghost in the shell" or ego is aware of an often arbitrarily conditioned fraction of those and places them on a "mental chessboard" that prevents optimal creative intelligence. One Dutch psychiatrist who worked with LSD and concentration camp survivors, Dr. Andersen-Hein, called psychedelics "conditioned response inhibitors."

An early focus of Leary's work was *game theory* – people play games composed of rules, roles, rituals, goals, language and values designed and managed to benefit whoever is in charge. Psychedelics seem to suspend the games and allow new and better ones to be consciously devised.

But beyond game theory, "The Serial Imprinting of The Eight Circuit Brain" was the primary focus of his work until his death in 1996. Sitting in solitary confinement in January of 1973 Leary wrote *Neurologic* – summarizing the last thirteen years of his drug work. His writing up to then had often been somewhat scattered and manic, his ideas often bizarre, like when they all started tearing up the concrete roads outside Millbrook with pickaxes preparing for a new society where all industry would take place underground. But now facing the rest of his life in prison, sitting in the hole with only half a pencil and an old legal brief to write on – he was ready to focus.

He described *imprinting as* a term borrowed from ethology, the study of animals in their natural habitat. It was observed that babies of a variety of mammals, during the *critical window* of the first moments after birth, would imprint as their mother, later rejecting their actual mothers, whatever moving object they were presented with. Ping-pong balls, jeeps and many ethnologists were imprinted in a tragi-comic melodrama as imposter moms to many confused newborn animals. Leary believed psychedelics were able to create a new critical window for a new imprint to be taken.

One tragic example of the power of imprinting involves a young man who was sexually abused by his uncle, who insanely dressed up in a cow costume every time he molested his nephew. In his early twenties this developmentally traumatized young man was killed by a kick to the head from a cow when he accidentally bit her udder while attempting to suckle. Less disturbingly there is the well-worn tale in sex psychology of the boy who grew up in a very crowded household without a lock on the bathroom door, forcing him to hold it closed while masturbating. He was later unable to achieve climax without holding a doorknob. Leary used to boast that he could tell when someone had their first orgasm by what music they listened to.

Based on the notions that consciousness is energy received by organized structure and that our brain and even pre-human life evolved through many distinct phases creating distinct structures, Leary proposed his eight-circuit model. The first four circuits are designed for terrestrial earth-bound life; the second four are designed for post-terrestrial space migration for which he advocated enthusiastically until his death.

These circuits will be discussed at length in the third section where they will be explored with the aid of modern psychopharmacology. "Theory Leary" was keen on integrating as many systems into his work as possible. Psychedelic pioneer Dr. Humphrey Osmond said of Leary that he was a "great entrepreneur of notions and at that he was pretty good, but some of the notions weren't." The eight-circuit brain model however has resonated with generations of neuronauts.

In the LSD documentary *Hofmann's Potion* Stan Grof condemns Leary for not "…giving people fair information. He said it makes your trillions of cells dance the dance of liberation. But he didn't tell you that you may go through hell before you get to heaven and you might stay there if you don't know what you're doing."

In an interview for *Playboy* in 1963 Leary said on LSD, "you and your lover's trillions of cells dance in liberation." He later admitted he was simply packaging his message for his audience, had the interview been for *Sports Illustrated* he would have "focused on batting averages and strike outs." To be fair, baseball's Dock Ellis, a few years later pitched a no-hitter on the drug.

Why was Leary so zealous? After WWII in "operation paperclip" the U.S. government imported many top Nazi scientists; this fact, coupled with the threat of nuclear annihilation influenced a generation of American social scientists to fear American fascism generally. A study by psychologist Stanley Millgram where subjects were encouraged by officious-looking scientists to give (pretend) painful electric shocks to strangers if they gave wrong answers on a test, proved ordinary people could probably be convinced to do just about anything by authority.

One slogan not created by Leary was "LSD: Let's Save Democracy." Some believed Leary viewed the widespread dissemination of psychedelics as a "calculated risk" to resist the growing threat of fascism. Robert Anton Wilson believed the real turning point for Leary came when Psychiatrist Dr. Wilhelm Reich was imprisoned and his books burned and orgone boxes destroyed in 1957 a few months before his death.

Conversely some believe Leary, who joined a veterans group in the 40s that turned out to be a CIA front, was actually a government agent all along using LSD to undermine the political left. Timothy Leary was an enigma of contradictions. As Leary's friend and Grateful Dead lyricist John Perry Barlow observed, "Leary turned more people on to spirituality than anyone who wasn't born in a desert, and yet he was a profoundly anti-spiritual man."

During the Harvard prison program one inmate commented that in all the years he had been receiving help from authorities Leary was the only one he "ever felt was entirely *for* me." Another long time friend remembered, "You could see your potential in his eyes." Virtually anyone who ever met him describes him as a brilliantly loving person, yet his relationships with his children and wives were often as chaotic as the rest of his life. His first wife and his first daughter both committed suicide and his son Jack had been estranged from his father for over thirty years when Timothy died. He was widely denounced by ex-Wife Rosemary for informing on associates and many people who were in the field of psychedelic research resent him to this day for selling psychedelics like a neurological hoola- hoop.

But turning on so many people didn't just prevent an American Reich – it also made psychedelics a permanent part of culture beyond society's capacity to remove from memory again. Maybe Leary hastened the demise of psychedelic research in the United States, but when Grof left Czechoslovakia he left a seventeen-bed locked ward dedicated to LSD therapy. Did the Czech communists end their LSD program because of Timothy Leary?

Leary believed if enough people tripped the world would be totally transformed – he simply repressed or denied any collateral damage and served as psychedelic pitchman until his second imprisonment in 1972. After that he repackaged his ideas de-emphasizing psychedelics but continued experimenting personally with drugs, particularly ketamine, a new synthetic invented in 1962 and classed as a "dissociative" professed to simulate a near death experience.

In 1977 Leary appeared before the Libertarian Party convention and described a future where "personal computers could share text, audio and video with other computers." One witness wondered, "How much acid has this guy taken?" Until his death in 1996 from prostate cancer at age 75 he was a tireless advocate for computers and space migration, summing up his philosophy with "think for yourself; question authority," and "SMILE – Space Migration Intelligence Increase Life Extension."

The massive consumption of psychedelics, especially LSD from '64 – '73 seems to have caused more social change than any other factor in history. At one civil rights meeting in the mid-sixties in New York City an entire bible was soaked in Acid. After a few speeches the book was consumed and the night rang with songs of righteous freedom. Psyche-delic culture's influence extended into every major social movement born during that era, environmentalism and gay rights especially, but of course every form of art and science was impacted and imprinted as well.

As I read presently his final book, *Design for Dying*, I feel the same sorrow that these are his last words that so many people suffered when he died – as he used to say "10 million people I made happy and only 100,000 have come by to thank me." His last writing concerns nanotech-nology and immortality and it is funny, educational and brilliant. "Just a few more riffs Dr. Leary." But alas this was his last public writing; his infamous last words spoken of course were, "Why not?"

Part II

Hollywood Hospital

Chapter 10

Delirium Tremens and
The Mysterium Tremendum: A Brief
History of Canadian Medical Mysticism

"Directly afterwards came upon him a sense of exultation, of immense joyousness accompanied or immediately followed by an intellectual illumination quite impossible to describe."
    – Cosmic Consciousness, Richard Maurice Bucke, 1901

By the end of 1961, a host of Saskatchewan government officials and addiction experts were championing LSD therapy for recovering alcoholics. Included in the roster was the Premier of Saskatchewan the Right Honourable Tommy Douglas and Jake Calder, the chairman of the Saskatchewan Alcoholism Commission.

The new shamanic technology spread across the prairie to his colleague in Manitoba at the Alcohol Education Service, Pastor William Potoroka, and across the continent to Alcoholics Anonymous co-founder Bill Wilson, as well as local chapters of the organization, and The Canadian Temperance Foundation. In Saskatchewan a trip to one of the province's five LSD clinics was standard treatment for the newly conceptualized disease of alcoholism. Had this been Ontario or California or New York it could have meant thousands of professional Acid therapists.

Earlier that year (1961) the Canadian Temperance Foundation held their annual meeting in Regina and the Saskatchewan psychedelic contingent presented their findings about LSD to the primarily religious audience. One member that was persuaded was Pastor William Potoroka from Manitoba. Potoroka actually tried LSD himself, saw alcoholics treated with it and endorsed it. Arrangements were made to begin treating alcoholics at Brandon Hospital in the western end of the province – the LSD cures alcoholism meme (cultural equivalent of a gene) was spreading.

But how had Saskatchewan become such a leader in psychedelic science? When Tommy Douglas was elected Premier in 1944 he promised socialism in government and medicine with an emphasis on research and innovation, which he delivered when his Chief Psychiatrist Dr. McKerracher hired Drs. Abram Hoffer and Humphrey Osmond to run the province's psychiatric research.

Dr. Osmond's interest in hallucinogens (he hadn't yet coined the term psychedelic) began with mescaline in post-war London when he and fellow psychiatrist Dr. John Smythies noted the similarities between the mescaline and adrenaline molecules and "der Meskalin rausch" (German for mescaline inebriation) and schizophrenia. They reasoned that perhaps an error in metabolizing adrenaline caused schizophrenia and for two years they experimented with the drug on normal subjects characterizing their results as "model psychosis" – the two British scientists published the first biochemical theory of schizophrenia in 1952.

When Osmond came to assume the position of Clinical Director of the Saskatchewan Mental Hospital later that year he brought his interest in mescaline with him. When LSD emerged capable of producing similar changes in consciousness at 1/2500ths the mescaline dose it seemed even more probable than an adrenaline error that a similar compound could be causing schizophrenia with auto-intoxication or inebriation by something produced within the body. Furthermore experiencing these drug-induced psychotic states would provide insight to those tasked with helping the poor souls who must endure them spontaneously and indefinitely.

The second researcher hired was Saskatchewan psychiatrist Abram Hoffer, a medical doctor with a PhD in agricultural biochemistry; the two doctors developed a list of chemicals with "schizogenic" qualities that they published in a paper in 1954. The next stage in their research into psychotomimetic drugs would involve giving them to experimental subjects again, but before that the doctors decided to try them personally, with their wives and other doctors, graduate students and family friends.

Two more years of experimenting appeared to indicate that these drugs drove you mad; any insights were into madness itself and apparently only rarely of a cosmic or ecstatic nature and even then carrying little impact, and after all schizophrenics certainly have transcendental experiences as well without it making much difference. But their paradigm would change when they expanded their research to a new cohort who, when it came to the brand new business of acid tripping, were born to fly.

Hoffer and Osmond went to Ottawa in the fall of 1953 to attend a conference held by the Department of National Health and Welfare; unable to sleep they were talking in their hotel room into the small hours. They discussed the apparent similarities between delirium tremens (acute alcohol withdrawal) and LSD intoxication. Although delirium tremens is fatal in about 10% of cases it often results in abstinence among survivors – perhaps if they induced a psychotic state in alcoholics with LSD they could frighten them into abstinence as well.

Upon returning to Saskatoon they gave LSD to two alcoholics and apparently cured one of them – what surprised them most though was the ease with which their new subjects achieved transcendent states – alcoholics tripped differently. This began a move away from the psychotomimetic model and towards a new kind of drug and a new word to describe it. LSD could facilitate peak mystical transcendental experiences.

Whether psychedelic therapy should focus on processing traumas like surgeries, accidents, abuse and neglect or by going for the full-blown white light mystical supracosmic void orgasm is a hotly debated subject. I asked the distinguished psychedelic researcher Dr. Jim Fadiman how important he felt the metabolizing of unprocessed trauma is to psychedelic therapy and he crushed me – "not at all.... If I take you out to the ecstatic cosmos when you come back the tight stitching on your shirt won't bother you a bit." He felt psychedelic peak mystical transcendence was the way to go. Unfortunately it seems for most of us you can't get there without going through the unprocessed superficial blockages first, but then things may be different in California.

In any case if the top of the mountain isn't reached and instead someone has a very difficult experience they might have been better off without taking the trip at all. By contrasting the bliss and liberation of the positive perinatal matrices with the despair and rage of the negative, Stan Grof is able to present a new context. Generally first negative COEX (condensed experiences) like accidents, abuse, surgery or neglect must be processed and negative perinatal dynamics must then be metabolized before accessing such exalted states, but they are intrinsically therapeutic and fulfilling even if just one side of an endless duality.

But is the psychedelic peak experience a glimpse into the ecstatic singularity *behind* the grueling duality? Are those ecstatic experiences toxic pharmacological artifacts seducing drug users into addiction and delusion or revelations of the underlying order of space and time?

Some believe the universe is a giant interconnected network and that this expansive and unitive fact can be experienced directly in a state called

Cosmic Consciousness in 1901, but Krishna Consciousness or Enlightenment a few millennia before in the ancient East.

Soma was celebrated as a means of achieving this state in Ancient India, but in the Buddha's time and place (circa. 500 BCE) austerity was the way to go and legend has it Buddha subsisted on half a grain of rice a day. However it was only later when he abandoned such severe practices and adopted a "middle way" between austerity and overindulgence, sat underneath the Bodhi tree and meditated for many months that he broke through to the other side.

Twenty-four hundred years later in his landmark book *Cosmic Consciousness* Canadian Psychiatrist Dr. Bucke compared the simple consciousness of the chimpanzee to the self-consciousness of the modern human and proposed another leap at least as quantum in the emergence of cosmic consciousness – simple, self, cosmic.

He describes his own Cosmic Peak Experience as occurring after a reading of romantic poetry in England:

> He (he writes in the third person) was in a state of quiet, almost passive enjoyment. All at once, without warning of any kind, he found himself wrapped around as it were by a flame colored cloud. For an instant he thought of fire, some sudden conflagration of the great city, the next he knew that the light was within him. Directly afterwards came upon him a sense of exultation, of immense joyousness accompanied or immediately followed by an intellectual illumination quite impossible to describe.

He goes on to catalogue others who attained these ecstatic states and spread the moral codes they inspired, like the Buddha and Jesus. The book was reprinted in the early seventies and became a standard part of the hippie canon and anticipated the coining of a new phrase in *cosmic consciousness*, for 56 years later Humphrey Osmond, corresponding with Aldous Huxley coined, *psychedelic* meaning "mind manifesting" drug.

Many experience mystical peak states spontaneously, Dr. Bucke was graced by reading Romantic poetry but American Psychologist Abraham Maslow proposed still another way – self-actualizing. Although Maslow believed everyone had peak experiences he felt they just didn't recognize them. He concluded that the highest sustained peak experiences require at least half a lifetime of hard work. He noted that people who excelled in a career and maintained a successful long term love relationship would sometimes, often in nature, report spontaneous experiences involving:

"Feelings of limitless horizons opening up to the vision, the feeling of being simultaneously more powerful and also more helpless than one ever was before, the feeling of great ecstasy and wonder and awe, and the loss of the placing in time and space." (From *Religion, Values and Peak Experiences, 1970 ed.*)

To reverse the logic if peak experiences were induced chemically would someone *become* self-actualized? After their experiments with chemical psychosis had evolved into chemical transcendence Hoffer and Osmond were ready to answer that question. And while romantic poetry, yoga, meditation, fasting, chanting, dancing, and drumming have all surely facilitated cosmic consciousness, psilocybin (and presumably LSD, mescaline and DMT) is scientifically proven to work in two-thirds of normally adjusted subjects in a single dose with appropriate set and setting. (randomized controlled trials, double-blind, active placebo, independent raters, peer-reviewed and replicated).

But facilitating the ecstatic vision is a demanding art form. In 1953 *Maclean's* reporter Sydney Katz wrote a piece called "My Twelve Hours as a Madman" after taking LSD with Osmond. In a picture from the spread Osmond is placing a towel on Katz's eyes knowing this will produce a kaleidoscope of breathtaking eidetic imagery or phosphenes. Most tellingly though, Osmond is holding his hand – the psychedelic reaction requires deeply human and humane therapists as an integral part of the setting – empathy would distinguish therapeutic research with it's military or academic counterpart.

After their initial success with their two alcoholics Hoffer and Osmond's colleague psychiatrist Dr. Colin Smith launched a study of 24 alcoholics in 1955 that also produced 50% abstinence at six months. Each potential subject had their adrenaline levels tested and those with high levels were excluded because, although Hoffer believed intellectual defensiveness and psychosomatic discomfort were both manifestations of *low* adrenaline reactions to LSD that might produce poor outcomes as well, the most excitable (based on adrenaline levels) were deemed too risky to even try.

In 1955 Hoffer met Al Hubbard, a shipping tycoon and psychedelic apostle from his own Sandoz Pharmaceuticals facilitated awakening in 1951, and invited him to Saskatchewan. Hubbard showed the prairie doctor what he'd learned about maximizing results with pictures, a rose, music, religious artifacts, mirrors and a gas called carbogen that produced intense but brief psychedelic reactions. We will meet the notorious Al

"Captain Trips" Hubbard later because he was one of the architects of Hollywood Hospital.

Around the same time Aldous Huxley had a mescaline experience guided by Osmond, which sparked the famous intellectual's *Heaven and Hell* and *Doors of Perception*. Next to Leary and Alpert's firings from Harvard almost ten years later, the publishing of these manuscripts introduced psychedelics to the most people.

At this point the drugs were still known exclusively as psychotomimetic or "madness inducing," but Osmond, in a rhyming couplet, sent in a 1957 letter to Huxley, would coin a new term that has become a permanent part of the cultural lexicon.

"To fathom hell; or soar angelic Just take a pinch of psychedelic"

"The term psychedelic is derived from the Greek words ψυχή (psyche, "mind") and δηλείν (delein, "to manifest"), translating to 'mind-manifesting'." Other words are less neutral, like "entheogen," which means manifesting the God within or psychotomimetic – but psychedelic implies that heaven *or* hell may manifest – a new meme was born.

The Saskatchewan LSD team had an excellent working relationship with Alcoholics Anonymous and members passed easily back and forth – LSD's spiritual experience and ego death re-inforced the AA aims of making amends to the community and surrendering to God. AA cofounder Bill W. took LSD a number of times and endorsed it until it became politically impossible.

In 1957 Osmond and Hoffer turned over the LSD therapy to colleagues so they could concentrate on their schizophrenia research, but for the next decade the work continued with 700 alcoholics (and about 1300 other subjects and patients) treated with a similar 50% success (abstinent or greatly improved) rate in five LSD clinics across the province.

Colin Smith published his study that produced a 50% improvement rate for alcoholics in 1958 and Sven Jensen, another Saskatchewan psychiatrist, replicated the results using control groups but not placebos and published in 1962. Meanwhile in 1959 collaborator Psychologist Duncan Blewett and Psychiatrist Nick Chwelos published the first trip manual with *Handbook for the Therapeutic Use of Lysergic Acid Diethylamide-25*.

By 1963 highly effective psychedelic clinics were operating in Holland, Germany, Great Britain, Czechoslovakia, Spain, Mexico, Argentina, Menlo Park California, Hollywood Hospital, maybe two dozen other clinics around the world, mostly in the U.S. and of course five LSD clinics in

Saskatchewan. Spring Grove Hospital was a center of psychedelic therapy since the late fifties but in 1969 the project moved to the Maryland Psychiatric Research Center that was originally planned to be completely focused on the new field with the third story totally devoted to the basic chemistry of psychedelic compounds. By 1975 Hollywood Hospital was the last one.

Timothy Leary was advised by Aldous Huxley to be cautious and circumspect, as the Alchemists advised – "do, dare, be silent" – however fellow American Allen Ginsberg convinced Tim that psychedelics were just too good to be the boon of the elite with the masses left in the neurological dark ages. In 1963 Timothy Leary predicted 20-30 million Americans would take LSD by the end of the decade (plus as many as 20 million others around the world) and they did – conversely from 1947-1975 only about 40,000 humans used psychedelics in therapy and as many as 10,000 in military and intelligence research – a thousand times more people turned on unsupervised and underground.

The establishment may have tried to suppress LSD anyway without Timothy Leary; there are certainly enough adverse reactions and pharmacological undermining of social convention for LSD to stir up plenty of controversy without him. But Leary, perhaps in a romantic effort to save the United States from fascism, pole-vaulted psychedelics into the mainstream counterculture – where they remain the defining element to this day. Modern feminism, ecological consciousness, gay rights and virtually all science and arts, particularly computer science benefited immeasurably from Leary's Utopian Psychedelic terrorism – but the psychedelic therapists working in projects like Saskatchewan's who were expanding knowledge and alleviating suffering would ultimately see their profession almost completely disappear.

By the mid-sixties significant momentum towards a psychedelic transformation of society was clearly underway and a classic moral panic erupted, and some scientists dutifully provided the data to make the case that psychedelic therapy didn't work.

Indeed, as the tide of LSD therapy rose equal and opposite resistance rose to meet it, mostly from the Toronto-based Addictions Research Foundation where scientists believed the drug was not responsible for the positive data but instead the environment and attention the patients received only were therapeutic. In their subsequent "study" alcoholics were given up to 800 micrograms of LSD, which was four times the average Saskatchewan dose or about 16 street hits, blindfolded, and/or restrained, and didn't interact with staff at all – the results were predictably negative. Of course if they really wanted to test their hypothesis they would have used the same inspiring comfortable environment with experienced and supportive staff and given half the subjects an active placebo like nicotinic acid or methylphenidate (Ritalin) or a low dose of the experimental drug. This method would be employed fifty years later with MDMA research and Post Traumatic Stress Disorder.

Most psychedelic scientists steadfastly refused to conduct double-blind tests of the compounds; the scientists who were willing to perform such controlled research were often indifferent or hostile to the new field. By the end of the fifties the therapists mostly felt the research was done and they were now busy applying it, doing more formal studies to satisfy the "squares" was only indulging their "hang-ups" – psychedelic therapists became the front-line of the culture war. And after all it is obvious when someone has taken a drug as powerful as LSD, if the experimental subjects as well as the experimenter correctly guess who got the active drug the blind is said to have failed anyway. This rejection of what would soon become conventional methodology allowed their work to be totally dismissed. At this time randomized controlled trials where subjects are randomly assigned to experimental and control conditions to ensure the isolation of the variables was becoming standard.

Once the studies were published technocrats in government approved them if enough replication with enough subjects generated enough statistical power to prove safety and efficacy (as it is still). This differed from how drugs had been developed in medicine for millennia and reduced the doctors to passive consumers of intellectual property ferociously marketed by pharmaceutical companies whose revolving door lobbyists are primarily ex-technocrats formerly employed by the drug regulator. Using the old-fashioned method LSD was sent out to doctors to test and report results – this would be one of the last drugs to be introduced this way.

On the popular 1970s TV show *Happy Days* the main character ladies-man Arthur Fonzerelli (Fonzie) was depicted in the third episode of the fifth season waterskiing and jumping over a shark, an unlikely event anywhere, never mind Milwaukee Wisconsin – the show went downhill from there. Subsequently when someone makes the wrong choice and ruins something good they "jump the shark." When the psychedelic scientists refused to use modern psychopharmacological research methodology they *jumped the shark.*

Unfortunately when sound methodology was applied ambiguous or negative results seem to be the trend from 1966 on with the notable exception of Spring Grove and later Maryland Psychiatric Research Center's work. Although the ARF (Addiction Research Foundation) study was outright dangerous (blindfolded, restrained, too much LSD, no support) generally alcoholics were given reasonable doses, left in comfortable hospital rooms, and nurses were nearby if needed – the resulting experiences were occasionally introspective and insightful but nothing close to a cure for alcoholism.

In 2012, however, the Norwegian neuroscientist Teri S. Krebs published a meta- analysis of controlled studies, including the ARF fiasco, pooling 536 subjects that proved LSD improved alcohol misuse in a statistically significant way. But, alas, 32 years before the Journal of Psychopharmacology published that story the sixties were over.

One of the reasons the Addiction Research Foundation disapproved of the Saskatchewan program was their affiliation with Al Hubbard. Hoffer made his colleagues furious when Hubbard bought a PhD from a diploma mill and Hoffer wrote him with congratulations. "God they were mad, especially my PHD colleagues," Hoffer reminisced in 2009 shortly before his death.

In 1955 Hoffer first talked with Hubbard on the phone, who boasted of his shamanic skills; the infectious enthusiasm of the pseudo-doctor Hubbard inspired Hoffer to have his three beds at the University Hospital filled with alcoholics and invite "Dr." Hubbard to Saskatchewan to see for himself.

"Al went to work and showed us what he did and it was very, very impressive." From his own initiation in 1951 until his death in 1982 Al Hubbard did little else besides shamanic drug work.

Chapter Eleven

Johnny Acidseed meets Ross Maclean

"It's easy to make people go crazy, what's hard is to make them sane."
— Al Hubbard

"In 1919 Hubbard represented the apparatus as being capable of extracting electrical energy directly from the air, but he admitted yesterday that this had been merely a subterfuge to protect his patent rights, and that, as a matter of fact, it had been a device for extracting electrical energy from radium, by means of a series of transformers which stepped up the rays."
— *Seattle Post Intelligencer,* (February 26, 1928)

When Al Hubbard was a boy of sixteen living in the Appalachian mountains of Kentucky he had a vision of a new battery. He built it in 1919 and the *Seattle- Post Intelligencer* reported that Hubbard's invention, "hidden in an 11" x 14" box, had powered a ferry-sized vessel around Seattle's Portico Bay nonstop for three days." He was awarded a patent which he sold half of for $75,000. Then during the 1920s he drove a cab in Seattle that served as high-tech communication headquarters for a rum-running cartel, which eventually earned him 18 months in prison.

His skill with electronic communication got him pardoned by President Harry Truman and he became Captain Al Hubbard with Office for Strategic Services, the predecessor to the CIA. He is even rumored to have applied his knowledge of nuclear science with The Manhattan Project that led to the first atomic bomb.

During World War II Hubbard, also a skilled mariner, was shipping weapons from San Diego to Canada, which was apparently illegal and he became the subject of a congressional investigation. He moved to Canada and became a citizen where he started shipping and uranium companies that made him a millionaire with his own island and fleet of airplanes and boats. One summer he had a second vision where an angel told him he would, "do something tremendously important for mankind." When he read about LSD in 1951 he knew this was it.

"Hubbard discovered psychedelics as a boon and a sacrament," recalled fellow acid apostle Timothy Leary, who wouldn't join the cause for over a decade until he first tried the drug.

Hubbard took it with Ron Sandison, a British psychiatrist and early researcher.

"It was the deepest mystical thing I've ever seen. I witnessed my own conception. I saw myself as a tiny mite in a big swamp with a spark of intelligence. I saw my mother and my father having intercourse. It was all clear."

With his personal airplane and satchel full of "wampum" (LSD, mescaline and psilocybin) Hubbard turned on 6,000 people before the laws were changed in 1966. "Cost me a couple of hundred thousand dollars. I had six thousand bottles to begin with." Alcoholics Anonymous founder Bill Wilson was among his subjects along with the Monsignor of the Catholic Church in North America, Aldous Huxley, the Beverly Hills psychiatrists who turned on their famous clientele and the scientists and engineers who would go on to start personal computing and the internet.

Whereas in Europe the trend was to use small doses and slowly work through the unconscious like peeling back the layers of an onion, Hubbard's approach was a single high-dose experience. His method included lying down with instrumental music playing, eye-blinders on and going within. Stroboscopic lights to change brain activity, religious artifacts and great works of art were all part of his system. If a subject appeared close to a breakthrough he would slowly turn up the volume of the music or shine a beam on the religious altar. Towards the end of the trip subjects were presented with a rose and a mirror and ordered to look into it no matter what they saw. It's impossible to know who truly created all these techniques, but Al Hubbard must have invented some of them.

"He also employed icons and symbols to send the experience into a variety of different directions: someone uptight may be asked to look at a photo of a glacier, which would soon melt into blissful relaxation; a person seeking the spiritual would be directed to a picture of Jesus, and enter into a one-on-one relationship with the Savior," another researcher rememberd.

There is significant controversy surrounding Al Hubbard's relationship to the CIA's MK-ULTRA, which was a mind-control program that probably funded the vast majority of early psychedelic research. Even the Saskatchewan LSD projects were visited by the CIA, as all researchers in the field were. To some, all psychedelic drug work was brainwashing even if the investigators didn't know they were being funded by secret intelligence, which was often the case not just in the United States but everywhere. What this ignores is the tremendous positive potential these agents possess and how unpredictable and inefficient a weapon they are.

Outraged, Hubbard said, "The CIA work stinks…they were misusing it. I tried to tell them how to use it, but even when they were killing people you couldn't tell them a God-damned thing." Army scientist Frank Olson committed suicide after taking LSD and Hubbard believed he was not the "only person who died as a result of the CIA's surprise acid tests," – where people were given the drug without knowing it.

Al Hubbard was definitely involved now and again throughout his life with every kind of espionage and intrigue imaginable but his passion for psychedelics was genuine. Near his death in 1982, he had an application before the Food and Drug Administration requesting approval of a study with cancer patients and LSD. The Captain's acid slogan was, "If you don't think it's amazing, just go ahead and try it."

When he met Hoffer and Osmond, Hubbard described his work with LSD and facilitating a "peak experience" – full-blown religious ecstasy and spiritual breakthrough. Osmond and Hoffer began to expand their horizons beyond the idea of "crazy pills."

Al Hubbard was the lone licensed Canadian importer of LSD. He met Dr. Ross MacLean, owner of Hollywood Sanitarium in 1957. MacLean had made a lot of money on Albertan oil, and also owned a cattle ranch and a geriatric hospital up the coast of British Columbia. Convinced by his own experience, MacLean built a treatment suite, complete with music system, a panic button and a chicken-wired balcony in case somebody tried to jump – exclusively for the administration of therapy with LSD and mescaline.

One of their first subjects was J.E. Brown, a Catholic priest at the cathedral of the Holy Rosary in Vancouver. In a letter written to his parish Dec. 8, 1957 he wrote, "We humbly ask Our Heavenly Mother the Virgin Mary, help of all who call upon Her to aid us to know and understand the true qualities of these psychedelics, the full capacities of man's noblest faculties and according to God's laws to use them for the benefit of mankind here and in eternity."

By now many projects were underway – in Toronto as well as Hollywood Hospital and Saskatchewan with about 3,000 subjects a year being treated worldwide. Eventually Hubbard started another clinic in Vancouver and many more groups following his "high-dose model" began working in California, especially Hollywood. "All my life," Cary Grant said in 1958, "I've been searching for peace of mind. I'd explored Yoga and hypnosis and made several attempts at mysticism. Nothing seemed to give me what I wanted until this treatment."

The British Columbia College of Physicians and Surgeons wanted Hollywood Hospital's psychedelic clinic shut down, so Dr. MacLean asked reporter Ben Metcalfe, working for *Vancouver Magazine,* to be a subject. He was treated by Hubbard himself and wrote a glowing series about his trip, which he says, "for a long time I took to be the great experience of my life." Metcalfe went on to co-found the environmental group Greenpeace. *Vancouver Sun* publisher Dom Cromie had a session. The Courts and The Salvation Army were sending clients off the streets, but the magistrates and reverends were taking the trip too.

While the work at Saskatchewan was totally government financed and asking for money from down-and-out alcoholics would have been considered heresy, Hollywood Hospital was private and charged $500.

MacLean moved in to what was then the largest house in Vancouver and was publishing important work in journals and books. Psychoanalysis required up to three visits a week for years, while Hollywood Hospital offered analysis in eight hours. Unlike most psychedelic therapy, which was done exclusively with LSD, most subjects took mescaline by itself or in combination. In early reports mescaline was described as being more visually stimulating with particularly more intense colour. Conversely LSD tends to produce complex kaleidoscope patterns and a more intellectual experience, to which the mescaline added both brilliant colour and raw feeling. Early German researcher Psychiatrist Dr. W. Frederking described "mescaline as producing more intense affect and LSD as producing a broader range of phenomena."

Generally mescaline combined with LSD produced not only iconic imagery but also full immersion into the fantasy narrative, helping the energetic process to run its full course. Psychedelic researcher Dr. Rick Strassman advises subjects, "if you see a door, don't just go through it – go through the grains in the wood."

Timothy Leary estimated 1 in 1000 would have a prolonged adverse reaction; others have suggested 1 in 400 or 500 but in all of Frank's notes there is *not one* catastrophe. MacLean managed to keep the government bodies at bay and the west coast psychedelic cowboys rolled on.

Unfortunately, Al Hubbard objected to the fees being charged, believing it should be free. In 1960 Hubbard briefly rented an apartment in Vancouver to treat subjects before heading for Menlo Park California where he helped start a similar psychedelic project at the International Federation for Advanced Study.

Hubbard's departure cleared the way for a new therapist to join the team. Frank Ogden had been a flight engineer during World War II and owned half of an airplane sales company when he read about LSD in *MacLean's* magazine in the same year Al Hubbard left for California. Blown away by what he read, he sold his share to his astonished partner and moved to Vancouver.

Chapter Twelve

Frank Ogden – Psychedelic Flight Engineer

"Many of them would say, (pulling off eye-mask), I just saw God. And a lot of the ones that would be depressed would maybe experience dying real early, then they'd be reborn and then they wouldn't have depression. So it was real magic, I'd say, Holy Christ, look at this one."

– Frank Ogden

Frank was an entrepreneur. He was raising guinea pigs at age seven and until his death at 92, he was still selling e-books and personal seminars from his website that he purchased in 1992. Dr. Ross MacLean was also an entrepreneur. Hubbard was an entrepreneur of another kind, more of a bureaucracy wheeler- dealer, of the "know whom to call to get things done" variety. Al, Frank and Ross were all united in an entrepreneurial mission of ego-transcendence – psychedelic engineers.

Upon arriving at Hollywood Hospital Frank walked up to Dr. MacLean and told him, "I'll work free for you for a couple of months, then see if you can afford me." The idea of someone from outside the field excelling was not unusual – Ross MacLean was not a psychiatrist but a General Practitioner – Hubbard was an engineer and businessman.

In addition to his Vancouver mansion Dr. MacLean owned an Alberta ranch, Hollywood Sanitarium and another geriatric hospital up the coast that required weekly grand rounds just like Hollywood did, so one day a week he would make the seven-hour trip. Frank, who had sold half of small plane merchant Vendaire to start his psychedelic work, bought a plane, wrote it off and flew him over once a week himself.

Any nurses or therapists who would be around psychedelic subjects were required to take two trips. This is Frank's "trip report" written a few days after his initiation.

• • •

Subject's Report

"I was part of an eternal striving upwards. I recall many times with different bands of people walking up mountains. We were striving, to do what many times wasn't quite clear. The "always upwards" feeling I can't explain. It seemed like plants we were reaching for the Sun."

The day was early, the room was nice, the witnesses pleasant, I had been conditioned to go. I was ready.

I placed the small 500-milligram mescaline capsule in my mouth and chased it with the 300 micrograms of LSD contained in a 4-oz. glass of what looked, tasted and smelled like water. I was told the normal reaction occurs in about half an hour. I waited.

Within 15 minutes my vision became slightly blurred. The curtains wavered although there was no breeze. A definite feeling that something was happening – something strange – passed thru me. My fingers tingled, grew cold. My posterior felt like it was resting on a slab of ice. I took off my coat and shoes and lay down.

A momentary fear gripped me as I felt my barriers evaporate. Barriers that had been both a prison and a fortress to the Inner Me. I remember the Therapist, saying, "Relax, you have nothing to fear, enter into this and do not fight or try to rationalize the strange feelings and the sensations will be far more pleasant" or something along those lines.

The thought entered my mind "Well, you are here for this adventure, let's go" as a swirling, multi-colored, clockwise vortex like swimming pool appeared. I hesitated then dived in. I've just been through a war what the hell's a pool? As I dived I dissolved.

The valley that appeared before me was one no human eye had seen before. The surface was a fabric with the warp and weft woven horizontally and vertically. It tinkled as I walked along no trail.

On the nearby hills deer-like creatures in iridescent translucent, pulsating colors gamboled along the hillside. Trees, beautiful beyond all comprehension grew, flowered and grew and flowered again. I felt the texture of this world's blanket, had undreamed of odors assail my nostrils. I saw a sky throbbing with ever changing colors of a thousand hues. I felt part of the scene. I was both there and I "was" simultaneously.

Scenes woven of pure beauty unfolded before me. It was Super Cinerama, with 3-D 360 vision. Breathless with wonder and delight I recall crying out to Dr. MacLean at the time "Oh thank you Dr. for bringing me here." I know I was crying profusely at the time over the sheer beauty of it all, yet later the Dr. remarked that these copious rivulets I felt running down my cheeks were not visible to him, at that time.

Then I noticed music. Not "heard" in the regular sense, as I knew the Hi-Fi was playing in the room, but "felt" and "knowing." It was more like I had been injected with soul music by some celestial Chopin.

For the next eight or nine hours – or was it centuries – or seconds, I knew a world that out-Disneyed Disneyland like Technicolor outdoes black and white. The colors were unbelievable and ones previously unseen. And the colors were not just colors but music as well. I felt that with brush and paint I could compose a picture that was both a scene and a song. The never-ending scenes changed with fantastic speed.

As the sensual sounds said strange things I dissolved again. I seemed to evaporate into the fragrance that was also the color. "Jasmine, what a pretty color," I thought. Then through time and space I went to Planet X of the Inner Mind.

My valley disappeared and I was at Independence Hall with Hancock signing the American Declaration of Independence. I was there! I was part of the crowd. I saw the tri-cornered hats, the long quelled pens. Saw the red, white and blue vertical bunting and stars in a circle. I saw each thread in the cloth, felt the cobblestones under my feet. I was so close. The individual hairs in each of the many Patriarchs' beards were as noticeable as coils of rope. The thrill of the crowd was my thrill, their joys my joys. I looked for Washington.

The scene changed. I had set sail on a strange voyage. I was high in the rigging of an old sailing ship with some ancient adventurer sighting new lands for the first time. I felt the burning of the rope rigging against my chest as I clung to it against the tossing from the ship as it rode each wave.

About here I took off my shirt and undershirt but that was rather vague. More of a momentary nuisance of something I had to do in another world. I remember feeling the hot sun against my bare chest. I felt an explorer's inner pride and satisfaction. Aquiver with desire to continue I sailed joyously onward.

Next I was on another boat, sinking somewhere off the Isles of Greece. I don't know how I knew where I was. I just knew. I was clutching for something, anything, to hang onto, reaching upwards. There were many in the sea around me. I tasted the ocean waves as they broke over me. I tasted the salt in the waves. A salt far saltier than any earth salt. I was clutching, gasping for air. The waves closed over me. I drowned. It was the first of many deaths.

Instantly I was in a land of many-tiered, subway-like overpasses. Not a subway really, not a freeway over-pass either, but a combination. The whole thing was a super bubble gum machine. Only it dispensed not gum, but candyfloss, banana splits, chocolate sodas, foaming root beer. Everything I had enjoyed as a child was there for me to taste. And taste I did. It was wonderful and I was crying with all the happiness of children of the world had ever experienced. The "taste" was expanded tremendously. Everything was – and was so much more.

Next I was in a fun or amusement center. I was laughing and feeling all the wonderful free emotions you feel as a child when you see something for the first time. I felt all that every child that has ever been born felt. The hope, the joy, the compassion for little animals and birds. The giggling, the awe, the pure fun. I recalled I had a good childhood.

Immediately I was moving rapidly over the ground in another scene. Not flying. Moving. The Caliph of Baghdad never had for transport a magic carpet like mine. It was knitted like an elongated doily. And substantial. It was made of pink sound.

Without being aware of change, I found myself leading a band of Turks across the sands of Arabia driving the Infidels back into the sea. I felt the exhilaration of the charge, heard the cries of my companions, felt and smelt the sweat of the animal under me, saw and swallowed the interminable dust, felt the stinging sand, felt the weight of my Saracen sword. I recall I seemed very proud of that sword. I especially enjoyed fighting the invaders. I don't know why but I have the impression they were Christians. "They are the worst kind," my fellow riders told me. Suddenly I felt the pain of burning wounds. I fell. Felt hot sand beneath my fingers, saw small streams of lovely red blood flow in changing patterns over the sand only to sink instantly out of sight. I felt myself sinking too – and died again.

In all the scenes the colours are just too much. Fantastic is a mild word to describe them. Like "good" in that other earth world I knew long ago. The colours move continuously. They change continuously. And they pulsate and glow like they were illuminated from within by a light of unlimited power and feeling. It is as though the colours were alive too, and something only a Dali could imagine. Sometimes they were of recognizable scenes but mainly of landscapes men of earth have never witnessed before.

The Hi-Fi in the room was now playing Bruckner I felt only Scheherazade – a Scheherazade of orange and green.

Next I was in an ancient temple, where a gamut of instruments played music that was a delight to hear. But the source of this lively sound was not visible. I mused "Could they have Muzak here?" The temple itself was a high well-built affair, mainly an off white but with some sections in smooth red sandstone. Yet where walls were needed for support, nothing but air curtains stood. The floors were warm. I felt "here are floors upon which happiness stood."

About here, I think I said out loud something about "Baal-The True God." But that was here. I was there! I felt the earth between my bare toes. I felt the sun. I made love to a hundred different – yet familiar – dusky tawny maidens. I felt the texture of their skin, looked into their eyes, kissed their breasts that felt like bombs of passion and caressed thighs of heated lava and experienced a thousand climatic moments of ecstasy. I was there.

I lived with them, ate with them, hunted with them. I felt the heat from their fires, ate their food – strange vegetables and fruits with unearthly tastes. Spices that man has long forgotten tantalized my palate. And those women!

They were dressed in what today I can only describe as a Daisy Mae outfit but, on them, there, it looked like the raiment of Goddesses. These Astartes of another land were full breasted, to understate the facts. Some of their clothing left one breast bare. They were dusky bronze in color with long sinuous legs and healthy, uninhibited sexual appetites. We loved in a million different ways. I too was a healthy, lusty pagan. And I loved it! Surely this must be the land theProphet promised the Faithful. I laughed. "Paradise of Pharmacology and the Prophet" – what a perfume! I thought of converts by the million switching to this religion. Baal's come back – and with the "strong" sell.

I then recall a ray of light coming thru the towel over my eyes. It was Dr. MacDonald, the hospital psychiatrist, asking me how I was. I felt like saying – in fact I did say, "If this is insanity – open up the cage I want to climb back in." Even as I said these few words a hundred thoughts, pictures, actions had come and gone while each vowel was passing my lips. No wonder so many find this 'experience' hard to describe.

Thru all this I was conscious all the time. Well at least most of the time. I knew that the earth world was out there. But this was so much better a world. Perhaps a world that could be if all men could remove their superficial veneers and see the beauty that abounds around them instead of constantly engaging in petty jealousies and bickering. I remember saying something about physical nausea but I was more interested in getting back to my other more real world. I remember my conscious mind thinking at one point "this is a hell of a time to puke when you are making love to this pre-Cleopatra Cleopatra on the lush green, green, green banks of the White Nile."

The many tiered subway thing returned. Only this time it was more like a subway with people built like boxes whizzing by. It reminded me of the old-time change system that department stores used to have where they shot by compressed air or cables the money up to the head office to be receipted and changed. The net result I felt from this was that in our present busy world you get on each days subway train, earn a dollar fight, argue, have a million little wars with petty bureaucrats, struggle, spend and at the end get off with – if you are lucky – a net of a nickel for the day.

I saw whirling, spinning doors, up-down escalators, but not earth types, here – there, everywhere, rush-rush. Very glad when that part was over. And about here I think I said "How much more? Can't we turn this channel off?" or something along those lines. My mind was already satiated with the impressions of a dozen lifetimes.

In a flash I had returned. Returned to more music. But now music that fell like waterfalls of thunder from Olympian crags bathed the land in all colours of my expanded spectrum. In the music river sapphires, emeralds, garnets and iridium lined the riverbed like baubles. These scintillating jewels sparkled and lived and glowed from a candle shine within. The water tasted blue although I never drank it. I just know it tasted blue. "Blue tasting water is the very best kind," I thought.

Then I heard a silence that sang in a primeval rain forest when the mist was violet and violet was Spring. And Spring was music. In this forest my raiment was made of ferns woven between the feathers of a Peacock and lined with the Cote de Azure of the Mediterranean. An exquisite pleasure, subtle perfumes of an all-encompassing love swept over me. A spiritual infatuation with life I thought. An affair of body and soul.

My heaven was jarred by a scratch on the record player back in World One. I thought surely the scratch must have been produced with a hunting knife – so loud the bounce of the needle.

Again the music. This time a symphony. But one missed by the priests in the Tower they call Capitol.

Next, and most vivid, I was leading a band of pirate girls, flying the Jolly Roger, conquering all who crossed our paths. The girls again. Dressed so seductively. After a few years of this, – or was it a mini-second, I died again. I mean died. I felt the cannon shell rip my side to bits, saw the blood loop round the doweled deck, felt the pain, felt the haze and comfort of death. I have always felt that death didn't worry me like it does some people but now I hardly think it will bother me at all. I now believe that those who are followers of re-incarnation would be forever convinced if their experience were anything like mine. I can also see how the founders of Hinduism, or of any religion for that matter, had some ancient, similar drug that gave them the "visions" they experienced. I can also see how a pro-religious Christian type could see Christ etc. I came away from the experience thoroughly convinced that Christianity is a sham. Christ a crook. With all this beauty to behold, "they," have earth people – at least in this unenlightened section of the Western World -- covering everything with cloaks and prohibitions. I felt like ripping every nuns habit to shreds.

Somewhere about here someone in World #1 said something about "fighting battles alone." Couldn't he see my pirate crew all around me? They were warm, loyal and a great bunch. I recall being annoyed by this petty questioning and the mirror that was held in front of me. I said something like "I have had a wonderful life." If I am supposed to have re-lived my life while under LSD I guess I did. I have had a wonderful life here and in that world too. I remember after saying this going back to a room in the rear of the ship to a wine and orgy party. It was a leisurely debauch. "The best kind," I thought. The fact that I had died on this boat, minutes, hours, years before, mattered not. Time was shuffled like a joker in the deck. First on top, then on the bottom, next in-between. Sounds confusing now. It wasn't at all then. Back to my orgy. It was wonderful. I saw most vividly the tossing around of the spoils of our captures. I can just not tell you how great a feeling it was. Civilization has its drawbacks.

Next, I became a tree. I was a tree. I was the trunk. My arms the limbs. I saw as a tree, I felt as a tree. I drew my strength from the ground as a tree. I exhaled through each leaf as a tree. I cuddled the bird's nests like a Mother and felt tiny feet on my boughs. And a thousand raindrops fell on my leaves.

Then I was the earth. I felt people and animals walking on me. I looked up between many blades of grass that I had fed. I fed the plants, felt the rain, felt the sun. I was the earth. I wasn't just next to Nature. I was Nature. I was a lily pad in a wooden glen, a gardenia soaking on a perfumed Polynesian shore.

Again, on a boat. This time with Vasco de Gamma rounding the Horn. Feeling the deck shudder with each lurch of the ship as it plowed through waves of the most beautiful translucent aquamarine. I saw the waves break over the bow. I felt the salt spray again in my face. Felt the salt on my lips. Felt the monotony of a long voyage. Tasted the same food, day after day. Picked the maggots out of the rotten meat. I was there!

Now in a tropical plain of long ago. I saw impenetrable bowers of luxuriant woven bamboo grass that rippled as it swayed. Here was an untouched realm "they" would forbid to mortal man.

The verdant field changed to arches of Jade in which a vine of butterflies spiraled in the breeze. A voluptuous enchantment swept over me, breathing colours in strange fruits that appeared like and yet unlike tropical papayas growing from a mangrove tree which was speckled with dainty chameleons of orange alabaster. The sunlight seeped down through the orderly tangle of growth in this primeval rain forest. Always I was walking. Walking, walking, walking, walking alone. Walking with other natives. Eating what we could. Birds, beetles (these were quite tasty – something like a big flying grasshopper with a furry-feathery covering) that we ate on a stick. I remember thinking "suburban bar-b-que a la Dawn of History." More walking. We were always walking. When I was later in the room assigned for me for the night my legs were extremely stiff. They were for a week afterwards. It was that damn walking. We struggled, we fought weird things, we were sometimes cold, although most of the time I was comfortably warm.

Next another temple. All my scenes, or at least many of them had girls. If this proves I have a pre-occupation with Sex I want you to know that I think that is just GREAT. The dresses – and I recall them exactly, were of a striped zebra skin, with one shoulder strap, a high slit skirt, that twirled as they walked yet would not fall apart when they lounged. In all my scenes I saw no chairs, not one motor, nothing mechanical, no cars or airplanes. I was either walking, on an animal or on a boat. I saw these things. I felt these things, I WAS THERE. Every emotion all people felt, I felt. I was part of an eternal striving upwards. I recall many times with different bands of people walking up mountains. Saw the sweat on my companions brow, saw the moisture through the fabric of their clothes, felt their struggles, felt their woes, felt their victories. We were striving, to do what many times wasn't quite clear. The "always upwards" feeling I can't explain. It seemed like plants we were reaching for the Sun. The struggles were for many things. Sometimes against oppression. Sometimes just against fate it seemed.

One scene was in the Himalayas. I just know that someday I will see that place again. I can describe the spot down to the last grain of sand. That seemed strange. Here at the top of the Himalayas – sand? I would have thought it would have all washed down hill. However, I doubt not that when I am there again the sand will be too. The rocks too I know.

Their position, their shape, their colour and size. I know the lack of vegetation. The dust. The barrenness, the strange sky. And we were always looking up. My neck was tired from it.

And here I recall the nurse coming over. I was sick and had spit into the bucket. Thanks for the convenience. I also noticed I had used quite a few Kleenex. My undershirt was soaking wet and it was on the floor. Yet I had taken it off long (?) ago. At this point I felt fear that I hadn't come out of it, the drug, and that the hospital staff were worried. Then I felt humor over the situation. "They got a problem," I thought. Then I felt sorry for having gotten them into this mess. It seemed like years and years had passed and I was to be here forever. When I looked at the nurse, she had a big scratch on her right cheek and it was still bleeding. I just knew it was from a tiger.

Then ghosts etched in my sub-conscious memory danced forth in cackling colours. And their dance! An extra-ordinary blend of vigor and the tableaus of the Damned. I was in a world of hobgoblins and witches. But these were funny, friendly people. I laughed and played with them. We ran into a few dragons and I whacked off their heads. It was fun.

All this could have happened in 10 minutes or a million years. Time is relative. It can be non-existent or an eternity. Each incident seemed so long – so short.

Memories of both the therapist John Holloway and Dr. MacLean questioning me with the mirror I recall annoyed me. I felt like saying "I am looking at myself, I'm that handsome guy up in the rigging" I looked real good to me.

What an educational tool I thought. Here a school where one acquires genius on the installment plan. I felt like erecting a sign paraphrasing Dante "Ye shall acquire understanding all who enter here."

I wondered if I had visited the emotional Mesa of the Muses. I find now my normal mind is but an old shed attached to a vast newer building. A building that houses, not machinery but thought. But "thought" of unbelievable complexity, incomprehensible simplicity and unknown warmth.

Why have I not been here before I wonder. Have other men? Certainly all should see "What could be." I felt fused into the Cyclopean eye of all souls.

The thought struck me. If Superior Beings from another world can use this "thought" regularly no wonder they pass us by. Does the Lion notice the Gnat? The whale the water flea?

I wouldn't have missed this "experience" for the world. It was decidedly most worthwhile. I could go on describing the other 14, 206 scenes but the world hasn't made enough paper.

After what I gauged to be six o'clock I was led while still dizzy to another room. During the first two to three hour stage in this other room the drugged condition was in effect about 50% of the time. It returned in waves. Now I was in World #1. Then I would go back to World #2. I could call this world Fantasia land but it was so real. Much more real than this world. Much more. I cannot emphasize too strongly that I WAS THERE. I can still see "us" striving, reaching, the storm beating across our chests, the rivulets of water running down our faces, the clothes soaking wet around our torsos. I felt the rain, the salt, felt the thirst and the passions. I recall afterwards in the private adjoining room checking to see how messy my ejaculations had been I was so certain I must have had hundreds. I hadn't. At least not in this world.

While this come-go stage lasted I looked at the picture of the mountain scene on the walls of this new room and the scene was moving. I took the picture off the wall and propped it up on my bed and watched it intently. As I watched the seasons would change. The snow would disappear and come again. The clouds change shape. Yet, I could look out of the window (I was annoyed at the heavy screening) and see the usual street scenes. With highly improved vision and hearing I could see so much more in the flowers, hear car doors closing blocks away, see the outside sky. Yet, back on my bed the picture still moved. I watched my leg. The skin would fall away and it would become emaciated. Then, while I watched grow back to normal. Moments later I would be all "Here." This went on for several hours. Half here – half there. Then more here and rarely there.

I was terribly thirsty by the time I went to the second room, I went to the washroom and urinated gallons. I should have weighed myself at that time.

For me the strangeness – at least some of it – was the lack of cars, of planes, of anything that contained a motor, as I know one. Had I gone ahead to a world that had unlimited power? Mental power beyond our comprehension? Or had I gone back to a land and time where such was unnecessary. Or was "there" a forward and backward?

I saw no cities, as I know them. Nor was anything upon which to sit over one-foot high. No chairs, no stools, just low divans.

In retrospect when I was "there," in many cases I seem now to feel that I was invisible. Yet, I belonged.

Was I the Present overlapping the Past while both overlapped the Future? I thought of the colour transparency overlays used to produce magazine colour plates. Each one is part of the picture – but only a part. Only by overlaying them all together – a separate transparency sheet for each basic color, does one get the complete picture, with all its clarity, its meaning, its shadings, its "feel."

Is the complete picture of Life – the Past, the Present, and the Future overlaid as in these colour transparencies of the lithographers etching table?

In retrospect I feel that outside of the experiment it was good for me as a person. I saw myself. It crystallized my own personal convictions – and changed some that might not have been right. I feel now I can show more compassion, more tenderness, be franker than I was before. For example I would never had said before I thought Christ was a Crook if I had felt it. Now I would. I believe it. I also now believe the Kingdom of God, any God, is within yourself. And you don't need an intermediary to get an appointment.

I thought before I was basically a good person. Now I feel more so. I could be humble before. More so now. I do not think that any body can go through that experience – in the "full" way that I did and not feel that someone pulls the strings. I am equally well convinced though that NO organized religion is the answer. I feel the less such religions the better. The less restrictions, the less taboos the better too. I would also now question if civilization – as we know it – is the answer either.

I also feel a great debt of gratitude to my parents for giving me such a pleasant childhood to enable me to have such a wonderful experience. My sights were mainly happy ones. I can well understand that others go through pure Hell because their early life was not pleasant. In the whole experience I do not recall having a material thing mean anything. Possessions were non-existent. For the past few years possessions haven't meant much to me any how. Now they will mean less. I always have for many years been quite capable of giving love. Now I feel like all the reserve of an emotional Hoover Dam is behind me. It's a good feeling. I feel I'm good. I feel cleansed. Not because I have been cleaned but because I now know there was nothing bad to be washed away. Of course, I never recognized "sin" in the accepted sense anyhow.

At one of the mirror-in-the-faces stages I remember a really symbolic trip up a mountain overturning every stone and finally at the top thinking "all that and nothing under any of them all the time."

I think this experience is a must for every writer, musician, painter and architect. I saw castles, bridges, buildings, the mind of normal man couldn't imagine. I heard music that flowed like blood in your veins, smelt odors, tasted tastes that were so unbelievable beautiful. I felt like shouting "Hooray, I'm LSD's first addict."

I believe this LSD has a wonderful future to help us understand the human mind. Both the mind that is sick as well as helping the mind that is well grow in perception. I can also see where it would be pure hell for some people. For me it was 99% wonderful. I wasn't particularly crazy over the sickness but it was nothing compared to how I benefited.

Once to the nurse I said something I thought was very witty at the time "I dreamed I took LSD in my Maidenform Bra." It seemed so right at the time.

This then was my impression of an LSD Experience. It had provided answers to questions I hadn't asked, raised questions I hadn't dreamed existed. Showed me sights my travels had failed to witness, gave me an emotional range I never knew. Re-informed a confidence I thought was too strong already, yet balanced it on a pivot of humility not common to Caucasian men.

Here endeth the adventure. An adventure surpassing the sum of life.

Frank Ogden
Hollyburn Mountain
May 2, 1963 West Vancouver, B.C

* * *

Despite declaring himself "LSD's first addict" Frank took the drug only twice more, once to complete the program required for all treatment staff and then again to test an LSD antidote supplied by the CIA. Rather than stopping the trip, "it extended it for an extra twenty-four hours and I could control the visions," he remembers.

MacLean was rarely in the treatment room during sessions, even though he was medically responsible for whatever happened. He, or Dr. MacDonald the chief psychiatrist would do an official write-up, screen out potential psychotics, recommend doses and then, hand them over to Frank Ogden who sat by their side through heaven and hell.

I only had two injuries, one guy fell off the couch and separated his shoulder and another guy who had issues around homosexuality and he saw me painted up with make-up and he belted me with a right cross, but he caught me on the way down.

The worst subjects were psychiatrists and engineers, because they're so rigid. A lot of engineers would tear the skin on their fingers while they tried to tear their iron rings off.

We were most successful with frigidity cases in women. I remember the first breakthrough, this woman, never had an orgasm in her life, and I put my hand on hers and (stroking his fingers down her hand) by the time I got there she had an orgasm. I saw her a few years later at a dinner party and she came up to me and said, you're not going to do that again tonight are you?

The original focus of the clinic when it opened it 1957 was alcoholism, although it soon expanded to anyone relatively sane with five hundred bucks.

"A lot of the alcoholics, a third of them instantly stopped drinking." By 1967 Abram Hoffer or a member of his team had treated 2,000 Saskatchewan subjects and reported half were improved – unfortunately they stopped using LSD that year, but Hollywood Hospital continued until 1975.

In agreement with Walter Pahnke's 1962 research and Roland Griffiths's 2006 work Frank reports, "everyone had a spiritual experience, it only differed in length."

"Many of them would say, (pulling off eye-mask), I just saw God. And a lot of the ones that would be depressed would maybe experience dying real early, then they'd be reborn and then they wouldn't have depression. So it was real magic, I'd say, Holy Christ, look at this one."

"Sometimes when they were at the end they would just be lying silently and I would write articles for flying magazines."

Frank would often sleep in Dr. MacLean's Casa Loma mansion, hanging out with the boss. "We were called, "the big bomb boys" because we would give such heavy big doses." Life was good.

"The hundreds of nurses that worked there didn't hurt either."

Frank was a great doubter of education's ability to keep up with accelerating technological change. His approach to LSD was similar to the rest of his life, "just do it." Sadly Al Hubbard or Ross MacLean never wrote a book describing their theory and practice of psychedelic therapy.

Or perhaps their methods were too simple to fill a book. In any case, the questions of how does it work and/or why does it work when it does and why doesn't it when it doesn't are never addressed. The Big Bomb Boys with a West Coast Zen surfer's mentality just went for it.

If Drs. Leary and Grof were at a restaurant in this analogy they might pull out their knives and forks and start cutting up and chewing the *menu*. Frank walks in with the food–

Psychedelic treatment room at Hollywood Hospital

Chapter Thirteen

Preparation

Before the Mystery Rite at Eleusis, aspirants gave a full confessional before a tribunal of judges and confession plays a big part in the Bwiti ibogaine initiation as well. But Hollywood Hospital went far beyond and asked the client to also consider who they wanted to become –

E ven if every word of the preceding section proves totally untrue, and psychedelic drug use is Russian roulette with permanent madness and the entire scientific field destroyed again, the Hollywood Hospital story is an extraordinary one. Unlike every other psychedelic project this one was entrepreneurial – a private hospital offering a controversial and "unproven" treatment for $500 – or about $3,270 today – roughly the same price as the recently re-opened psychedelic clinic The Iboga House near Vancouver, using ibogaine.

If Leary's 1 in 1000 adverse reaction rate for LSD is right Hollywood Hospital beat even the safety record espoused by the drug's most fevered advocate. Out of the thousand plus souls who took the drug there none required serious intervention.

Some of the subjects had displayed severe psychosis requiring hospitalization in the past but were given the golden ticket anyway. How many were turned away is unknown. Subjects were given a physical, a huge personality test still in use called the Minnesota Multiphasic Personality Inventory and asked to write out their autobiography in an eighteen-question format.

AUTOBIOGRAPHY

1. State reasons for taking LSD, what you hope to accomplish by it, and the problems confronting you now.

2. Describe your birthplace, date, and circumstances surrounding your birth.

3. Discuss early development, temper tantrums, bedwetting, nightmares, illnesses and other unusual feelings or circumstances.

4. FAMILY

a. describe Father- his age; if dead, at what age did he die, and the circumstances of his death. Describe his physical and mental characteristics as a Father, husband and person. What was your relationship to him and how did he affect your life.

b. Mother – describe as above

c. Brothers and Sisters – describe similarly

d. Any other individual concerned with your care and development living in your home.

e. What effect did you have on your family (i.e., your family's response to you).

5. EDUCATION

Discuss all aspects of your education, formal education and age accomplished. Describe your passes and failures, reasons and feelings re leaving school. What was your goal in getting an education – if any.

6. ECONOMIC

Discuss jobs held, and your relationship to others at work, your ambitions, successes and frustrations. Number of times promoted or fired. Why? Etc.

7. MILITARY HISTORY

Reasons for entering. Age of entry. Service. Ranks. Promotions, demotions – why? Experiences and attitudes in the Services. Time of, and reason for discharge.

8. LEGAL HISTORY

Any imprisonments? Charges, fines, etc? Reasons for such and results. Attitudes to courts and police. Any other legal involvements such as divorce, lawsuits, accidents. Describe circumstances and outcome of each.

9. AMBITION

Goals you desire in life.

10. INTERESTS

11.RELIGION

Describe your religious beliefs, conflicts, concept of God, Heaven and Hell and Death, philosophies, prejudices, and the influence religion and philosophy have on your life. Have you had any religious or mystical experiences?

12. HABITS

a. Tobacco – Amount. When started – problems associated with it, etc.

b. Alcohol – When started, amount, problems associated with it, and how it influences you when under it, and the problem it poses you, your family and society. Any unusual experiences.

c. Drugs – Same as alcohol

13. SEX AND MARITAL HISTORY

Describe attitudes developed towards sex, and whence they came. If a woman, describe age of onset of menses, pain associations with it, irregularities. Attitudes, concept of pregnancy, fears, etc., associated with it. Attitudes to change of life, etc.

Describe sexual experiences, circumstances under which they began with whom, at what age, their age, reasons for it, and feelings associated with it.

Describe masturbatory and homosexual experiences, and relationships with the opposite sex. Elaborate on this paragraph only if you wish to.

If married, describe courtship, age of spouse, and reasons and circumstances of marriage, oppositions to it, and conflicts surrounding it.

Describe spouse in detail, your relationship with spouse, attitudes and relationship sexually. Describe attitudes to children, desirability, their acceptance, ages and present relationship towards them.

14. Describe all past illnesses and their effect upon you. Describe any fears or phobias, their onset and attitudes towards them. What effect do you think your ego or personality had on the production of illness?

15. Discuss any chronic or hereditary illnesses in your family – emotional, alcoholic, other.

16. SELF-DESCRIPTION

What kind of person are you? How do you see yourself as a

person? Do you like yourself? Why? Describe your moods, sensitivities, jealousies, adequacies and inadequacies, complexes, fears, guilts, philosophies, capacities for self-deception, your role to other people, your family and yourself. Concept of honesty, sincerity, rejection, etc. – describe in full. What is your ideal of the personality you wish to become? How could you become this ideal?

17. HOW DO OTHER PEOPLE SEE YOU?
     Their attitudes toward you, their acceptance of you and their expectations of you, etc.

18. Describe any other outstanding experiences or feelings that have played an important part in your life.

• • •

Before the Mystery Rite at Eleusis, aspirants gave a full confessional before a tribunal of judges and confession plays a big part in the Bwiti ibogaine initiation as well. But this went far beyond and asked the client to consider who they wanted to become.

Unfortunately, Hollywood Hospital did not use an experimental methodology but a therapeutic one. Research in psychoactives requires placebo controls because the mere expectation of a psychoactive effect can cause a cascade of chemical changes in the body. One study of alcoholics revealed that just putting a little vodka on the rim of an orange-juice glass for "the first of the day" would produce all the body changes associated with being drunk. It is not merely a matter of cognition but organic changes in the body as one anticipates the effects emerging.

The placebo works well, for example, with antidepressants that take weeks to start working, but with psychedelics it's usually obvious to everybody right away.

Walter Pahnke and Roland Griffiths's research proving psilocybin can facilitate "religious or mystical peak experiences" did use "active" placebo controls, employing nicotinic acid and Ritalin as decoys with neither experimenters nor subjects being aware of who had taken what. Another example of placebo-controlled psychedelic research is the MDMA Post Traumatic Stress Disorder (PTSD) study by Dr. Mithfoer; this project uses a very low dose of the drug as an active placebo.

The kind of critical self-analysis required to write the autobiography is intrinsically therapeutic and the notion of answering the question of "who do I want to become?" represents psychotherapy at its most romantic. Paying out an enormous sum of money also primes the mind for results. Hubbard first tripped in '51 and had obviously been experimenting very carefully and innovating brilliantly ever since.

MacLean also performed a complete physical to screen out serious liver damage, epilepsy, severe heart problems and overt or latent psychotics. Even this demonstrates a commitment and a level of honesty and thorough optimism as though the neuronauts were really astronauts.

A psychologist was hired to administer and score the Minnesota Multiphasic Personality Inventory (M.M.P.I.) for each subject. Frank believes he "was right every time" about how someone's trip would basically unfold. My first year psychology professor said, "LSD could make you go crazy at any time, the first time or the thousandth."

Yet, in the years since LSD and other psychedelics became popularized in the 1960s, schizophrenia rates have stayed the same. However many cases of madness being *triggered* by psychedelics, most spectacularly by LSD, are well documented. Almost always some form of mental illness would have manifested anyway, but this is little comfort to parents who blame psychedelics for their children's suffering. These kinds of subjects were screened out.

About two-thirds of the subjects were considered "neurotic," the largest minority being alcoholic, but every contemporary form of mental anguish was well represented.

In psychiatrist Dr. Sydney Cohen's 1960 review of 5,000 subjects who had received psychedelic psychotherapy 0.2% (one in 500) had an adverse reaction requiring at least 48 hours of hospitalization. Hollywood Hospital's score of zero puts them in the elite in the field of the 42 teams that Dr. Cohen contacted.

In the early 1960s Freudian psychoanalysis was the entrenched ideology and biochemical theories of the mind the young upstart philosophy. The M.M.P.I. personality test, a version of which is still used today, avoided the ideologies of the day and simply compared a battery of 567 true-false items with the answers of those suffering various forms of psychopathology. Depressed people tend to form one pattern of answers, the paranoid a different pattern, etc.

Number	Abbreviation	Description	What is measured
1	HS	Hypochondriasis	Concern with bodily symptoms
2	D	Depression	Depressive Symptoms
3	Hy	Hysteria	Awareness of problems and vulnerabilities
4	Pd	Psychopathic Deviate	Conflict, struggle, anger, respect for society's rules
5	MF	Masculinity/Femininity	Stereotypical masculine feminine interests/behaviours
6	Pa	Paranoia	Level of trust, suspiciousness, sensitivity
7	Pt	Psychasthenia	Worry, Anxiety, tension, doubts, obsessiveness
8	Sc	Schizophrenia	Odd thinking and social alienation
9	Ma	Hypomania	Level of excitability
0	Si	Social Introversion	People orientation

Validity scales further assess the subject's sincerity.

Abbreviation	Description	Assesses
?	"Cannot Say"	Questions not answered
L	Lie	Client "faking good"
F	Infrequency	Client "faking bad"
K	Defensiveness	Denial/evasiveness

This handout dates back to back to 1959 -

INSTRUCTIONS FOR PATIENTS TAKING L.S.D.25 OR ALLIED MEDICATIONS
Between now and the treatment session I would like you to think over what you consider to be your main problems. If there are any questions about these to which you would like to find answers write the questions down in a list. You will find that during the drug experience it may be very worthwhile to check the list over because then you will likely be able to find the answers.

A day or two after we will want you to write an account of your experience. This will help you by making it easier to remember later on.

The drug that you are going to take is given in very small quantities. You will be taking only one ten-thousandth of a gram which is almost microscopic so it has been made up in a pill (or capsule) form for ease of administration. You will take a pill or a drink of water – there are no needles or anything like that.

You will notice certain physical symptoms and rather peculiar feelings particularly at the beginning. How you react to these is important. You can make them both pleasant and enjoyable or, if you let yourself become alarmed by them you can make them unpleasant and painful.

You can ensure that they are pleasant by simply relaxing and enjoying them. For example you may feel your body becoming weightless and may feel that you are melting. Accept such changes and enjoy them as novel sensations for they are part of the treatment and will offer you a chance to explore new areas of experience. If you fight against them you not only make them disturbing but also tend to lessen the benefit you can hope to gain through this treatment.

This is true of all aspects of the experience that you are to have. Accept what happens and how you feel with as little questioning as you can. Later, after the experience you will have ample time to think about it and you will be able to recall what you felt and thought but during the treatment itself remember to relax and enjoy the feelings, thoughts, images and sensations for themselves. If during the experience you try to make everything fit into your every day experience you will cheat yourself both of the good effects of the drug and the pleasure you can find.

At times during the experience you may feel much like laughing or crying and you should not try to hold back these expressions of feeling. Nearly everyone who takes the drug finds himself moved to laughter and to tears several times during the experience. Actually these feelings will bother you less if you accept them as a normal part of the experience and do not try to fight against them.

The day will be quite informal and we will listen to music, talk about various things, read, and look at pictures and so forth. The drug makes music more enjoyable and increases your appreciation of pictures. If you have records you would particularly like to hear or pictures you would like to look at please bring them along. Photographs are very interesting since one seems to understand the pictured people very well and often becomes aware of new aspects of their personalities.

It is unlikely that you will feel much like eating during the day but we will have plenty of candy and fruit juice on hand.

The physical symptoms tend to fade away after about two hours. However, if you begin to question the reality of the experience or to become dissatisfied with the experience or with yourself or with other people, the experience may become confusing and unpleasant. Or you may find yourself growing extremely suspicious and afraid. At these times some of the unpleasant physical feelings will be likely to return.

You may feel at times that ideas are being put into your mind to make you think various thoughts. This is not so. Most people feel this during the experience from time to time and it is mentioned to you since when the idea occurs to you it is a sign you are losing trust in yourself, or in us.

This is very important. During the experience we must trust each other, because if we do not the experience cannot fail to be unpleasant so long as the mistrust lasts. If you find things becoming unpleasant simply concentrate on the bond of trust and understanding between us – and you will find that the unpleasant aspects of the experience will fade away.

About five or six hours after you take the drug you will feel that drug effects are largely gone and the experience is over. This is usually not so, rather you have learned how to use the drug and it is in this period that we can exchange ideas with remarkable ease.

It is not wise to begin to worry about getting out of the experience and having it over because this phase is a very useful one if you do not worry or upset yourself. This is why it is best to be well rested to begin with since otherwise you tend to get tired and find the later stages of the experience less enjoyable.

After about seven hours the physical symptoms will all be gone with the possible exception of a slight difficulty in judging distances, which may last into the following day. You will most probably feel as though you had gone for some time without sleep and had arrived at the state in which you were no longer sleepy.

You will probably feel physically tired but mentally clear and alert.

We know that you can find this a very valuable experience. There is really nothing to be concerned about from the point of view of your health or of any bad mental effects of the drug. Thousands of people have taken it without any ill effects, while nearly all of them have found its effects remarkable and wonderful.

The important things to remember are these:

During the experience accept the novel feelings as real and true. You can question them and apply the usual forms of logic to them at your leisure in the days that follow but for the few hours that the drug is operative simply accept and enjoy them.

To the extant that you trust yourself and trust us the experience will be pleasant and our understanding and fellowship very close. To the extent that you mistrust yourself and us you will find that you are growing suspicious and withdrawing and the experience is becoming unpleasant and confusing. In this experience you control your own feelings and you can stop the development of these unpleasant aspects by simply concentrating on the level of trust we can have in each other and the bond of affection and understanding that the experience can generate.

The Medical Staff, Hollywood Hospital

During one early session Al Hubbard and Ross MacLean had an interesting exchange that illustrated their "bedside manner" well:

Mac: He is not likely to produce much more in this session, is he?

Hub: Not much from our point of view but lots from his, as time goes on many of the things he has thought of will be clear to him.

Mac: There may be some type of <u>delayed </u>reaction due to realizations he has not voiced?

Hub: No delayed reaction is likely as he is doing fine now.

Mac: Best to let him go as far as possible without any night sedation like tuinal? Hub: Let him go as far as he likes he could not go psycho if he wanted to now. Mac: I am going to see him early tomorrow am – I will phone tonight and I'll order what is necessary.

Hub: O.K. good, suggest no sedation until 11 or 12 tonight. We can go at 3 if you like as Dr. Byrne had used to do it this way. The principle this works on is the L.S.D. has done its work after 6 hours, even if the effects last for about 8 to 10 they handle it with ease, but the 250 mg of mescaline will keep him working but is not very strong as it takes usually 400 mg.

By 1966 only six U.S. LSD projects survived, down from 210 a year before; however underground psychedelic therapy has continued uninterrupted. High- tech pioneer and psychedelic researcher Myron Stolaroff wrote of one such therapist in *The Secret Chief Revealed,* where he discussed the pioneering work of Dr. Leo Zeff, who treated some 3000 subjects in individual and group settings working with a variety of psychedelic medicines.

In 1975 a research chemist named Sasha Shulgin synthesized MDMA and told his now-retired therapist friend about the drug's potential in therapy. Leo Zeff came out of retirement and over the next ten years an international network of therapists became skilled with using this substance until it too was prohibited in 1985.

Dr. Zeff would have his clients read the following prayer before picking up the chalice and beginning the voyage.

By Francois de Salignac Fenelon, Archbishop of Cambray, 1651-1715, AD:

Lord, I know not what I ought to ask of Thee;
Thou only knowest what I need;
Thou lovest me better than I know how to love myself.
O Father, give to Thy child that which
he himself knows not how to ask.
I dare not ask either for crosses or for consolations;
I simply present myself before Thee,
I open my heart to Thee,
Behold my needs that I know not myself;
See and do according to Thy tender mercy.
Smite, or heal; depress me or raise me up;
I adore all Thy purposes without knowing them;
I am silent; I offer myself in sacrifice;
I yield myself to Thee: I would have no
other desire than to accomplish Thy will.
Teach me to pray.
Pray Thyself in me.
AMEN

One psychedelic researcher, psychiatrist Dr. Oscar Janiger, worked with hundreds of subjects and computed the three most frequent occurring statements describing the experience.

"It's all alive."
"It's all connected."
"It comes in waves."

• • •

"If you started in the wrong way," I said in answer to the investigator's questions, "everything that happened would be a proof of the conspiracy against you. It would all be self-validating. You couldn't draw a breath without knowing it was part of the plot."

"So you think you know where madness lies?"

My answer was a convinced and heartfelt, "Yes."

"And you couldn't control it?"

"No I couldn't control it. If one began with fear and hate as the major premise, one would have to go on to the conclusion."

"Would you be able," my Wife asked, "to fix your attention on what The Tibetan Book of the Dead calls the Clear Light?"

I was doubtful.

"Would it keep the evil away, if you could hold it? Or would you not be able to hold it?"

I considered the question for some time. "Perhaps I could – but only if there were somebody there to tell me about the Clear Light. One couldn't do it by oneself."

Doors of Perception, –Aldous Huxley

Chapter Fourteen

Hollywood Hospital: *Listening to Acid*

"I had a pleasant dream last night and thought I had a plan whereby I could change all things, and return to a new life and to see and visit the many one's I dearly love, and am forced to leave."

In 1993's *Listening to Prozac* Dr. Peter Kramer describes an elderly patient who suffered a severe depression representing a worsening condition that Dr. Kramer believes was long masked by the serotonin system, but after decades of stress it too had finally succumbed. The elderly patient turned down prozac but what would he have said to LSD?

In *The Use of LSD in Psychotherapy and Alcoholism,* a chapter written for a psychedelic medical textbook for an alternate universe but published in this one in 1967, the Hollywood Hospital crew describe a similar patient who first suffered a depression at age 65 "which responded readily to treatment" (ECT). Six years later however the depression returned, this time with an obsession regarding digestion that remitted again, for four more years this time.

But then in 1959 at age 75, emaciated, obsessed with a delusion that because of an ill stomach he could not eat, the depression became psychotic with "definite auditory hallucinations with delusions of guilt, unworthiness and impending physical punishment." In a disturbingly melancholy letter to the staff, a week before his session he wrote, "… my stomach has killed me. I had a pleasant dream last night and thought I had a plan whereby I could change all things, and return to a new life and to see and visit the many one's I dearly love, and am forced to leave."

Similarly to Peter Kramer's elderly depression sufferer this man had a heart problem, but not only that, the Hollywood Hospital patient was also showing symptoms of acute psychosis, on his third hospitalization, and 75 *years old* – but nonetheless on April 10, 1959 he took 400 micrograms of LSD-25 at Hollywood Hospital.

"He did not speak during the experience and at the end of 7 hours he stated he had been travelling but did not wish to talk about it. An hour later he was resting quietly, and said he wished to thank all the staff for their kindness to him."

The next day he said he "had seen the end of the world... Two or three times he felt he was dead – at times in heaven and at other times in hell. The messages during the experience were more vivid than the original commands not to eat. He stated that the pain had now disappeared from his stomach."

He gained his weight back and left the hospital, depression free until his death from cancer four years later. When Kramer listened to prozac he heard that the drug enhanced hedonic capacity, heightened affect tolerance, reduced rejection sensitivity and quickened thought. What can we learn from listening to LSD?

It seems the suffering in your life is reflected in the amount of suffering in your session and the neurotic suffered most. Such subjects had very long days indeed; the quagmire of the biographical and perinatal unconscious is much deeper and wider. Conversely healthier people are much quicker at working through the energy blockages in the unconscious.

There is some controversy among psychedelians regarding the importance of biographical and perinatal sequences in therapy. Al Hubbard and that school perhaps aspired to the facilitation of a cosmic consciousness so transcendent *any* abuse, trauma, surgery or even birth experiences will be dismissed as trivial. At most, in about one-third of abnormal subjects and two-thirds of normal ones this mystical peak experience seems to have been achieved, although sometime some negative biographical or perinatal material is present as well – so it's better to prepare people for the darkness – for 99% of subjects some of the experience was very difficult.

Carbogen, also called Meduna's Mixture after the psychiatrist inventor is a mixture of 70% oxygen and 30% Carbon Dioxide (although more formulae have emerged) that has a profound psychoactive effect after a few inhalations, which Dr. Meduna believed changed the brain in a way similar to antidepressant drugs or Electro Convulsive Therapy (ECT), also ignoring any dynamic content. Here is one subject's report:

"After the second breath came an onrush of color, first a predominant sheet of beautiful rosy-red, following which came successive sheets of brilliant color and design, some geometric, some fanciful and graceful.... Then the colors separated: my soul drawing apart from the physical being, was drawn upward seemingly to leave earth and to go upward where it reached a greater Spirit with Whom there was a communion, producing a remarkable, new relaxation and security."

However almost invariably even with carbogen, if these fortunate characters continue to have sessions the dark side of the cycle must be entered. Perhaps advancements in psychopharmacology will eventually produce drugs that deliver the peak mystical state in all or almost all subjects and the pain of our lives can be forgotten. As it is for us now and was for them then, life is hard.

I have divided the stories into three chapters, the first dealing with cases of defensive and incomplete reactions, the second composed of successful liberation reactions in those suffering abnormally (neurotic) and finally the breakthroughs among those suffering only normally – "subjects" instead of "patients."

Chapter Fifteen

Character Building – Incomplete Reactions

"As if wanted to die but couldn't." – S77Y5

"Wretch but no vomit" – Alan Watts

As time went on it seemed people learned how to trip, how to go with it and let go at the same time. Frank generally considered engineers, priests and psychiatrists the most resistant, activating little and resolving even less. The subjects in the first of the three groups were either overly defensive or unable to complete the emotional material evoked.

S45H6
"It's a fucking battlefield"

This subject was a 34-year-old successful interior designer from Toronto. At age 16 he confessed to his parents that he was thinking about killing his stepfather and he was committed to a psychiatric hospital for three months where he underwent ECT and insulin therapy. He had suffered depression, anxiety and problems in his relationships ever since but according to Dr. MacLean, S45H6's psychiatrist at the time and the "HOD" or Hoffer Osmond Diagnostic test (designed by psychedelic researchers Humphrey Osmond and Abram Hoffer to asses perceptual disorders related to schizophrenia), he was not considered schizophrenic even though he had been labeled psychotic at 16 when he was committed.

Despite his career achievements he felt his life had been wasted and was pessimistic about his future as well. His father died when he was thirteen months old then he moved to Toronto to live with his grandparents and an unmarried uncle. His mother retrieved him at eight and moved him in with a strict and aloof new husband (his stepfather) in Boston. He had no sexual contact until 18 and although no homosexual experiences, he is obsessed with the fear of being gay. He also suffered from severe joint pain that doctors advised him to take 10 – 16 aspirin a day to treat.

Treatment Day

9:05: 300 mcg LSD/400 mg mescaline

9:35: patient told to put on mask chest pounding

10:00: "I'm glad you're with me doctor, don't leave me doctor" nauseous

10:30: sees colors – "I'm not leaving me yet"

10:40: "Does my Father love me? I'm going to be okay – they're getting threatening"

10:55: puts both hands on penis area very briefly

11:00: kisses right index finger, tempted to touch genitals, restrains self

11:35 "I'm seeing women and men. I must make a choice – I love you Dad – I'm your son Dad – I love you Dad –I'm a man tear me loose, dr. tear me loose – let me go – carry me Father I didn't kill you"

11:45: "Grandma where are you? L. (his girlfriend) I love you – my woman; love me L. (girlfriend); Angry, take me, rip me apart, show me my Father; Hamlet (birth-Father), Hamlet what's the matter with your head?"; Screams

12:00: "God why did you take him away from me?; I loved him and I killed him; I'm Catholic, I'm Catholic, I'm a man Homosexual feelings are from my Daddy My stomach hurts; Some of that old junk; Had my doubts about you and the doctor No more fear, I have no fear; I am his son, no girl child"

12:30: "Didn't mean to hurt my Daddy, see I was just playing, Daddy don't die Was uncle putting it in his mouth – in his mouth?; How could he do it, he's only a baby, not my uncle; Dr. – uncle did it to me and what did he do to me? A little boy Uncle how can I ever forgive you?; Its me that's sick not M. (uncle)" Stands up "I'm standing up"; Feels like a young man "Uncle you stupid ass"

12:50: "I'm free, I can sail, I've come a long flight today; Do you think I had an orgasm with Uncle as a baby? Long way to go"

13:00: "it's a fucking battlefield Was uncle playing with me? I was brave today wasn't I?"; You have to be masculine," throws pillows against wall. "Such a little boy"

13:45: "I killed him he hurt my mommy Help my Daddy up he's bleeding"

14:20: "There's still more shit to be shed -; I have to urinate but feel it's sawed off and blocked off"

14:55: "Want to be able to come and give myself to you Daddy,; I'm your son – there's an awful lot burning in there I'm scared of sickness; I don't need to kill him; he's a duck quacking.; I have to come – this is a birth ritual"

15:50: "M. (uncle) I love and trusted you, how could you have done that?"

19:30: having an awful battle; Feels sordid in his body, looks at mirror, "its not so bad"

23:10 : "I'm Catholic, I'm a man and its all over"

Post Treatment

I feel a certain amount of disappointment in that the experience seems incomplete.

I saw spikes and needles falling on my (birth) Father, I covered his body with wine to protect him…my Stepfather was having intercourse with my Mother and I pleaded with him to stop hurting her.

The part that seems most significant and yet most difficult to believe was an apparent homosexual attack upon me by my uncle. I wonder whether it was a figment of my imagination.

Comments

At ten months old, this subject's dad died at age 30. He moved to Toronto where he was living with his grandparents and an unmarried uncle who sometime between thirteen months and six years apparently sexually abused him. It would appear he witnessed either his stepfather or his real father having sex with his mother and this generated some hostility, Freud called this uncovering the "primal scene." "Hamlet" is an invented name but the subject did use the name of his birth father and seems to be accurately reliving his death at 30. At sixteen he felt murderous rage toward his stepfather that was likely displaced from his repressed abuse by his uncle.

In 1896 Freud published *The Aetiogoly (origin) of Hysteria* where he described sexual neurosis as being caused by abuse. He later changed his mind and categorized the "abuse stories" as fantasized solutions to his patient's Oedipal or Electra complexes. It appears here his first answer may have been better.

S45H6 says repeatedly that he "still had a long way to go." Although he was planning another trip, unfortunately it didn't happen. Psychedelic researcher Dr. Gary Fisher worked with severely disturbed children and LSD during the early 1960s in California. Nancy, a totally uncommunicative nine year-old girl who was permanently restrained because she would gouge out her eyes and was fed with intravenous tubes because she refused food, was his first subject, because it seemed "she was going to die anyway."

Nancy had never spoken in the years she had been at the hospital. A few minutes after taking the drug she began screaming. This went on non-stop for hours until Dr. Fisher couldn't take it anymore. "Nancy for God's sake would you stop screaming. I can't stand it anymore."

Silence. "Leave me alone, I have a long way to go," she answered before returning to her "burning karma." Nancy was treated many times and eventually returned to school and thrived. S45H6 wasn't so lucky.

S77Y5
"As if locked inside a great hell that changed in time with music. As if wanted to die but couldn't."

This subject was a 49-year-old Jesuit History professor from the midwest. He suffered severe depression that drove him to seek therapy for three years from a psychology professor at a nearby University with little success. The two decided LSD might help. His Father was a Protestant traveling salesman and borderline alcoholic unhappily married to an Irish Catholic woman controlled by her family. He had no "direct" masturbatory experiences whatsoever, but a few ejaculations had been allowed and some Homo and heterosexual fantasies had been enjoyed. While an unquestioning believer his feelings for the priesthood were ambiguous and he wondered what his life might have been like otherwise.

Treatment Day

09:20 – 500 mcg LSD

09:50 – abdomen quivers, possibly crying

10:10 – starts sobbing quietly

10:30 – seems ashamed for crying

11:55 – no more tears, legs writhe a little

15:40 – patient begins to sob again listening to religious music

19:00 – refused to more than glance at mirror

Post-Treatment

I Hated hearing "Onward Christian Soldiers" which reminds me of "old time religion" which I loathe. Smelled and still smell peculiar odor that I took to be a crayon set in kindergarten. Relived having an orgasm at age 4-5 and felt deep shame for it. I saw a boy peeing his pants over and over.

Later in evening I saw very clearly self as little boy in sailor suit – he is smiling, kind of cute, with blue eyes open and confident…felt sorry for the little lad, this is the closest I have come to some kind of self-acceptance. I had no male figure to identify with. Visualizing a baby crying and seeing a near-fetus wailing, at any rate I cried out all my infant sorrows whatever they were.

I saw myself twisting down caverns. Feel that I should explore the sensual richness of the world with the little kid that smiled at me. But who am I supposed to be? Feel that I still don't know.

Treatment Day II

08:55 – 500 mcg LSD, 200 mg mescaline

09:25 – said he went into priesthood too early. "<u>Of course I wasn't ready for marriage at 21!</u> marriage to the church or God?" eyes and body covered felt more nervous today than before first session used b/r twice in about 20 minutes talked about a man he met at a bar with children

11:20 – small patch of perspiration maybe holding back tears

12:10 – more perspiration

13:50 – *Bolero* 3x at start of record shakes head, moves around, whole body writhes pants have been unzipped for some time grabs pants near crotch with left hand writhing of body continues goes to bathroom and has a very satisfying pee

19:00 – When I told him *Bolero* caused a person to move his body with the music he said "but you're married" and laughed

19:10 – religious music and tears

19:20 – said he wouldn't ask anyone else to take the vows; If he hadn't become a Jesuit he probably would have gotten married crying, talked about his first kiss which occurred the night she was to enter covenant – told her he loved her, talked about college girlfriend

Post-Treatment

E xperience of winding down tunnels towards increasing darkness, all alone with threatening power. Deeper and lonelier.

During Bolero going faster and faster down caverns completely surrounded by sounds, odor of semen. Smothered by pulsing noise. Terrible feeling of suffocation as if buried alive. As if locked inside a great hell that changed in time with music. As if wanted to die but couldn't. When music stopped as if new lease on life. Felt pressure in groin and had a pee like a geyser erupting from my body, penis seemed unusually large, thought to myself there go all my baby tears. Then *Bolero* again but this time no tension, instead I stood as a spectator and relaxed – even enjoyed the ride as if battle was over.

I saw Image of myself as a little boy in a sailor suit and a young man in baroque costume asking a girl to dance. I saw other images of couples courting.

Made a Jesuit right out of high school, never gave sex life a chance – feel brainwashed. The last images were of walking around mountaintops looking for hope.

Comments

The precocious orgasm at 4-5 may be a manifestation of sexual abuse. The *Bolero* sequence is most illustrative of the inter-related dynamic matrices, dealing thematically with his own conflicts over sexual identity and celibacy combined with the progress from the second to the third Basic Perinatal Matrix (BPM). This subject was very defended and controlled and more sessions would activate and discharge more of the unconscious. It is interesting the pervasive fear of being homosexual – is that simply a manifestation of the times or would similar frequency be found today?

S56T5

"I thought I had caused a nuclear holocaust"

This subject was a 36-year-old actuary or insurance technician from Minnesota. His Father was a multiply abusive man who threatened to withhold his college tuition days before school started each year and constantly criticized him; even begging his fiancé not to marry him behind his back! His Father also beat him and when S56T5 was only three years old the owner of a hardware store molested him and when he told his Father about it, bizarrely his Father just shrugged and said quietly, "I think I know who it was." The oldest of four children, he was his Mother's favorite and deepening the Oedipal dynamics further, she also undermined the subject's faith in his Father's manhood with her attitude towards her husband.

In kindergarten he witnessed a girl get cut in recess and refused to go outside thereafter. He became convinced he had a body odor and bathed excessively through high school; similarly he combed his hair compulsively as well. During the war an angry mob assembled outside looking for Jews. In high school he bought a switchblade and accidentally stabbed a student, he was paralyzed with guilt and his studies suffered – coming in 7th from the bottom. But then he became a top student after meeting some new friends with more academic interests, apprenticed as a statistician and began a top-flight career in the insurance business, perhaps using his obsessive nature as an advantage. He got married and had children.

He is described as having a sharp depression, a non-masculine orientation, hostility, strong insecurity and as being socially withdrawn. At the time he is diagnosed as "chronic psychoneurotic anxiety reaction."

Treatment Day I

09:10 – 400 mcg LSD, 400 mg mescaline

09:55 – "there are flowing colors that disappear if I try to control them" becoming a little frightened or just tense

10:00 –"strange to feel myself out of my body, yet still move around in it"

10:05 – "feel things clutching at me – got to let them tear me apart so I'll find me – whoever I am how awful to feel evil. Yes I'm afraid to feel evil. I feel like an evil empire bat"

10:15 – "got to let myself go, to feel, know I'll get back; Is it you Dad? Dad! I feel so alone, Dad I was trying to find you. Can see monsters, but I'm going to find you when I find the strength. Why couldn't I have been a beautiful person, why so ugly?"

10:25 – "This is what one calls a bad trip" reassure pt. "Get back 'cause I feel hostility coming on" pt. pounds couch several times

10:35 – "I feel evil. Dad, are you the evil bastard? I've got to find you, I'm going to feel real evil. I've got to face you. Is it homosexuality I have to face? I have to face it! Can feel there's a feminine part of me. Can feel you hostile bastard grabbing at me. Dad, Dad why are you always critical?"

10:50 – "It's homosexuality. Got to face you Mother. Ok I'm attracted to you. Big deal. You are an evil homosexual!"

10:55 – "It's T. (Wife) and kids that are real! I can be a man, I don't have to be stifled by this homosexuality. I just have to admit it. I love my Wife and kids!"

12:50 – [Bolero] "I want to vomit because I'm homosexual." Tried for last 40 minutes to keep mask on with 50% success

13:55 –"I've got to feel"; pt. writhes on sofa

14:25 – "I'm afraid if I let myself go, I'll go insane" Encourage pt. to experience insanity

16:30 – hate for Father still there, wants to get rid of it

17:30 – "I feel like I know myself for the first time"

Treatment Day II

09:30 – 400 mcg LSD/400 mg mescaline

10:00 – pt. complained of nausea – shivering violently

10:45 –"I'm getting wrinkled – I'm awfully cold"

11:00 – asking for reassurance

11:15 – "oh God – God!"

11:45 – "can't we start all over"

12:15 – "I'm very frightened"

15:00 – pt. has been pacing room for ninety minutes – repeating "at least I'm alive" pt. for many years had fear of catching cold in his testicles – pt. discussed homosexual fears and Father in detail

15:30 – pt. feeling sick – feels there is something inside him that must get out

Post-Treatment

Perspiration was the first perceptible sign. It flashed through my mind that I was in the womb – then I left my body. I started decaying and I think feces started collecting on me. I was no longer a magnificent stag but a defeated shell of a man – without dignity, without pride and without manhood. I had disgraced my children and I didn't care enough to fight.

If I couldn't even see bright colors under LSD then I was hopeless – Hollywood Hospital had lost their 1001st case – I saw a funeral.

Then I felt great, I felt masculine. I felt affection towards Frank. I was sure I wasn't insane, I was sure I wasn't homosexual. I felt love for everyone I thought of. I couldn't wait to take up the mainstream of my life.

Then I started to feel slightly nauseous – like I was covered with feces again.

I knew I was a homosexual – a complete queen. I knew if I looked in the mirror, then irrevocably I was a queen. (I'd do anything but die rather than being a homosexual)

I knew if I couldn't experience true hostility there was no hope. Frank offered some sleeping pills – I felt that if I took them, I'd failed the test. I left the treatment room and saw a man who I couldn't decide whether or not he was my Father. I saw a nurse and my first thought was she was my Mother.

After Frank went to sleep I left the room and told a nurse I was homosexual. I demanded Frank be woken up and we met back at the treatment room. I thought everything was a test of my homosexuality. I thought if I first confronted my homosexuality I would then begin to feel.

It's further clear to me that I'm really a bit of a coward. Bravery is a quiet confrontation.

Treatment Day III

09:45 – 400 mcg LSD/200 mg mescaline

10:05 – started to feel nauseous – eyes and body covered

10:20 – "wow"

10:30 – "I'm not a homosexual, it's crazy; if I want to be a homosexual – be one; yeah Frank there's nothing to lose, I trust you – fuck you Frank; I love my Wife, I love my Daughters and we don't need anyone else I'm not a homo – if I were so what?; fuck humanity – I don't need it – I'm a nice guy"

10:40 – "feel like throwing up"; knees drawn up – grimaces

11:35 – told pt. just face the horror and you'll be through with it 12:00 "I'm in permanent hell"

13:00 – believes he is God – "honesty is sinful"

15:00 – "I knew I wasn't a homosexual"

15:25 – "you have to get out of here – I must know that I faced this by myself"

Post-Treatment

The afternoon and evening before my session I consciously spent time trying to trust myself more. As it happened, I was calm after ingesting my LSD and mescaline. I took off my robe because I was afraid I was using it protectively.

As in the previous experiences I became nauseated. This time however, I barely trembled, my body wasn't rigid and I didn't feel extremely cold.

After the mask was placed on pastel colors started swirling. There was no fear of not being able to get back and I just went with my feelings. There wasn't a direct confrontation but I seemed to know that I wasn't a homosexual. I knew I could go it alone and felt affection for Frank. I felt love for my Wife, children and parents. There was a small portion of the universe that was marred however – that part that made me feel "dirty." I became concerned about the form in which I might return, dead, homosexual, insane? I thought I was hurting other people by working things out and feeling.

The feeling that I was somehow harming others started to increase. I started getting a feeling of power – it frightened me. It was ugly. It kept expanding as though it were a nuclear reaction.

I felt the hospital had made a mistake giving me the drug. I felt that I was the ONE person against whom humanity had been protecting itself. I thought I had caused a nuclear holocaust.

I thought Frank had left the room to tell Dr. MacLean what had happened and that everyone was going home to spend the last few moments with their families. I felt the hate of everyone. I was the insane destroyer of the world and could no longer pretend to be working things out for myself.

I thought of Jesus and said to Frank that it might sound crazy but maybe there was still hope. I was thinking in terms of my accepting punishment from God for what was done. I couldn't be humble and it was already occurring to me that I might be God. Then I realized there was a God (Father) waiting to punish me. Then I was the devil in hell. I sat in a chair and was about to say let's get it over with but then realized it would never end.

At a later point, when it was dark outside and Frank was no longer in the room, I began to wonder if I were homosexual – I thought that I might not be homosexual and though the conflict had been partially resolved I perhaps felt "dirty" for another reason.

I felt a fear of the bathroom mirror – which I confronted, then the dark, then the floor.

The following day I walked around in a slight depression and didn't want to think but wanted to "live" the depression – the bad feeling. When I went to sleep that evening I realized what a selfish person I had been and that I had hurt other people and cried. I realized my Wife was the most important person in the world to me and I trusted her.

I had been resigned prior to the experience to face things that were threatening me directly but had not been prepared to cope with hurting other people. There was a clash – if I faced things then more destruction would occur to everyone else.

I suspect the God I feared was going to punish me represented my Father who used to tell me how selfish I was. After returning home I feel more relaxed and relate better to my Wife, children and everyone else.

Comments

During the second experience at ten at night he is offered a sleeping pill and was roaming around the hospital confused as to whether the people there were really his parents (transference), so on this trip a week later he is given only 200 mg mescaline with his LSD. At the beginning he has a superficial positive experience that gives way to the second and third perinatal matrix. The ascending tension, violence and feelings of nuclear annihilation did not reach the self-organizing critical state necessary for catharsis. He fears he will return dead, homosexual or insane the classic ego death triad. His experience does illustrate the deepening and intensifying affect that must be worked through to release energy blocks and activate positive governing systems on the perinatal level.

One of Grof's trained holotropic breathwork practitioners told me, "Stan believes you should let it get as big as possible." The notion that he was harming others may have been an ego defense against the impending annihilation that he doesn't quite realize. Some therapists might have used methylphenidate (Ritalin), Methamphetamine or more LSD/mescaline to accelerate his transmodulation.

S77F5

"Not doing anything at the moment why don't I shave?"

This subject was a 50 year-old successful Floridian businessman and functioning alcoholic with a long list of fairly serious health problems. He had two grown Daughters who he and his Wife had ideal relationships with but an eighteen year- old son who was apparently becoming a sociopath. He is described as having a "non-masculine" orientation that the psychologist interprets as possible "sexual immaturity." Four years prior he had a heart attack and was hospitalized for one month, but again the treatment is considered to have a wide margin of safety.

On the treatment day notes Frank refers to a "strobe session" an hour before he took the mescaline. Sound and light frequencies can be used to induce changes in the electrical activity of the brain. They may have been priming the brain for optimal visualization, this is apparently yet another innovation introduced by the infamous Al Hubbard.

Treatment Day

10:00 – 600 mg mescaline/ 200 mcg LSD

10:55 – "what is the youngest age you have administered this to?"(12)

11:00 – pt. quiet and still

11:25 – "I feel like I'm suffocating"

11:35 – "I can't breathe. I can't swallow. I'm so dry." What are you really thirsty for?; "Does everybody have to go through this?"

11:45 – *Bruckner 9th Symphony* side II is playing; "Tell M. we should have our tin pans back from; Dr. T. in about two weeks" pt. talking about business

12:00 – pt. advised to try and talk less

"I'd lose control." Then lose it

12:10 "They are nightmares."

12:15 "Not doing anything at the moment why don't I shave?"

12:30 "I'm suffocating. Turn off the music. I feel like I'm dying. Can't we stop the music?" pt. told he must face himself; "I doubt I have the courage to face myself." pt. goes to w/r

12:45 – "I have to go the w/r again." Goes; "I feel nauseated." Pt. perspiring profusely mask up mask down

13:00 – "this is the darnedest thing I've ever been thru."; Pt. slaps own face; "When do these uncomfortable feelings stop?; Isn't there ever any feeling of well being in this treatment?; I must have been hallucinating to have ever gotten in here in the first place. I'm a coward, let's call it off."

16:00 – pt. quiet and still 19:00 pt. studying mirror

20:00 – pt. shook up "doesn't know what to think"

21:00 – "I've gone through a day of agony to find out I've been selfish all my life. I'm sick."

Post-Treatment

My first sensations were ones of thirst. My mouth and throat became very, very dry, my throat quite sore, this passed then I had the feeling of being suffocated, and my heart began to pound with the shortness of breath. Every time I removed the eye shield Ogden promptly restored it.

...I had the sensation of being tossed around, quite gently, in air; I saw scenes that reminded me of Dante's Inferno. My mouth would get very dry and my lips seemed to swell. I smoked a cigarette – Mr. Ogden informed me that we still had hours to go.

I looked at two pictures of Jesus that seemed to be moving.

I remained in the therapy room for some time while the effects of the chemical wore off, but it left me with a feeling of nausea. At about 9:30 p.m. I was returned to my room to sleep. I couldn't sleep all night, as I felt quite sick. Everything I drank tasted like orange juice, which I had drank in the late afternoon. I remember thinking that if it didn't stop me drinking Scotch, at least it had orange juice. Breakfast was served me about 8 am, I had a few mouthfuls of eggs and was violently ill. After this I felt better and calmer. At about 9:30 am Dr. MacLean ordered me a sleeping pill, which I took and shortly thereafter fell asleep for about five hours. On awakening I felt much better and quite calm. I stayed in the hospital Friday night and returned home on Saturday.

Comments

This subject's whole experience is dominated by defenses – talking, smoking, taking off the eye shield, what does manifest seems to be BPM II. The only positive transmodulation or shift he achieves is the next morning when he throws up his eggs, which suggests his experience was very poorly integrated and unresolved. He apparently imprints orange juice during the end of the trip and can't shake it afterward. This is not an example of successful psychedelic therapy but of the capacity for defenses to prevent resolution; this guy needed more sessions.

S21S3

"It's no mere accident Brahms, Strauss, Wagner, Tchaikovsky, etc are musical geniuses. That junky music has no business in the LSD room."

The next subject was a thirty year old European ballerina, successful but self- conscious. She was extremely resourceful and at one point wrote the Hollywood Hospital crew bragging of selling her first painting. About a year prior to the following trip she had her first two experiences with experimental ecstasy at Hollywood Hospital and spread the word far and wide across the entertainment industry. As if LSD needed any more endorsing at the time with Cary Grant the unofficial spokesperson.

Treatment Day I

09:30 – 700 mg mescaline, 250 mcg LSD, 30 mg methedrine (methamphetamine) 11:00 pt. quiet *Music For Relaxation* playing

11:30 – pt. respiration increasing – slight, moan, once

12:00 – pt. breathing rapidly, fists clenched tightly

13:30 – pt. opened eyes – stared wildly, hands opened in claw-like grip; pt. staring at floor while pure sound of waves washing against shore playing – "I understand."

13:50 – "Daddy" – pt. holding head over waste basket moaning

15:00 – pulling her hair with claw-like hands

16:45 – pt. looking in mirror, making murmuring noises

17:20 – pt. returned to D4 by Dr. MacLean – left with mirror

Post-Treatment

My memory of the images I saw and the exact words that went through my head during my LSD experience seems to be very poor, far worse than the other two experiences I had.

I do remember that I had one image all in red of watching with D. (boyfriend) dressed in red tights, then changed into little mice and scurried away. I also saw a funeral and several images of babies. I remember wondering if I were consciously evoking i.e. forcing myself to see certain things or if they were coming entirely naturally. I had many visions where there was little or no emotion involved and I shall elaborate on this later and explain the reasons why – I hope this will be of benefit to all future LSD subjects as I have something very important to say about the choice of music and the handling of same, which makes all the difference in the world.

I remember a great longing for my Father and feeling I needed him terribly – I wanted him to love me. Then I had a similar feeling for my Mother only not as strong.

I also had a feeling that I had said something wrong at birth and that I was suffering the consequences all my life. It came to me just what it was I had said only it wasn't in English. I remember also thinking one had to rip one's body apart for God, and I kept digging at my scalp to try to make it hurt only I couldn't feel the pain and thought I was worthless. I had images of dandruff, pus and other unattractive things and, as in my first experience felt I was lying in broken glass and blood and was disfigured. I remember feeling ashamed too.

I remember again the feeling of lying in hell and repeating all the worst things over and over as I held my head over a bucket. This image was strongest.

When I once looked in the mirror I thought I was breathing out poisonous gas. Also when I looked and saw the nurse I thought she was my fourth grade teacher, and Frank I thought was Mickey Mouse – Dr. MacLean weighed two tons.

At one point I felt very ashamed because the tape had stopped and everyone was staring at me. I thought everybody knows all about me and I'm worse than anyone else. I thought I was the worst person in the world and there was no hope for me.

When I left the room I felt very incomplete as in "is that it?"

Now for my criticism of the music – I could hear the record changing, clicking several times so I know for sure that I was given several records of the "candlelight and wine" type music. Ugh is all I can say. If I were to buy a ticket to the La Scala opera in Milan and then arrived only to hear Frank Sinatra and Dean Martin I would be very disappointed.

What a difference in the emotional content during the ENTIRE experience a year ago and this time. That Junkie cocktail music does nothing. You can't imagine the difference once the really stirring music was played – only there weren't enough of them. It's no mere accident Brahms, Strauss, Wagner, Tchaikovsky, etc are musical geniuses. That junky music has no business in the LSD room.

Treatment Day II

08:50 – 500 mg mescaline, 200 mcg LSD

09:05 – *Mahler Symphony #1 in D flat*

09:40 – pt. murmured

13:30 – pt. making claw like gestures with hands 14:00 pt. slid herself off couch on to floor, lying on floor murmuring – pt. walks over and puts her arms around the nurse who leads her back to the chesterfield – same action again

15:30 – pt. lying quiet listening to religious music 16:30 *Mahler* replaying

17:00 – pt. still looking in mirror

19:20 – pt. watching Academy Awards with nurse

22:00 – pt. in bed smiling

08:30 – pt. in bed still smiling

Post-Treatment

I liked the music much better this time. It seemed as though I took a long time to settle down, though I kept tasting the coffee and wishing I hadn't had it, feeling a bad taste in my mouth and feeling sick – also no visions happened for some time and it worried me to hear the records click and people moving about. By the time *Bolero* by Ravel started though, I was seeing gorgeous colors and felt like I was sinking with D. (boyfriend) into wonderful worlds. I also saw L. (nurse's daughter), who had played the record the other night and said it was monotonous – however it didn't appear so to me; each portion was a distinct world of its own, with the music and colors completely distinct and individual. She looked very pure and lovely and white.

I also saw my Mother trying to aid me in getting sick and saying, "oh I wish you weren't sick" and also later balling me out (as a baby) for wanting to play with feces. She kept criticizing me until I thought I'd go crazy and I saw all sorts of visions of hatred and thought, "oh how I hate you! I hate you!" And then there were a couple of times when the hatred turned to love, yet it was nearly always thwarted by the knowledge of my being so bad and never being able to please my Mother.

There was a portion where I developed a hatred for all functions of the body and all parts of the body and I wanted to rip my body apart – I thought how ugly vomit, bile, blood, phlegm, urine etc. are and I couldn't stand the thought of them – although I kept seeing them and hating them more. Then too I was afraid of dying and afraid of being mutilated. At one point I was sure somebody had cut my eyes out – that was really awful!

Later on I noticed I was alone with the nurse and I asked where all the men were – I got scared – at that point I thought I must have been left alone with R. (nurse) for some "delicate feminine" talk and I was furious – and when she said, "you can tell me." I thought for sure I'd done something awful but I didn't know what.

Then Frank came back and I again associated some of the visions personalizing Frank and R. (nurse) as my parents. I thought I was reenacting an event of my childhood where I was about ten or eleven and had been scolded because I was curious about sex. Again I thought I'd have to vomit up all my badness only I was afraid of getting sick. I tried to take my socks off at one point, as a beginning because I thought my parents wanted me to. Then I lay down on the floor and moaned – Frank and R. (nurse) looked so ugly – all covered with sores and funny lights and they had claws. So did I for that matter – bloody claws that were also dirty. At on point I thought I was lying in a pool of blood – I tried to embrace R. (nurse) at one point and also to sit on Frank's lap but they made me go back to the bed! I thought they were mean. When Frank came and sat down on the table next to me I thought I was a sick patient first and he a doctor only, I didn't quite trust him – then I also thought he was my Father – I wanted to bite him all up as I thought he was a meanie. He also seemed a toad, but not as my Father.

When Dr. MacLean came back in I felt that he thought I was bad and wasn't having a good experience. Several times I got anxious about that factor, being able to hear movements about the room and even the bus outside at times – I kept thinking people were trying to deprive me of something. Then at one point I didn't know what was real anymore – I kept saying, "I wish they'd tell me the difference." Several times I really felt myself sinking down deep though it always infuriated me when the notion came that I was being wrought with outside influences and that people were trying to get in my way. It made me feel even sicker to my stomach and have a worse taste in my mouth.

I saw Ross (MacLean) in a blue shirt with his hair combed back and some hair tonic on it and he had a very merry twinkle in his eye – I had the feeling that he could say anything and even if it weren't true I'd believe him. Then he changed into a canary and flew off.

I saw all sorts of ugly forms on the wall, and crawling all over Frank and the nurse. Also with my eyes closed I saw the same ugly creatures, which I couldn't rid myself of – these were in part specters, skeletons, phantoms and comic strip characters.

I also heard the same childhood language as before, usually telling me how bad I was and how everybody hated me for being so bad. I wanted to scratch and bite the nurse's sores and pustules, also to eat the bunions off her feet.

I think Frank and the nurse told me several times to cry or get sick – also Frank referred to the fact that I could "neither cry nor get sick" and I thought he was saying there was something wrong with me – whereas I had been feeling wild and frightened before then, with this statement, I entered upon a period of indifference, a humph, "who cares?" attitude – I bit my lips and picked my nails at the same time I wished I could summon forth some emotion of caring but I couldn't – I felt I was a fraud, a poseur, kidding everyone – that in reality I was a dilettante playing games and wasting time. It was a terrible thought that I'd wasted years of time, and again my Mother came to my mind.

I also remember when I first looked in the mirror how stupid I looked, like I remember looking in the fourth grade at a show-down with my teacher or as a child in camp with a stupid grin on my face as I was being bawled out, or at certain movies and for sad occasions of my childhood where everybody was weeping and I was grinning and laughing.

During the experience several times I had the feeling of running away and also of being lazy, or taking the easy way out, or at least looking to find it. I felt I wasn't up to the hard way, even though I would like to feel I'm not a time-waster but someone who is useful and productive.

When Dr. MacLean held the picture up the first time all sorts of funny red things were creeping around it, like followers or martyrs hovering and moving in the background. The second time there was no movement.

Sometimes in the mirror I looked fairly clean and nice and other times I was my aunt and my Mother, my Grandmother and others but mainly my Mother – with sores around her – she was very unhappy and pained.

At one point I saw another aunt and I felt I'd been mean to her and I was sorry, especially because she was so old and a spinster and is now dead. I also felt disgust for being a woman and wished I wasn't one. My Father always eluded me. Every time I thought he was going to be nice something awful happened instead.

All in all, despite all the notions of "interference" and the upset stomach and bad taste in the mouth, which plagued me, even for hours afterwards, I had a very satisfying experience and came out much happier this time than last. Thank you Dr. MacLean!

Chapter Sixteen

Liberation Reaction I: *Abnormal suffering*

"It seemed a hell without end. I was fighting and running trying to do this or that in a mad frenzy, feeling that each path or door would provide the answer. Finally stopped running to accept what was." – S31F7

Most of the people willing to shell out five hundred bucks (about $3500 in current dollars), write out the eighteen-question autobiography and undergo an experience regarded even by its advocates as arduous had some kind of problem they wanted fixed.

S44T6
"J.C. just walked in the barn!"
"I can't describe this but it's as if the whole world has lifted off my shoulders"

This subject was a fisherman and alcoholic who had been sexually abused by an older brother as a child, this same perpetrator later kicked him out into the streets to "ride freight trains and sleep in jungles." He was 46 and married, but his Wife forbade his friends coming over because she believed "they were all a bunch of queers." He had apparently been drinking daily since fifteen and smoked three packs a day.

Treatment Day

09:00 – 100 mcg LSD – 250 mg mescaline

09:18 – Lies down covered with blankets, eyes covered; "How come I can't see the face now, that's laying in bed all the time"

09:30 – pt. occasional head tremors "she eeps calling me a rat"

09:30 – "Don't be so mean Mama I helped you when you were down"

09:40 – "It's working"; that's the donkey we had our picture taken on"

09:42 – "How is it Grandmother's here?; It wasn't nice to do that"; Hands trembling, makes reaching motions as if trying to grasp something

09:50 "So many funny places I can see – St. Evan's School"

09:55 strong agitation in solar plexus area

10:00 music of *Ketelbey Persian Market*

10:20 pt. muttering, mentions speed of changing pictures; "the face won't come out of the heart"

10:25 "ah mom please don't"

10:35 "there's a room and a chair – a small church – I know that preacher"

10:40 responses more intense clenching hands body spasms 10:45 "its cold" – shivers – music – *Near My God to Thee*; "beautiful – We're in the barn – J.C. just walked in the barn! twelve years old"

11:35 doing a lot of re-evaluating personal relationships – Brother – Sister – Wife; many gestures – some with finality

12:00 *Just a Song*; "this is my life and that's the way its going to be" making decisions; motions of dismissal – some of acceptance "that's it! that's it!; going backwards gets you nowhere – you've got to go ahead" occasional smile

12:30 I've got it right here now" shakes his clenched fist – "and right here too" pounds his heart – great determination expressed

12:45 "I know what's right – hell I'll fight for it too!!"; Hawaiian Music

13:00 pt. sighs deeply makes expansive gesture – smiles "what I've got now I'll hang on tight with both hands" expression quite happy; "it's right here in my heart!"

13:05 "this is wonderful – what a load I got rid of – what a relief"

13:15 pt. shown mirror – "you'd never recognize me as the same guy that came in here this morning"; pt. face shining; "the Old Man upstairs is the One. He knows.; I don't have to care what anyone thinks of me anymore I'll do what's right.; I wish my sister knew what happened to me today she'd be very happy -; I can't describe this but it's as if the whole world has lifted off my shoulders"

14:00 "what were all those funny faces I saw part of the time"

14:10 *Music for Relaxation – Three Suns*

14:15 "I have never felt so relaxed before"

18: 00 pt. shaving – in good spirits

Post-Treatment

Later that evening he ate a piece of a sandwich and some milk and at midnight began vomiting, he then woke up at five am, sweating so much he needed his pajamas changed and vomited again. The next day he ate normally and was fine and as Frank described him – "general disposition very cheerful – reiterates the feeling of having had a great load lifted from him – appearance bright more alert."

A few months later Frank writes that he "has gained 8 pounds of weight, has new dentures – uppers and lowers- this after having gone ten years without them.

Domestic relationships greatly improved this from both husband and wife; happiness established that was completely absent. Took one drink of vodka after an upsetting visit from his Mother in law but instead of continuing old drinking pattern – he called me. Attitude wholesome – visited his brother whom he'd refused to see for twenty years and re-established relationship – harmonious."

Comments

It is easy to see with results like this why investigators were so optimistic. It is impossible to know if he abreacted his sexual abuse trauma at all, let alone whether in symbolic or literal form, but the positive perinatal dynamics don't get much clearer than they do here.

S75G5

"'You may help me carry my cross." I was so happy – I pushed with all my might that I might lighten the load and even though I felt turned inside out with the strain of it I was happy. Then a huge shadow of the cross appeared on the face of the earth…"

This subject was a forty-year-old Mother of four children. She was an extraordinarily resilient person and maintained a relatively healthy disposition, despite two very chronically traumatic events. The first occurred when she was five and her Mother died suddenly. Her Father was overwhelmed and joined the Army leaving her and her two siblings with his Grandmother. This was interrupted when the Grandmother was hospitalized and the children were given up for adoption. Potential parents would look at her apparently much more attractive siblings and say "these two are beautiful but we're not taking her."

She is rumored in her circle to have "psychic powers" which prompted her Catholic priest to remark, "If this was the fourteenth century you would be burned at the stake."

After a few years the children were returned to the Grandmother and life resumed normally until she fell in love with a man who later became a paranoid schizophrenic. After she had twins he started to hear voices and this marked the advent of a new man – delusional and violent. She was ultimately forced to leave her husband who was too afraid of being "kept" to get treatment.

Treatment Day

08:30 500 mg mescaline, 125 mcg LSD

08:55 pt. laid down on chesterfield, body covered with blanket, eyes covered with double cloth

09:55 pt. reported feeling of nausea,

10:07 pt. sick

11:00 "can't get hands untied – I'm seeing all sorts of things"

11:45 pt. agitated, alters position several times, appears cold; huddles under blankets – *Bruckner* playing

11:50 raises herself, "heavens" – resumes lying position

12:50 "we just had an awful fight, you won"

14:35 "are you trying to trick me? Stop it" – pt. crying

17:00 pt. shown mirror; "I look good," crying, "I didn't ever think I would look good again"

21:00 "we sure traded thunderbolts – you were strong – I'm glad – I needed you then"

Post-Treatment

It seemed like a long time before anything happened at all – but it probably wasn't. I first noticed sound – the loudness of it, when I ran my finger over the chain on my neck, I could hear it – it startled me – I rubbed my fingers together and then my feet – a great delight seized me and I thought "I'm stereophonic" and burst into a million pieces of reds, crimsons and purples.

I went through a time of some confusion and feeling that my hands were bound together. (I have always had arthritis trouble with my wrists and so decided I wanted to explore this) Immediately I was plunged into a vast crowd of mocking, jeering people – my wrists were tied together and a few of us were being pushed and pulled down the street – I had the feeling of being a young Christian on my way to the lion pits. I felt no fear for myself just a sad helplessness that these people wouldn't understand – they wouldn't listen – I wanted to help them and for this I was to die.

Then I was in a different scene – the word Salem leaped into my mind. I was in a cart this time – with a few others, my hands were tied together again and the coat was woolen and rough and so was the road. The crowds were yelling, "Witch!

Witch! Burn her!"

It seemed as if the cross around my neck became alive and turned into a sword and started in on the crowd making a singing hum – as it did it wasn't thrusting pain – but truths, but it was hopeless. I was tied firmly and they set the torch to me. I could feel the heat of the flames – the pain and the smell but it didn't compare with the agony in my heart that I hadn't been able to help these people – I began to cry for the hopelessness of it and I felt myself covered with tears other than my own and it seemed that for a brief instant the face of Jesus was mingling with mine and his tears were mingling with mine. He said, "So too I have wept" and then I was plunged into darkness.

A deep vast womb of black darkness of which I had no fear (this amazed me because I find myself terrified for no reason in the dark) – the darkness was soft, warm and comforting and I wanted to remain there. But then I felt something thrusting me out – I didn't want to go – I hung on – but the pressure became greater and greater and I realized I was being born. I had to pull my huge over- self into this small body I felt inhibited already in a way. And then I saw my Mother's face and I was sorry for the trouble I had given her – I just hadn't wanted to be born yet.

Then followed a period of where different loved ones appeared to me and I was either happy with them – amazed at them or sad.

There were so many scenes and violent explosions that I'll just write as I remember them now – though they may not be in the order that they happened.

There was one scene that was two in one – quite confusing – one was of a music box – but to me it seemed like a merry-go-round. Full of laughing children, fun and excitement but I couldn't get on – I even tried – but couldn't, I just had to watch. Then they were all reaching out and grabbing golden rings, which if they got one, would give them a free ride, I was filled with envy and then a voice said to me, "but someone has to give out the rings." Then it seemed like the merry- go-round was faster and faster until I could no longer stand the laughing and I wanted to smash it and I did! Immediately I was filled with great sorrow – I hadn't meant to destroy it – I hadn't meant to hurt it. I lay down by it sobbing, "give me one more chance" – a voice answered me – "I have given you these and you can have the joy of sharing and tending over their childhoods." And the faces of my fine children swam around me.

I lived many scenes of trying to help people all around the world – in dungeons, deserts, and sometimes so many people I couldn't even move, some trying too, others scoffing. There was a lot of pain and torture and heavy weight – many falling by the wayside. And ever present in my mind was "why?" Finally in desperation I cried out, "I want to be like Jesus – I want to help – I'm strong, but what is the ultimate end? – Will we ever get anywhere? – Give us something.

Then I knew the word I had been searching for – inspiration.

But much to my dismay He turned away and said, "Where is your faith? You're not strong enough after all." Horror struck me and I went running after him (though this was only his voice I knew the way to go). I went through deserts, fainting in the sun but still managing to keep onwards. "Look at me Lord, I'm strong. I don't give up." It seemed as though all the elements were let loose upon me and I fought them with all my strength.

"You may help me carry my cross." I was so happy – I pushed with all my might that I might lighten the load and even though I felt turned inside out with the strain of it I was happy. Then a huge shadow of the cross appeared on the face of the earth and I was filled with deep awe and reverence.

Then I saw a series of cartoons. I thought perhaps this is our front or our shell that we present to everyone.

Then I was an Amazon of a woman – huge and golden like a Goddess out of mythology – I was increasingly aware of Frank following me – I felt he had no right to do this and I launched an attack on him. But he gave me back lightening bolt for lightening bolt, thunderclap for thunderclap. The heavens whirled with our battle and the earth shook – he won, I collapsed in amusement.

I was angry at Frank – I started to accuse him – telling him it wasn't fair to look inside me and pull these things out – how did he know? But I couldn't get up enough effort to speak. The music caught me up in a swirl of blacks and reds and I gave into it completely and became a voodoo priestess but one of the drummers was incessant and getting wilder and wilder – he didn't hear me tell him to stop – so drawing myself up to full height I pointed my finger at him (actually it was the Stereo) – he gave one yelp of pained surprise and all was silent – I was fascinated and then my next thought was half reality again and I got on my knees to peek over at Frank to see if he was mad because I broke the stereo.

I went through many sorts of pain – the burning of the witch, the terrible heaviness of the cross, childbirth with full pain seven times! I felt as if I was being torn apart, at one point Frank told me I was going to be okay now and I agreed, but I wanted to ask him how we were going to hide the whole in my stomach – but again words failed me and I slipped into more experiences.

At different points I was at different places in the world – one minute Egypt pulling a great load with many others to make a Pyramid. From that immediately to laying on a great couch being fanned with palm branches, very regal and proud – then to France back in the old days – running through the streets hand in hand, laughing filled with indescribable joy and happiness.

At times I felt myself getting very isolated with the music and wishing he would put on something I didn't know and then I felt I was all music and knew all music and could find myself anticipating the next movements and getting cross with one cello player because he was a bit flat. Often the music took on (singing) voices of the greatest grandeur and sounded like a massive choir.

I found myself once more on the ocean side walking through the water along the shore, tired and a bit lost – rain pouring down on me – I fell to my knees in weariness but arose again and felt the rain was from heaven and a cleansing of my very soul – I felt very humble. My thoughts turned to God again and I asked him to let me help bear his cross, I felt I could with better understanding.

When Frank showed me myself in the mirror I didn't want to look but when I did I saw many things – Mary Magdalene – peace, goodness and as I looked deeper and became afraid because it started to change, Frank held me there to keep looking, I calmed myself and saw only a shadow of a cross on my face and then just my face – I realized that perhaps I wasn't so bad at all.

There are some things I know I've left out – my feeling of being able to communicate with Frank when he was sitting by me, without words and having him answer me.

How different people coming into the room affected my session – there are probably 1001 things more I could write that happened – but I believe I covered the greatest and most meaningful parts of my session. I could never express what this has meant to me and what I feel it has done for me. I can only thank you for the new concept on life and the biggest experience of a lifetime!

Follow-up

One thing that has bothered me physically since my LSD is headaches. Before LSD I had a headache every now and then but not too frequently. During one of my sessions I started to go into an experience that was interrupted by another doctor in the room – it seemed I was unable to go into the experience while he was there, as I did not feel the same understanding in him as I did in Frank Ogden! Right after this I developed a terrible headache which I didn't think too much of at the time because I had already experienced so much pain.

However on my discharge from the hospital the next day I had a terrible headache. The funny thing is I wake up with them in the morning. Now – I don't know if this has anything to do with my session or not – but thought it best to mention it.

I must say the benefits and assets I received and the self-knowledge that keeps increasing from my sessions are priceless!

I find I still have many of the same problems and even a "few" of the same fears but I also find that now I understand them and I'm better equipped to handle them rather than becoming depressed and building them up to mammoth sizes. I am able to shun bad characters and accept the fact that someone good and kind could want me – that I'm not wicked or evil and that good things can and are happening to me. And to be able to accept this – you can't understand how big this is to me and how it is changing my whole life.

I also find my memory has really stepped up – as a matter of fact I amaze everyone at my part time job by being able to remember the names of over a hundred customers.

I'm spending more time in outdoor life –learning to fish, hunt – etc. I find great satisfaction in this and being in the outdoors away from the hustle of the city is a new and different life for me – one I didn't have the courage to explore before. I find the mountains and rivers awesome and feel very close to God and the awareness of the universe.

Comments

The more verbal the client the easier for them to relate their experience and this person was a very gifted woman – a remarkably spiritual and emotionally generous subject.

This exclusively Christian mythology differs from other reports that people experience religious archetypes often from traditions totally unfamiliar to them. It is possible more sessions would have manifested a richer vision of the collective unconscious.

She suffered severe arthritis in her wrists and her experience of being a witch with her hands tied behind her back is interesting. Some might argue that the arthritis represents non-integrated traumata from a past life and the complete experience of the witch burning would resolve the symptoms. Studying the experiences of children who believe they have been other people in the past gives credence to the ancient notion of re-incarnation. However, another approach to the witch burning sequence is to consider the possibility that in such a state of consciousness as this subject attained she was "tuned-in" to infinity and eternity and therefore capable of accessing anything including this narrative. The hardcore materialist might assert that the fantasy was simply a manifestation of a medical condition and any improvement would be merely the result of suggestion – this debate will likely rage for generations.

A friend of mine had a serious problem with his foot that lasted for years starting with the day his biological Father died and ending when he traveled to Peru to spend a month with Ayahuasca Shamans in the jungle. During one session a shaman pulled out pieces of bone apparently right out my friend's foot and threw them in the fire – the pain has been gone ever since. To the jungle shaman and Hollywood Hospital what was important wasn't how it worked so long as it worked.

I included her reference to headaches because it illustrates clearly the basic principles of this psychotherapy. Negative biographical, perinatal or transpersonal material was being expressed through a severe head pain, the doctor entered the treatment room and interrupted the integration of this material but since it had already been activated the symptoms will likely persist until the discharge is completed.

Once again there was an explicit mind-meld between Frank and the subject, which was a common occurrence in psychedelic therapy. Among the purposes of psychedelic use by specialists is predicting the future, finding lost objects, figuring out which sorcerer put a hex on somebody etc. Master Yogi Patanjali advocated the use of "light-bearing herbs" as a tool on the path of enlightenment that brought siddhis or psychic powers.

S74R1

"I felt that God is Love and God is I and He and I are part of all creation. I could see this and felt that I was a very small, although important, part of all creation."

Amiddle-aged, very wealthy, Ontario social worker with a drinking problem will be considered next. His family had a lot of mood disorders and alcoholism and his Wife had left him because of his drinking and took their young son. He had used antabuse (which induces vomiting when mixed with alcohol), joined Alcoholics Anonymous and in the late fifties became addicted to barbiturates, thereby managing periods of sobriety of up to one year but always reverting back to the bottle. He says that when drinking "he does things he would never normally do." He has had two "spiritual experiences" both followed by bouts of sobriety, but had been drinking heavily again at the time of treatment while managing to find a new girlfriend. If a sociopath is indifferent to the suffering of others but a psychopath enjoys it, this subject is definitely a mild sociopath – today he might be described as having a personality disorder. Apparently the subject's girlfriend was opposed to the treatment "for obvious reasons" and he is considered "above average material for an integrative experience."

Treatment Day

07:30 900 mg mescaline, 350 mcg LSD

08:35 "I'm fighting it – I don't want to."

09:40 pt. quiet arms folded on chest

10:30 *Mahler 1st Symphony*

11:20 "gets pretty basic doesn't it?"

11:30 *Beethoven 9th Symphony*; <smoking a cigarette every hour, but occasionally Frank refuses>

11:45 Pt. opening fingers of upraised rt. hand like petals of a blooming flower, "I might be innocent yet."

14:30 "I sure have been kidding myself, haven't I?

15:00 pt. lying quietly listening to religious music

16:30 pt. looked in mirror, discussed Wife, girlfriend, drinking etc. "There is a God and He does care. I feel humble and fortunate to come close to Him."

17:30 "I know what I have to do but I don't know if I have the strength to do it."; pt. reassured

Post-Treatment

The first sensations I had were bodily – a slight tingling of the extremities and a "clamminess" of the skin. I did not see any flashes of light or geometric shapes. My auditory perceptions were sharpened and the music seemed to have a great deal of meaning and was somewhat distorted. I found it difficult to "let go" and experience the emotions to the fullest at first, but later I think I did. I recall that one piece of music triggered the visual impression of God in his temple and moving from there out over the earth and into the cosmos. This was very vivid, in colour, and this vision reappeared, each time stronger, whenever that particular piece of music (or something I thought similar) was played. At one point my extremities seemed to grow and I was praying to God to take me to do his will. I felt lifted up by someone but was then put down. I could see my life from a very tiny baby to far into the future and realized that today's problems were a small part of my whole life and perhaps relatively unimportant.

At times I found the music disturbing because it seemed to break-up an experience I was building. At one time I felt my mind coming apart and this was mainly a series of very strong emotions, which I can't describe. I also felt my body flying apart and this I could see. I kept returning to reality and then drifting off again. I couldn't seem to control my thinking.

I felt and could see myself crucified with the Lord and also could see myself above the Cross looking down on the scene. This occurred twice. I felt that God is Love and God is I and He and I are part of all creation. I could see this and felt that I was a very small, although important, part of all creation.

The recording of *Corinthians I:13* had a great deal of meaning for me and I felt very strongly about this. I felt also that some of the singers and some of the music had genuine feeling and that others were insincere. Later in the afternoon I seemed to come face to face with myself and could clearly see my faults and how they caused my present difficulties. I realized and felt strongly that it was time to do something about my immature behaviour patterns, but I did not then have the strength to do anything about it.

After I returned to my room, I considered some of the experiences I'd had and the feeling grew that I did have the strength and I could do something about myself. I could see clearly that the only way I can live is to avoid doing anything that makes me feel even a little bit guilty, as this guilt seems to be cumulative and inevitably results in drinking or an excess of some kind. I realize this is a day-to- day struggle that most people are engaged in as well and this seemed to help. I know I can only be happy if I do what I think is right. I don't know what the future holds but I feel it can only be better than the past because of my new insight and feelings. I want to get started properly discharging my responsibilities and I don't think I'll be happy until I do.

Comments

There are two ways to change governing dynamics for the better – either through the abreaction (transmodulation) of negative material or the direct activation of positive matrices. This subject strongly activates BPM I and possibly to a lesser extant BPM IV but seems to avoid the abreaction of any negative material whatsoever – a feat that is virtually unheard of among the thousand subjects.

Although Frank does occasionally refuse him a cigarette, he smokes continuously, sometimes lying down with the blindfold on, perhaps this control of his affect allowed such a rarely apparently uniformly positive trip. Unfortunately no follow-up is provided but it would be cynical to question the authenticity of his religious experience, although I wonder if he doesn't reveal a Freudian slip at the end when he describes, "properly *discharging* my responsibilities."

To the team at Hollywood Hospital the transformation of alcoholics was routine –

S52Y6

"I was actually experiencing the making of my own body."

This subject was a 34 year-old bank manager from a small town in rural British Columbia, Canada. He came from a reasonably prestigious upper-middle class family, his Father managed a mill. Although the family struggled during the depression he and his only brother ultimately lived in a mansion and were driven by a chauffer. His childhood was reasonably happy although he does recount a familiar tale of surgical trauma, "I can still see the cold leather of the operating table, see the trolley with the surgeon's instruments laid out and the doctors and nurses in their white gowns and masks. Ether was administered through a cone of gauze placed over my nose and mouth by an anesthetist that I could see upside down as I lay on the table."

His Father was a self styled Victorian patriarch who still lived with the subject's Mom although he treated her less like a Wife and more like a Mother, likely suffering from symptoms related to his service during the war. The subject and family moved to Canada after his Father left the military and S52Y6 started working at a bank about ten years before his session. He was a disciplined student of eastern meditation although fairly agnostic generally. While successful in his career in banking he was sexually ambiguous, suffered from low self- esteem and sometimes felt isolated.

Treatment Day

09:45 700 mg mescaline, 200 mcg LSD

11:10 pt remained quiet for total period since 10:25 expressed feeling of "nothing happening" 500 mg mescaline

11:40 pt. sat up for five minutes said "nothing happening but feel tightness in the pit of my stomach" smoked pipe for one min.

12:25 pt. very restless, tossing and turning constantly, "unnamable tension" building up; pt. talked for five minutes

13:00 "now I've told you I'm a homosexual what more do you want?" pt. very restless; Bruckner's 8th

13:05 "I thought this was an unreal world with apparitions but its real, its REAL! It's too real!

13:10 pt in throes of torture

13:20 pt. reports intense pain in his groin

13:25 "now I know what hell is. Two thousand centuries of torture I'm torn apart!" Pt. has legs drawn up with rt. arm between – Constant talking with majority of words indistinct

13:30 "I want to be clean. I'm nothing anyway."

13:40 "I'm more aware than I've ever been before"

13:45 "I float in space – studded with heavens. Is this God?"

18:30 "I feel like a small child again"

19:30 "Am I in this world or the other?"

Post-Treatment

I had been told that the first symptoms might be the apparent movement of the curtains in the room and, whether or not by this suggestion or by the first effects of the chemicals – I did in fact see such a movement in about 15 minutes.

There were times when I thought I saw through closed lids apparent geometrical shapes and some colour but nothing very definite. In the mean time tension grew and I became more and more uncomfortable. I rubbed my hands together and twisted my fingers and tossed and turned while I rubbed the foot of one leg against the other leg. This tension was beyond belief and I had never imagined that psychological tension could reach such a pitch.

Dr. MacLean then gave me another 500 mg mescaline and I resumed my position on the couch. Mr. Ogden told me that in his estimation it would now take another eight minutes for further effects to develop and for release from this tension to be noted. Again I writhed on the couch for what seemed like a long time. I finally dragged myself up onto the arm of the couch and said to the therapist, "Frank if this is hell there must be a heaven too."

"Sure there is – all you have to do is look for it." I slid down on the couch on my back with my arms spread and in seconds experienced the first of two powerful ecstatic and completely inexpressible religious experiences.

I was looking up into the heavens at night and the canopy above was studded with stars. It was extremely peaceful. Then it was as if the lid of this gigantic canopy was pealed back or lifted off and I looked straight into eternity and infinity. The stars blazed – each a dazzling point of intensely white light while around the rim of the heavens and within my peripheral vision was an ethereal, celestial

blue-green light. At this moment the whole heavens rang (I can use no other word) with the sound of a choir the likes of which this world will never hear.

I must note at this point that this was a total experience. I did not just see. I experienced this with all my senses and all senses were tuned to a hitherto unbelievable pitch. This is quite inexpressible but every fiber of my being was electrified and every fiber screamed, "yes" in affirmation of these words that I understood. The ecstasy of this splendid moment was indescribable. And yet I knew that all this that I beheld was real, was true and was mine. It always has been and it always will be. More of this experience I cannot say, it was literally that which passes all understanding.

I then began what seemed to be a descent – not physical but rather biological. I was in the position of feeling that all that I possessed that made me a separate personality was being assaulted and demolished by these two implacable chemicals. My ego defense mechanism was crumbling. At this time I heard the music of *Mahler's First Symphony* and again I understood with my whole being. I was one with him and I knew that he had experienced what I was going through. I asked him by name for help and, at the same time it seemed that I went down on my knees and begged the chemicals, also by name, to "take it easy on me."

I have omitted to say that during that time of extreme tension I did most emphatically notice that I had been castrated. This is the very first thing that I had been deprived of. I could no longer prove my manhood. Now as I descended the scale of life I was being robbed of my personality, the image I had built up and which I showed to the outside world and finally my intellect. I knew beyond all doubt that I was going insane – becoming psychotic.

My eyes were closed but now I looked at the left hand and to my unutterable horror it had turned all curled up into itself and was, in fact the hand of a baby. I still knew that all this was real. I knew also that this was my hand. I had seen it that way before – so long ago. This was too much for me and I pressed my hands to my face and covered my eyes. Incredibly it was the face of me as I was as a child. It all came back to me. This was as I had been perhaps at the age of three or four. I touched my face this way when I was a child and it had felt this way. I had merely forgotten all this in the intervening years and was reliving it.

I continued what I must call for want of a better word, my descent down the scale of life. And I come now to a portion of the experience that is particularly hard to describe. It is hard to verbalize because I returned to a time in my life before I had the ability to speak. My impressions have never been caught and crystallized in words.

The scenes were varied but they fell more or less into two groups. There were scenes of pearly white moving shapes not unlike maps of continents in geography. These were however constantly moving and changing. Sounds accompanied these movements. Then there were scenes of a lattice like substance made of golden brown material not unlike ragged thin elastic bands. I must point out that during the time that I experienced all this I did not think about it objectively. I was not capable of any thought –

I was merely reliving it all in fantastic reality and clarity. Something which had all happened before which I remembered clearly. In retrospect, I now realize with a man's intelligence that I was wrong if I had thought that these were scenes from earliest childhood. I now know in a way that I cannot somehow doubt that these were scenes of a pre- natal state. I was actually experiencing the making of my own body.

The experience went deeper. I was now at the very bottom of the scale down which I had descended. I saw what looked like a watery scene as though I were at the bottom of a body of water. Bright objects like fireflies swam around it – each was a slightly luminous bulb that trailed a thin wisp of light behind it. I cannot tell how but I knew I was witnessing the very beginning of something that I can only say was myself. I now believe with absolute assurance that I was seeing my own conception.

I must discuss my feelings about this hell for so it was. After the horror of my hand turning into a baby's, what I call the pre-natal state, I felt "un-nice" but not horrible. The conception was made bearable by the knowledge it was an act of love.

I returned then to the prenatal state and, it seems to me looking back, that I must have begun some sort of upward trend. I became conscious again of the room even though I was still a child.

The nurse became a Mother or she somehow embodied the word Motherhood and that was all that mattered. First her face became a mask that was the epitome of kindness, sympathy, understanding and Motherhood. Almost immediately it changed and assumed an expression of sternness and discipline. These changes took place one following another with fair rapidity but not so fast that I could not clearly see each one and understand what it meant. It was as though each expression remained just long enough to give me the full import before it changed again. Strangely, this neither puzzled nor frightened me.

I closed my eyes again and returned to my childhood – for how long I have no idea. Time meant nothing to me then or later.

My next recollection happened with startling speed. In what seemed like a flash I was fully conscious, a full-grown man and I was standing on the opposite side of the room from the couch upon which I had been lying. I looked back at the couch fully expecting to see my body lying there, for in this instant I knew with not the slightest possibility of doubt that I was not in my body. In fact, I did not see my own body upon the couch and this frankly disappointed me. I was shaking like a leaf from head to toe but I did not feel frightened.

I now returned to the other room, looked around it, noted the door, which led to the outside passage and decided to go "exploring." As I put my hand upon the doorknob I became smaller in stature and felt more like a child. Like a child also I opened the door and peeped out into the passage. It was rather a child-like world – an "Alice in Wonderland" world of childish delight and adventure.

This world I was in was a plastic world. Dimensions can and do alter and change and to some extent one can control these alterations. If things appear distant you can bring them closer by simply desiring that they become closer. The colours of the passage and room I had left were the same but sharper and more real in some way.

I decided to go downstairs and took about three or four steps. I stopped momentarily because I saw two men talking to one another at the bottom of the flight of stairs. Their heads and shoulders showed clearly and solidly against the wooden paneling of the wall behind them. I shall break the narrative at this point to mention that the flight of stairs is not unbroken. In reality the stairs descend in one flight to a small landing, turn one hundred and eighty degrees to the floor below. In normal consciousness this view would only have been possible had I descended to the first landing and then looked down and this I had definitely not done.

I descended the last flight of stairs and saw the lobby of the hospital. Everything looked perfectly normal and I distinctly remember seeing the sunlight streaming through the translucent glass on the front door of the hospital. At this moment, from an office situated to my left and below, a girl appeared. She was dark and attractive looking and she looked up at me and flashed a glance in my direction which conveyed the impression of some surprise, mingled with understanding – as if she understood instantly all about me and the condition I was in. At once she darted back in the direction from which she had come. I received the impression that she had gone to fetch someone and almost instantaneously with this thought came the knowledge that the front door of the hospital would open and that Frank Ogden would walk in. The thought was no sooner formed than this, in fact, happened. He came into the lobby, saw me and hurried up the stairs. He put his arm about my shoulders and led me back upstairs. I was very confused and kept explaining to him that I was unable now to say which dimension or world I belonged to.

Now some more music was played and I asked the therapist if could look outside. Accordingly the curtains, which had covered the windows

all day, had been drawn back. I went through the door and out the veran-
dah to look at the garden. The day had been a dull one but now the sun
was just showing from time to time and I asked the therapist if this was
really so or if it was my imagination. He assured me that the sun was just
beginning to shine. The garden below me looked perfectly natural and in
no way distorted. The colours were bright but not unusually or unnatu-
rally so. They were warmer and more meaningful. The whole scene was
suffused with a rosy glow. It was rather as if I saw the world through very
slightly, rose-tinted glasses. At the same time I was happy and contented. I could hear the trees exceedingly clearly as well as see them in much
sharper focus. And again the whole scene was somehow more meaningful. If our vision can said to be "stereo" normally then this was like having
"stereo- stereo" vision.

During the rest of the evening I went again several times to the balcony
overlooking the garden and enjoyed the more meaningful view. I exam-
ined the therapy room and on one occasion stood close to the cabinet of
HI-FI speakers. I put my hands on it and looked <u>into</u> it and experienced
the music it was producing. The music itself filled me and caused me to
vibrate inside in harmony with it. I can only say that one does much more
than simply <u>hear</u> music in this state – one <u>experiences</u> it totally with one's
whole being.

During the evening I again experienced the same religious ecstasy that
I had felt during the morning. The therapist at this time returned and was
once again playing music to me. I don't know whether it was Mahler or
Bruckner or what it was. But the transcendental experience was the same.

Comments

This subject reports a return to his meditation practice with improved
results and feeling greatly benefitted by his session. He in fact in-
vites Dr. MacLean to speak on psychedelics where he works which Dr.
MacLean accepts, sadly no talks from the eminent physician exist to my
knowledge.

As the tension built early in the experience they gave him more mescaline and Frank suggested, "In eight minutes that tension will release."
Which it does – he then experiences a religious ecstasy and "becomes"
his prenatal self. Then in a far from smooth procession he returns to his
current adult body.

This is reminiscent of renegade psychiatrist R. D. Laing's experimental
therapy for schizophrenia and other disorders practiced in the late sixties

and early seventies at Kingsley Hall in London, England. Dr. Laing proposed:

> "1. Whatever it is that clinically is diagnosed as acute schizophrenia or schizophreniform breakdown, may itself be a resource a human being calls upon when all else seems impossible.
> 2. If the *set* and *setting* can be changed (from the mental hospital model), the experience may be so transformed, that it no longer need be regarded as "psychotic" at all."

People left the hospital, stopped their medications, moved in and just "let go." One lady felt she had lost herself somewhere along the way and, "felt she had to go back to where she had lost herself and find herself again. A few days after coming to Kingsley Hall, she was going back quite considerably, in a way that I have never seen anyone do. As she went back she became completely helpless to the extent that she had to be fed with a baby's bottle every two or three hours." Eventually she became emaciated and suffered a uterine hemorrhage but she persevered nonetheless and "went back to before she was born, before she was even incarnated. She wanted to abandon her body completely."

Many people believe they must go back to their own conception before they can start to return – a process he describes as "neo-genesis."

"This woman came back over a period of five to six weeks. Each day she was a little older and a little more organized." She became a minor media sensation and remains the "signature patient" of R.D. Laing's radical therapy.

Returning to our psychedelic subject it's clear that if the regression at Kingsley Hall bears any resemblance to the Hollywood Hospital psychedelic version, the latter was a lot faster but a lot less complete. The Kingsley Hall approach is like clear-cutting a diseased tree at a lower point than an infection so that it can grow again normally, conversely the Hollywood approach integrates the gnarl into the system fully and grows around it.

At one point Frank had left the treatment room, which would only happen at the end of the trip when the subject was hopefully coming down. At this point however S52Y6 was not internalizing his experience but in fact was roaming the hospital worshipping his own superpowers. It must have been a shock to Frank to see him wandering around but the intrepid therapist managed to resolve the trip well and it even ended with another "ecstatic religious experience."

S18H5

"I always thought the world was stinking. It was me."

The next subject was a 32 year-old single teacher with what would now be considered social anxiety. She was highly introverted and had never been in love with a man but reports no history of homosexuality. This they accept much more readily than when male subjects have similar problems. The clinic attracted many homosexuals, whose therapy now would focus on accepting their sexuality rather than changing it. However two prominent homosexual "psychedelians" Richard Alpert and Allen Ginsberg both advocated the use of the drug for improving sexual health. Ginsberg even claimed he felt "heterosexual urges for the first time on LSD."

According to one study, 2-4% of men are exclusively homosexual, 1-2% actively bisexual and 20-25% engage in fantasy and experience some homosexual attraction (the numbers are about half for women) – the sexual revolution obviously isn't finished yet.

Treatment Day

09:50 250 mcg LSD, 600 mg mescaline taken

10:10 pt. nervous and anxious

10:35 pt. reported feelings of nausea

10:50 "why do my legs shake?"

10:55 pt. counseled to drift with music in fantasy

11:00 pt. shivering

11:15 *Mahler 1st Symphony*; pt. caressing couch

11:20 "I can see myself."

11:25 "I really am rigid, aren't I?"

11:35 pt. yawning continually; pt. thighs trembling; pt. constantly rubbing back of chesterfield with left hand pt. shaking head "no"

11:40 pt. stiffens whole body; pt. stretches arms out fully

11:45 pt. showing ecstatic look on face, stretching; *side II Mahler's 1st* playing

11:50 pt. moving lower jaw extensively; pt. shaking head "no"; pt. hand lifting in air – lower jaw trembling pt. yawning sighing

11:55 pt. pushing sensuously at back of chesterfield

12:00 *Bruckner's 8th* commencing

12:10 "I don't want you." pt. sighs frequently

12:30 "It's coming back" "I know" crying; pt. struggling with self; "I don't want to be helpless"; much struggling and movement and crying

12:31 "I just don't want to be like that – helpless"; pt. beats couch with fist

12:35 pt.'s hand icy cold; "I seem to be in the same pattern" pt. squirming violently; "I don't know which way to go – which way am I supposed to be. I don't know."

12:40 pt.'s arms flailing in every direction

12:50 "I never thought it would be like this. I should never have taken it. I just can't get out. Why can't; I get out"; (have feeling pt. is experiencing life as a lesbian)

12:55 "everything I'm pushing away is soft and feminine"

13:05 "I'm afraid to let myself go – I'm afraid to be feminine"

13:10 pt. writhing like snake all over couch; pt. sits up, goes to stand, falls back on couch "I don't trust you guys; I don't trust men; I never thought it would be like this. LSD."

13:25 "I hate you. Don't laugh. Stop it.; I'm afraid" pt. screaming at top of lungs; "Don't keep laughing. Macdonald don't keep at it everything is trying to take me. I'm in another world. Macdonald's laughing. He's laughing because I'm crazy. Everything's beautiful and I don't want it."

13:35 "I hate men. You are always working against me."

13:40 "Are you giving me shock treatments or something?"

13:50 "I'll just be."; pt. falls back exhausted; "take me out. I don't want that tunnel again." Frank puts arm around pt.; pt. relaxes; pt. gets excited again Frank relaxes again

14:35 "I know I must break out of this shell."

14:40 "He presses me down."

14:50 pt. faced with mirror; pt. alters her view of herself as she looks in mirror "stupid little shell. Aren't I?"

15:15 *Scheherazade* just finishing; *Grand Canyon Suite* starting; pt. has angelic and passionate look on face simultaneously

15:30 "I want to just be a little girl. I don't want to face anything; I just want to be a little girl.; Why aren't there any women around here? Always men.'; Pt. screaming, "I need something to hang on to something solid."

15:50 "I know it's me inside a stinking shell; I'm going to be sick.; Everything is snow now – everything is nice. Where is mom and Dad? I love you all."; Strauss Waltz; pt. lying on back eyes closed – arms outstretched "I sure like that Dr. Macdonald.; It all boils down to just what I wanted. I like myself."

16:05 "I thought you meant sexual, just sexual but now its spiritual," said softly; "I know I've been in essence – everything is so wonderful. Life is wonderful. I see it all now.; I must love.; I'm so glad I went into hell." repeated; "I'm going to stay up here amongst the trees. It's just like when I was a child. I hated things about my Dad. He never rose above all this. I love him." pt. crying

16:15 "I want to tell everybody. Write it down."

16:20 "I want ants and spiders to be free. I want men to be free."

16:30 "I'll never see myself the same way again.; I went to heaven. I know what paradise is. I know myself now."

16:35 "I know I have to come down and help too.; I was afraid of all that sex. I never knew men like you, like that." pt. crying; "I'm God"

16:50 "I always thought the world was stinking. It was me."

Post-Treatment

Near the beginning I experienced Egyptian or other ancient monuments on parade, which I liked – kind of a rust colour. Next I was swimming in an aquarium, then things seemed to close in on me – but the water felt nice. Then from the lovely music I saw really lovely women so soft in their colours but didn't seem to want to be so helpless or weak or something to that effect. Then for what seemed to be a long time I kept trying to find out what and who I was.

When the others in the room said and asked certain questions I went into all different weird proportions. I didn't seem to know how to be as soon as I said a wrong thing the proportion would unbalance. I didn't know where I was and had the sensation I had been hopeless and in there for days trying to get a right proportion. I just couldn't break through as I felt so heavy and I was so ugly at times.

Then I could feel all souls blended together through each other – dainty exquisite green and clear crystal all across the sky – then the ceiling lamp was multiplied into hundreds revolving and blending in – with a delicate blue through the center of each moving in and out of them. All the sky was a harmony of perfection.

Then I, or my soul, blended in with the white as though my soul had reached perfection. Then I got the sensation I was God – however I said it wrong, as I suddenly was conscious of myself and was going out of proportion – so then I knew I was just part of it all. Then I looked at the white light and it stood silent and beckoned me to come and stay there. Then I knew it was me that was the one to make the decision and I hesitated. I wanted it but I wanted the earth too.

Follow-Up

The main benefit I derived from L.S.D. was being sure of God and a pattern in the universe. And when feeling low no one will help me unless I help myself and only through this will I grow.

With music two months ago I again experienced God and the feeling was so <u>strange</u> and so perfect. I knew this had always been my true home. All there was, was simply a state of being (just being companion with God; nothing else). Now I understand the meaning "God is." Nothing else is needed. I also feel that no one can explain God but that God has to be individually experienced. I also never really knew that God was so lovely. I didn't see God as a symbol but just everything in one. I guess as being God yet not being God, but a true part.

Since L.S.D. I've learned I cannot skip and be a yogi but have to live through life. Now I have an ideal, which gives life its real purpose. Also by loving someone I will find my balance.

Now I feel so much closer to nature and have the desire to study the thoughts of painters and musicians.

I only started really seeing myself a few months ago and it is depressing but I think that as I gradually blend my ego into the real law I will have a good life.

Thank you Doctor MacLean and Frank for your help.

Comments

The problems of sexuality and identity are primary once again. She was likely lesbian and now therapy would strive to help her accept it, nonetheless the abreaction of the negative perinatal unconscious and the activation of the positive is truly textbook.

At one point she complains of all the sitters being men, in the late fifties Betty Eisner and Sidney Cohen noticed then when patients were dealing with their most difficult experiences having a therapist of each gender helped moved the process forward faster, this has become recognized generally as ideal.

S74H6

"Mother I love you if only you wouldn't beat me so much. Mother why do you hate me? You shouldn't hate anyone. God is kind and God loves…. I think God is listening to me."

In the next case a 53 year old lobotomized, schizophrenic alcoholic with suicidal tendencies, who took five thorazine and two stelazine (two closely related anti- psychotic drugs) daily, and had been severely physically abused by her perfectionist Mother – was given 100 mcg of LSD and 400 mg of mescaline. She showed severe depression and other pathology but was "far from the most disturbed patient studied." After experiencing severe depression in the 1940s she was *lobotomized,* she also had received insulin coma therapy and the theoretically similar electro-convulsive therapy.

Treatment Day

10:30 400 mg mescaline/ 100 mcg LSD

11:05 pt. expressed hostility towards toward her Mother who she describes as a "perfectionist"; pt. explained how sometimes she doesn't go into the laundry room (she lives in apt.) because someone else is there – she won't get mail either if someone is there

11:25 "Oh I wish I was home." *Songs of the South* playing

11:30 pt. shaking violently

11:35 trembling subsides then returns "Oh dear God." repeated

11:40 pt. clapping hands together (in terror); "Oh dear God please help me. Show me how to help myself.; Oh please dear God show me the way" hands in prayer; "I want to make my husband happy. He's doing so much for me. I'm so thankful."; loud clap, more violent shaking, rapid clapping "Our Father who art in heaven. Dear God" much screaming; "Don't hurt me; Mother please don't hurt me; Oh Mother don't do it to me. I beg you. I love you."; loud screaming; pt. slapping hands together; "Oh Dad don't let Mother hurt me. Dad I love you don't you love me? I know you do."

11:45 "Pray to God Dad that she will stop; Mother I love you if only you wouldn't beat me so much. Mother why do you hate me?

You shouldn't hate anyone. Mother why don't you ever kiss me? Why don't you love me?"; *Mahler 1st Symphony*; "God is kind and God loves." Pt. repeats Lord's Prayer

11:50 "dear God I love you. Please make her understand.; I'm drunk all the time.; I don't call her unless I'm drunk, she said I know my husband loves me.; I'm so thankful he doesn't beat me."

12:00 "Dear God in heaven take me home."

12:05 pt. now apologetic towards talking mean to her Mother "Dear God make her happy physically and mentally.; Dear Mother why can't I tell you I love you."

12:10 "It's because she hurt me! Oh help her to become good."

12:15 pt. loud screaming at the crescendo peak of *Mahler 1st*

12:30 "My Mother keeps me from telling others that I love them."

12:35 "I don't go to church every Sunday, why don't I?; Please God help that little girl that takes the needle" (girl she met in hospital)

13:10 "Dear God, why does my Mother hate me? What did I do?; I want to be forgiven." 13:30 *Bruckner's 8th* side III; "Something's getting in my mouth"; pt. pulls at mouth – pt. trying to blow something out of mouth

13:40 "Oh God, I'm tired.; I think I know then I don't know." 13:45 pt. repeats love for husband

14:20 "Am I acting? I'm mixed up. I want to forget, that is why I like shock treatment it makes me forget. I know what; I want but don't know how to ask for it."

14:25 "I'm sick."

14:35 "I want to be normal."

14:45 "How long does this test go?; My head is going to ache in a moment"

15:00 "Have I been running away from myself and don't know it?; I've got to get that out of my mouth."

15:45 "Is it cold in here? It's in my heart isn't it?; This day will end won't it?"

15:50 pt. crying; *Ava Maria* playing

16:30 pt. crying; "I think God is listening to me." 17:15 pt. faced with mirror; "I'm ashamed of you (herself) because you didn't make the proper home for your children and now it's too late."; Pt. told she could still make a home for her husband

19:00 "I learned. I am going to tell my Mother I love her. I never could.; I'm so happy."

19:30 pt. left alone – candle lit

Post-Treatment

I have a happier perspective, see situations clearly, and do not have the tension that I had and have lost the depression.

Follow-Up

A week later she was sent home to Florida to the consulting psychiatrist. Dr. MacLean writes "there is little doubt that her immediate post experience condition was vastly improved over that on admission. It is likely that she has recognized and accepted her alcoholic problem realistically."

Comments

What makes this case so amazing is the degree of disturbance and the confidence they demonstrated in giving her the treatment. Once again they have apparently produced another breakthrough. It is obvious how important her relationship with her husband is and how therapy is well served by focusing on strengths in addition to addressing weaknesses.

Thorazine and stelazine (anti-psychotics) were being prescribed at almost one full gram of synthetic chemicals *daily*, 365 grams a year by ten years is 3.65 kilograms of "stuff." In insulin coma therapy, the blood sugar is reduced to a level where convulsions or seizures occur, in 1938 the Italian physicians Ugo Celetti and Lucio Bini began using electricity instead of insulin because it could be controlled better. This subject described severe memory loss from her still regular ECT sessions. S74H6 was subjected to massive "heroic" interventions to save her and yet the criticism of psychedelic therapy was how dangerous it could be. The removal of parts of the brain, chemical or electrical induced seizures, the consumption of kilograms of synthetic chemicals however is considered good medicine.

This is particularly salient regarding drugs because psychedelic therapy at most usually involves only up to ten sessions (ten doses) whereas hydraulic oppositional mainstream medicine requires indefinite if not permanent doses. In other words if using only LSD you could have ten 200 mcg (2 mg) sessions with the equivalent weight of one tenth of *one*

day's worth of prozac (20 mg) in a whole lifetime. Partnership For A Drug
– Free America and the rest of the drug warriors may someday embrace
psychedelic therapy as a way to lower overall drug use.

S67H4

*"This molten metal I'm floating in – purple and orange cold fire – You've
got make do with what you have."*

This subject was a 46-year-old slightly neurotic and depressed social-
ite from Philadelphia with a schoolgirl crush on her psychiatrist. She
was unable to achieve orgasm during intercourse and feels a lack of meaning that sometimes contributes to serious bouts of depression. There is a
hint of possible promiscuity and even infidelity combined with fantasies
about a "prince charming" that will rescue her – what would now probably be called histrionic personality disorder.

Treatment Day

08:45 400 mcg LSD / 200 mg mescaline

09:05 eyes and body covered said her legs felt rubbery, crying says
she misses her psychiatrist most

09:15 "can't move, can't move"

9:35 – "I'm burning, I'm burning" – hand on abdomen. "I'm on
fire" laughs – "it's not funny at all, roars with laughter. Sobs; I'm
dying, God I am dying.; How can it be so tremendous when nothing is happening?"

09:45 "I'm melting, I'm melting; It's all Dr. L. – How can I ever
love anyone else? That's right, I'm frigid.; All cosmic, there it is. It's
purple, it's everything. Poor old Freud, he was probably a nice guy.;
Hope somebody is writing this all down"

10:05 "This molten metal I'm floating in – purple and orange cold
fire – you've got make do with what you have – human beings are
so beautiful, my children -; Why do I waste all this love and energy
on dr. L.?" roars with laughter, "help him he needs help – I have
seen and tasted colour – no one can every take it back"

12:15 pt. vomits large quantity of fluid

13:35 "I'm somebody here, am I here? Are we all here?" Curious
about time

14:15 wants to hear *St. Paul's Message* again

16:00 "I'm doing very well"

18:45 "I think I've found what I was looking for and all I need is patience"

Commentary

After the trip she is ecstatic and full of admiration for humanity, the Rockies, the oceans and all creation. During the experience she seemed to resolve her destructive infatuation with her psychiatrist. She wrote a letter a month later and told them how beneficial her experience was and how great she was still feeling.

S45G1

"... some of the patterns looked like Mother and some of the patterns looked like Dad as very young people and they would appear interwoven in the very patterns. I felt them very close to me. At one point I recognized Grandmother's bed throw pattern!"

Although only in her mid-sixties this next subject is referred to as elderly, which nowadays seems preposterous. Hers is a common problem at Hollywood hospital as she was romantically isolated all her life. She was a deeply shy and inhibited person and had developed an obsession with counting numbers when stressed. The prevailing attitude was well summarized with, "at her age I wouldn't hope for much personality change."

Treatment Day I

09:45 500 mg mescaline, 150 mcg LSD 11:20 pt. throwing up but settled again

12:00 pt. lying quietly

13:00 pt. sleep shade is still on; *Bruckner 8th Symphony* part 1

21:00 pt. very quiet from 4 to 8 – around six lay down with eyeshades on and stayed that way until 9 am

Post-Treatment

I believe the first thing I saw were fish – some beautiful swimming swiftly, some ugly and without form opening and closing ugly mouths. Then snakes – very swift pictures.

I saw a beautiful white bird with a collar of something very fragile and with brilliant coloring. I saw swift pictures but vividly recognized Mother's house's woven bed throw patterns. I used to feel as a youngster that some of the patterns looked like Mother and some of the patterns looked like Dad as very young people and they would appear interwoven in the very patterns. I felt them very close to me.

At one point I recognized Grandmother's bed throw pattern!

I saw a dance going on (must have been the very first dance I saw when I was 7-8 years old). My uncle, Dad's brother dancing with a very pretty young girl, beautifully dressed in that day's frills and flounces, dancing very fast as in those days. I got the feeling the floor was crowded and the dance was going on in great tempo. But recognized only uncle and this girl whom was the town's flirt and loose living as the talk went. I think I used to feel sorry for her and hoped I would never be talked about like that.

I saw one picture of many of my relatives, mostly Dad's people, seemed to be in the same vicinity. At two different times the music had the effect where I had the urge to get up and dance. Occasionally I had the feeling that I was losing control and my head would be disconnected at my neck. This didn't necessarily alarm me – I took it as part of the treatment.

Through the whole treatment I suffered pain especially in my head – I thought I would force my teeth through my gums. At first I didn't think I could endure the music so loud but as the treatment proceeded I still felt it was terrifically loud but enjoyed it.

Treatment Day II (eighteen months later)

> 11:35 pt. ingested 200 mg mescaline, 125 mcg LSD
>
> 13:35 pt. 500 mg mescaline
>
> 16:20 pt. quiet through wide range of music
>
> 18:25 pt. quiet – religious music played

Post-Treatment

As soon as I lay back on the pillows I had an uncomfortable spot under my left shoulder blade, thinking it was a corner of the pillow causing it, I would move then pull at the pillow, but by the time I got the second pill it was so sore I asked the nurse to give my pillows a shake, still didn't get relief but figured it was part of the treatment.

The first thing as I drifted off I was driving my car in a snowstorm, I drove fast and the snow became more and more blinding until I drove into a snow-bank or slide but I kept right on digging the car into it as far as I could. Then I saw colorful patterns, many of the same patterns I had seen in the first treatment. I felt as if I saw my parents as very young people again. Seemed to get glimpses of ancestors very far back. Seemed to see Grandmother (Dad's Mother) stranded in the woods with three little boys.

I saw a group of rather horrible eyes peering at me. Then after more colorful patterns I was shown a beautiful child with the most perfect features I've ever seen with flowing golden hair.

Then I saw a dance going on at a ladies place where I've been helping out. Even my own folks attended all dressed in glittering evening dresses in silver or gold.

One perfect figure was more outstanding than the rest.

The day I was all ready to leave the hospital my nurse came and spoke to me, I nearly exclaimed, "you're beautiful." Arriving at my friend's place when she opened the door again I wanted to say, "you're beautiful." She is nearing seventy and has quite a wrinkled face, but I seemed to see right through the wrinkles and saw her as smooth and beautiful, I was quite startled and still am at seeing the improvement in so many people.

The first week after the treatment I was tired, weak and nervous. This last week much stronger and have noticed very peaceful, restful periods.

Comments

The vision of her whole family dancing at a huge ball appears in both her experiences even though they were eighteen months apart; this might prove very appealing to those facing imminent death. At the end of her report she describes seeing two females as beautiful and this may be simply reflecting the positive aspects of the perinatal domain but what is more likely is that her sexuality is finally emerging freely.

S63W5
"I ask myself now why didn't I keep him and stop drinking?"

This subject was a 54-year-old wife and mother from Toronto with a severe drinking problem so serious that her 15-year-old son was sent away to a relative. Born in rural Ontario she worked like a slave on a farm where she picked up ringworm from a cow she was milking and missed two years of school due to infection stemming at least partly from her Father's mistrust of doctors. She left home and began cleaning houses at 14, all this during the "roaring" twenties.

Treatment Day

10:00 pt. given 400 mg mescaline, 150 mcg LSD

11:40 pt. bursts into heavy sobbing

12:00 "Where is he? Where is my baby boy? Can I see him?; I lost him through drinking. He is such a good boy."

12:40 *Mahler 1*ˢᵗ *Symphony;* "I'm afraid. I don't know of what, but I'm so frightened."

13:00 pt. clutching back of couch then of hair

13:05 "My head is so sore, it's so itchy. Oh momma." pt. briefly scratches and holds head

13:15 "Mom, my head is so sore" pt. holding head pt. crying; Bruckner 8ᵗʰ

13:25 "oh no" pt. jerks violently, pushes up mask

13:30 pt. tears off mask but keeps eyes closed; "It's better now Mom. Yes its better now. Doesn't hurt as much. Gotta be tough.; When he lanced it, it hurt. That's why you gotta be tough."

14:00 pt. wraps blanket tightly around her, still running hands through hair

14:55 "oh that was a bit much" – after *Bolero*

15:40 pt. screaming "stop it"; music stopped, pt. opened eyes to be faced with mirror

17:15 pt. wants to see her husband. Pt. freezing (room temp 78 f); but when shown "Veronica's handkerchief" she felt warm "why is that?"

18:30 tea provided

20:00 pt. visited by husband. Pt. very pleased.

22:00 pt. hungry, hamburger and chips provided; pt. feels she won't drink again

Post-Treatment

The first thing that I remembered was, when I was about 9 yrs old, the boat that used to run on the lakes. It would come down three times a week around 7 pm and back up the lake around midnight, of course if the trains were late in arriving at Yonge St. then the last boat would be later. If there were anything ordered from town my brother and I would have to meet the boat and sign for whatever was coming for us. This particular night it was around 4 am when the boat came. It was midwinter, lots of snow and very cold we had our horse and sleigh with us. We got part way home and our horse refused to go any farther, we knew that there was some wild animal around that the horse could smell. We finally coaxed him along and later we found out there was a cougar up in a tree at the side of the road. We were both so terrified it was horrible.

Then I went on to when I was around eleven years old, I got ringworm on my head from a sow I used to milk all the time. It formed a scab a good ½ inch thick that had to be cleaned off every so often in order to treat it. My Father didn't believe in doctors so there was a friend who looked after it for me, she knew a bit about nursing. It was terribly sore and itchy. I could hardly stand it. My oldest sister had to take me to the doctor on Yonge St. three different times to have it lanced, of course there was no anesthetic or at least I didn't have any. It really hurt. My mom was always there to comfort me. I was out of school 20 months with it.

I then went to last summer when I sent my son (now 15) to live with my brother because my drinking interfered with him.

I ask myself now why didn't I keep him and stop drinking? I must overcome being so stubborn. I intend to leave him there until June, then if he wishes to come home I'm sure things will be different, I miss him so very much.

Comments

The subjects always evoke a lot of empathy but when this one says, "it's okay Mom, it's getting better," it is truly heart-breaking. It's bad enough living as a pioneer but when a child's Father doesn't believe in doctors, which causes a serious infection and she had to watch her Father beat her Mother, even the hardiest dispositions among us may take to the bottle. Alcoholics respond so incredibly well to this therapy it was a devastating loss that this was discontinued. Generally they present no defenses whatsoever, sail through even the difficult experiences and feel different about their lives generally and alcohol especially. "We never cured one tobacco addict," Frank reports.

S31F7

"By finally succumbing to the snake it was also a great relief to have the fear terminated."

A temperamentally shy middle-aged carpenter with a checkered employment history and a drinking problem from Calgary will be our next subject. Once again issues surrounding homosexuality are prominent and while serving in the navy he had many such experiences. He feels his Wife dominates him in a similar way that his Mother dominated his Father. At age seven a leg infection almost required amputation but homosexuality and alcohol were once again the focus of therapy.

Treatment Day

11:00 800 mg mescaline, 200 mcg LSD; pt. underwent 15 min. strobe light earlier

11:20 pt. thinks music sounds "like a funeral parlor."

11:40 pt. eyes covered with sleep shade; "the music is beautiful"

11:45 "I feel like I'm being born.; I feel like I do when I look at my children."

11:50 pt.'s whole body jerking, pt. reports feeling bands breaking all over his body; pt. feels he is suffocating

11:55 pt. has hand on his privates; pt. moaning

12:05 pt. shuddering, apparently in great ecstasy "whee" "yi-ee"; above accompanied by much pelvic movement

13:20 pt. clutching privates

13:40 activity noticeably diminishing

14:15 pt. turns crying and wraps arms around F. pt. comforted pt. pushes F. away,

14:30 pt. tries several times to re-enter treatment room; some invisible barrier appears to be preventing re-entry pt. alternately smiling and scowling

15:45 pt. too active for past half hr. and 15 min to record. Pt. tried; a dozen times to leave room into hall partially succeeding one time. Pt. removed all clothes one minute after above entry made – pt. tried to undo wire screening (the porch was screened to prevent jumpers flying or fliers jumping or either landing); Used head as battering ram against screen. Pt. kicked door jam at one point violently – hurting foot.; On several occasions all energies of Dr. MacLean and F. needed to keep pt. in treatment room; Pt. frequently expresses love and hate toward F. and JRM simultaneously or at least in rapid succession

16:05 *Surf Sounds;* pt. requested quiet

16:10 pt. given mirror, looks for few moments and then drops it

19:40 "I always felt if I got rid of my penis my Dad would love me more I guess he wanted a girl because she'd be no competition."; Pt.

shown pictures of family.; "I never saw her like this before." (sister) pt. crying over picture of Father; "he was weak, poor guy."

22:00 Pt.'s Wife visited. Coffee served. Pt. in excellent spirits.; Wife highly pleased

Post-Treatment

It is 11 am the day after treatment. I feel very good at the present. I am feeling more optimistic every minute. A few hours ago I felt panicky, anxious. But now calm.

My overall feeling now is to love everyone. It is wonderful to feel relaxed. I feel I want to go with the current of life rather than to the buck the stream.

I communicated with several people in the recreation room in the last hour. I felt very empathetic towards all there. They seemed very friendly and happy to talk to me. I feel momentary pangs of self-doubt and inferiority but I do not resist them and soon it passes. I feel that by continually loving and accepting others I will make wonderful progress toward liking them and myself more and more.

The experiences of LSD were very shocking, traumatic ones, seeming to be like Dante's Inferno. It seemed a hell without end. I was fighting and running trying to do this or that in a mad frenzy, feeling that each path or door would provide the answer. Finally stopped running to accept what was and accepted instead of everlasting rejection.

Sex and all sensuality seemed to be embodied in the condition of the snake – probably a cobra, which would eventually suffix itself on my genitals and I would die. Dying this way seemed to come as a relief. A termination of running and dodging, twisting and turning. Death was me returning to dust! Then another scene would start.

It seemed that all scenes were similar in that there was the confrontation of vultures, clawing birds and ghastly animals persistently perusing me until I lay down and surrendered myself to them.

Many times I was an old shriveled up man gradually decaying and eventually dying in the desert in the searing sun. Then I would be a chick, cracking its way out of its shell. I would look awfully scrawny, bony and sticky wet. I would be crying. This could be experiencing birth. I also felt I was in my Mother's womb choking from suffocation.

My penis felt very very cold most of the time and I felt that I must hang on to or it might freeze or fall off.

I saw all types of people, all ages. I felt I was each one of them for so many moments. Becoming them I felt great compassion for them and understanding. I had the feeling that each was wonderful and a part of life – the same as me. I felt nothing to fear from anyone because I became them and loved them.

It kept reappearing to me that the greatest and most necessary force is to love others and then yourself. This is all beauty and heaven on earth. It seemed so easy. Running downhill instead of up. Life was the easiest fun and love resulted. It was so and is so wonderful to love others, to hold no defenses against them but to just let them feel your warmth and that you love them and want them to love and be very happy.

I have previously felt unloved and unloving. This created depression. There seemed no purpose in life. Now each circumstance can be evaluated calmly and with love rather than tension, apprehension and fear. Fear is to run away. To hide your face from the world. Love is to be exposed and to accept this exposure and to love it. It is openness and love of life.

This has been an experience to show that man is everything but love is eternal. The motivating force that encourages life and happiness. With love life is heaven and the things in it.

I feel I want to tell everyone the good news. The secret to life is loving. Why don't they know this? I hope I never forget.

Looking at my Father's picture I could see I was him. My face transposed into his. I could tell he felt inferior the way I had and I could understand and love very much. Looking at myself as a young boy I looked quite sad it seemed. By staring at the picture I felt I could say, "don't feel sad little boy, Daddy loves you because you are also Daddy." Daddy was just too afraid to express his love, but under his fear was tortured love.

The vultures and clawing birds were probably my self-doubts. Always after me making me run ever faster and more and more of them appearing. By letting them devour me I finally realized that by dying this way it had become a relief. Perhaps an ecstasy. These self doubts have always been ugly repulsive things to me – making me seem more and more worthless – making life seem so difficult hence the ugly personification in these animals. The deaths were gratifying because I felt reunited with the earth, a part of the universe rather than an alien entity.

By eventually molding myself with all other people I felt again reunited in the world. By feeling a part of them I felt human and warm again.

The symbolism of the snake appears either to be my Mother's constant protection by wavering constantly over me or my Father's penis. My constantly trying to hang on to and protect my penis from the snake may have been my determination to hang on to my masculinity although constantly threatened by my Father's jealousy towards me, or my Mother's insistence on not letting it grow so I would not stop being a little boy. By finally succumbing to the snake it was also a great relief to have the fear terminated.

I remember now as a young boy my Mother was always fiddling with my penis and I kept pushing her hand away. Since I can now stop trying to hang onto my penis I can entrust my Wife with it and be a better lover.

Comments

HOW DID FREUD AND JUNG MISS THIS!!?!?!! Freud died in 1939 and Jung in 1961, mescaline was isolated from peyote in 1897. Jung did comment on psychedelics suggesting they brought up, "too much, too fast," but Jung had more visions before breakfast than most psychedelians do in a lifetime.

The dying narratives may represent unfolding of perinatal cycles that visualization allows expressing through stories. LSD seems to supply the cerebral content and outline of the visual patterns while mescaline provided the raw feeling and colour to produce the highest quality hallucinations. Although since the eyes are closed the visions are better described as a waking dream than as hallucinations.

It's clear too that the Freudian emphasis on family dynamics was practical and early sexual experiences and the fantasies surrounding them are an important part of the more superficial types of neurosis.

Chapter Seventeen

Liberation Reaction II: *Normal Suffering*

"I was in <u>Hell</u>3/4. This was the ultimate suffering. Everything I had suffered in the real world or any thing I could suffer in the future was as heaven compared with this paranoid hell…finally exhausted from my efforts, both verbal and physical, I gave up the struggle. As I gave up the fight, things seemed to become more pleasant." – S28D7

The last group would not have qualified for any diagnosis but were simply adventurous.

S99X2

"It was almost as though everything that has hurt me was happening all over again…. I never realized the amount of hate I carried for my Father, when I came out of the LSD all the hate I was carrying was let out. I can't explain why but the hate is all gone and I am so glad."

This subject was a twenty-four year-old Mother of two from Vancouver. The only exception to her normality was an abusive husband who had recently committed suicide, leaving her to raise two children. This is a rare subject where LSD was administered alone – perhaps less risk was acceptable given the absence of psychopathology.

Treatment Day

09:00 200 mcg LSD

09:25 pt. laid down on couch w/ blanket and eye shades

09:30 seeing forms "like those brass plates you can buy"

09:35 pt crying

10:45 "I'm back small as a baby and I can't breathe again"

11:50 "I have had no fear since it started"

12:45 "why is sex so important to me?"

13:30 "If we all are all the same why is it so important where I came from?"

Post Treatment

When they say you blow your mind it's true! It was so vivid yet so fictional, so real but unreal, so beautiful and yet so ugly. I never realized before the amount of resentment, hate or distorted childhood ideas I still carried around with me.

When it first started to affect me I started sobbing, but I had no tears and I just ached throughout my whole body. It was almost as though everything that has hurt me was happening all over again.

Then I left my body and it was as though I couldn't get back in until I accepted myself just the way I am, then I was sort of put back together. Then I started back in my life. I always felt unimportant to my mom and Dad because I was adopted, but it was never discussed. But I am in no position to judge.

I never realized the amount of hate I carried for my Father, when I came out of the LSD all the hate I was carrying was let out. I can't explain why but the hate is all gone and I am so glad.

The feeling of restlessness I've had for the past few months is also gone. Life all of a sudden seems so important to me.

Life is so good and man is so good, at least we are all born pure, if we try to apply only good to our lives and society then that should give us the satisfaction I'm sure we are all looking for. It is a struggle but if life weren't, what would be our purpose?

Comments

Although adopted and suffering from the suicide of her estranged husband this subject was extremely well adjusted and progressed through her issues and negative unconscious material easily. This is an example of the use of psychedelics outside medicine and in the realm of spiritual recreation and a new politics of ecstasy where recreation involves the re-creation of the self.

S45J1

"I contemplated the idea of Life playing a game of hide and seek with itself, and that it comes up in each of us so it can be known to itself in a particular way (for me, Life wanted to experience itself with a hearing handicap)"

This subject was a forty-eight year old divorcee and Mother of two grown children who worked as a secretary but also had a large inheritance. She is summarized as a "quietly composed person" and with a phrase rarely heard in psychology "entirely normal."

Ever since reading the literature of Zen and mysticism she has wanted to experience Satori or "cosmic consciousness." Both her parents were dead and she had divorced her ex-husband – an emotionally needy sailor who wanted to dominate her affection entirely. Her and her siblings were often ill as children and one of her brothers died from pneumonia.

"I guess it's clear by now I only want to find and become more what I am behind the blocks, and that I hope LSD will help adjust the errors in my self-image. I want the infinite variety of responding to the infinite variety of life. "

Treatment Day

08:45 700 mg mescaline, 200 mcg LSD

09:17 Pt. talked about her 21-year-old son fathering an illegitimate child. She seemed surprised he would "climb in bed with a girl" and said it in those words.

09:18 Pt. laid down, body covered with blanket, eyes with cloth. Pt. quite calm and looking forward to the experience.

09:57 Pt. reported seeing "roads and an abrupt chasm"

10:10 Pt. breathing heavily then crying

10:20 Pt. "maybe you didn't give me enough" pt. crying "I'm just a person that's all – whatever we are, we are caught in the flesh – repository of the senses. I think I want to be a phrasemaker I don't think I'm going to see the clear light."

10:40 pt. crying "there is life and you spoil it; I'm getting so cold – what are we seeking? Are we looking for ourselves in someone else? We need each other."

10:50 pt. crying in F's arms "we are so alone – we play these stupid games – human life is wasted on human life – what can we do with it? All we can do is just go through it." pt. sitting up (Yoga position) "What's the reason for us to be separate?" meaning all people; pt. crying

11:55 "need each other to reflect to each other – take that down" crying continuously

12:15 pt. quiet – breathing heavily, hearing aids removed

14:35 pt. "I'm lying here feeling so sexy – it was nice music, but to me it sounded sexy"

Post-Treatment

After miscellaneous, meaningless, to me, displays of color and surreal landscapes, and me wondering where the Clear Light was, I suddenly seemed to see the poor, small Self struggling forward over the wind-eroded rocks and barren plains, and I cried for the pitiable and noble self who tries so hard and is so alone. I cried for the separateness of each of us and wondered about Life and why we're born to go on this lonely journey. Then I could see Life for each of us coming up like a golden bubble in a pool, whatever the circumstances of birth, fresh and pure each time. I contemplated the idea of Life playing a game of hide and seek with itself, and that it comes up in each of us so it can be known to itself in a particular way (for me, Life wanted to experience itself with a hearing handicap) and we're born into a body because the body is the repository of the senses. This phrase seemed so significant that I asked Frank to write it down.

Then I wondered why, if we were meant to be separate, we needed each other, and the answer came that it was to reflect each other to each other so that Life could see its game of particularity. Like, for instance, without someone to hear it, there is no music. And when Life is over, the bubble drops back into the pool.

I felt much better, somehow, when these things seemed clearer to me. Then I got caught up in the music and was going on a hard, fast journey on high, unreal plateaus, a mad journey to no place. I was wishing I'd get out into space, but I couldn't make it happen.

Then and I don't know how it began I got feeling terribly sexy. Frank changed the music and left me alone and I got on the floor and moved to the music – I knew just what to do, although I'd never been able to move to that kind of music before. It seemed to go on and on and I got very tired and finally went and lay down.

When Frank came back he had me look in the mirror, I found myself incredibly sweet and incredibly sensuous. And I was terribly hungry.

The rest was mostly return. It seemed like such a hard journey and I was so tired.

I couldn't imagine why I'd wanted to go on this journey, which struck me as terribly funny. Why under the sun had I had such a big thing on LSD? But thinking about it, I realized that I'd had insight into myself – I wasn't intellectual and I wasn't mystical – not even a nature mystic (Nature had always seemed beautiful to me and she was still beautiful in the same way) but now I could stop seeking and let myself be what I was – a very warm, good, loving person. I had seen into my nature.

S45I8

"I felt I had experienced so much agony and loss that I had been re-born again and I danced around and jumped up and down and wanted my family to know all about it. I seemed to see my life fitting together as a jigsaw puzzle. I felt absolutely exhausted in every way."

This subject was a thirty-seven year old Wife and Mother of three small boys, experiencing significant "personality clash" with her family. She survived the blitz (WWII) in England and still had fears of loud noises.

She was a sickly child; her Father was not emotionally involved with her and left the family when she was 8. Her Mother was still alive and they had an excellent relationship. After her Father left S45I8's Mother married an American lawyer, who when she was 16 had tried to seduce her.

"I feel the whole effect of the war in England had a great deal to do with the anxiety I feel today. Seeing a German plane suddenly swoop out of the sky – machine gun down the road over the rooftops, as I went to school, will never be forgotten."

Treatment Day

10:05 800 mg mescaline, 200 mcg LSD

10:25 pt. removed glasses and slippers and laid down on chesterfield – eyes covered with sleep shade and body with blanket

10:50 pt. "if I could only get a clear picture of my childhood what my Father was really like."

11:00 "I can see the house I lived in when I was three. I want to see our other house."

11:05 "Oh dear, I'm sick of something. Sick of the music, hate this mask, I feel sick right here."; points to stomach

11:10 pt. bursts into heavy sobbing "I'll just die"

11:20 "you know I have a heart condition – and it has effected me, my legs – it's terrible I think I'm going to die – maybe you gave me too much"

11:35 pt. lying on stomach, left arm dangling

11:40 pt. falls to floor "I'm really going to die"; pt. moaning constantly "This is why I am like this?; I always thought it was a physical thing"

12:00 "Oh why have I taken this thing?"

12:10 pt. now sitting up on floor "It's perfectly all right isn't it? I'm so happy I went through; I'm so pleased." pt. pounding floor and laughing "I want my husband right now!; I'm so happy. Goody, goody goody! That was wonderful"

13:25 pt. clutching and pulling hair. pt. violently pokes head with right forefinger. "I'm going crazy"

14:15 "I'm scared of everything now"

15:40 pt. highly active and aggressive for over one hour 16:15 "I'm so happy" pt. joyously tosses mirror in air; "I feel wonderful -; after being in the depths, I'm flying over the moon."

17:30 pt. relates how she is now free from "mommy" and; "loved her more for it"

Post-Treatment

To begin with I did not like the mask on or the loud music. Then I began to feel terrific body sensations in my thighs, hips, legs, back – I felt like an old, old woman and crouched over on the chesterfield to the floor, I felt a terrible weight on my back. Then I got on the floor on all fours, and then lay on my stomach. I groaned aloud and worried what other people in the hospital would think. I think I called for a nurse or doctor as I thought I might die. Then said, "No, I don't need a doctor." I wanted someone to lean on. Once I was back on the couch lying down on my side and felt terrific pain and saw a machine grinding and twisting and felt a limb being cut off – I think my leg.

Someone made me lie on the couch again, and I guess I kept talking and Frank kept saying, "be quiet." I kept taking off the mask and couldn't understand why I was there. Then I got into the state where I thought I had entered a new mental life all jumbled up – rather mosaic like – the colours seemed bright and I had my mask off but I kept saying "I can't understand it" and someone said, "Don't try to understand it. It's part of the new you." And I said again "but I don't" and "I can't understand it." I felt so lost and lonely and terrified at what I had done to get into this state. I thought I heard someone say "this is the way you wanted it" and I was just horrified and had lost touch with my motives for L.S.D. and really felt this was a new jumbled life to which I had damned myself forever. It was still the room I was in but my personality couldn't control anything anymore. The colours on the chesterfield cover seemed to stand out considerably.

Then I realized people were telling me to stop acting like a child and that I was just trying to draw attention to myself. I kept saying, "Mommy wouldn't mind would she?" Then the floor carpet and coffee table with my purse on it began to go into a lifeless state that I could no longer control. I wanted to get up and go and all the time everything stood rigid and I could no longer be a part of my environment. I felt as though I was going mad and couldn't remember what I was taking L.S.D. for and I was frightened – terrified – and Frank tried to hold me up as I literally felt my mind and life ebb away and I knew I must now be crazy and said, "Won't I ever get them back –(lists her sons and husband), Mummy?" I thought Frank said, "this is what you wanted, you can get them back if you really want to." And I felt very guilty that I had never loved them enough and had always thought only of myself – this was now my punishment. I felt nothingness and alone and afraid I thought I could not get back my sanity. There was a veil between me and the other people in the room now and I could not see. I could hear breathing and noises and I thought everybody was just waiting to see me collapse and be shut up in a mental hospital for life! Then I thought I must be dead and the music played "Ave Maria" and I thought "How stupid because I have always asked for cheerful music to be played at my funeral." I felt I was dead and I was hovering over my home and could hear doors being shut and even the odd sniff!

I was now one with the ages and all those who had died before and this was how Christ must have felt. I felt I was in the darkness of space and over the mountains of the world and I knew I must now keep moving and if I was dead I must do something. I think I felt I was some sort of saint too.

Then at last the room would keep vaguely swimming back into focus and I saw a woman's face – I knew she was the nurse. Someone still said, "You can do it for yourself." Then I realized I was looking out of the window at the world again and gradually I knew how much the world held for me and how much I wanted every part of it and I felt overwhelming relief and joy that I had come home to my dear family and everything familiar and great joy and happiness that all I thought I had lost I had once more found. I felt I had experienced so much agony and loss that I had been re-born again and I danced around and jumped up and down and wanted my family to know all about it. I seemed to see my life fitting together as a jigsaw puzzle. I felt absolutely exhausted in every way.

I feel as though I was a miserable cranky old dog before but now I am a lop-sided pooch! I was very happy to see my husband and I know I made him happy too.

Because I was able to let myself free of my old self in this experience, I shall be able to love my family more as I am more satisfied with myself.

This verse has come to me:

> *The Joy of Love and how to seek it*
> *The Joy of Love and how to find it*
> *The Joy of Love and how to keep it*

Commentary

A classic, efficient rebirth of an emotionally well-adjusted person, however this subject's story contains one of the truly disturbing qualities of psychedelics – even after a powerful transmodulation and integration of a negative BPM, a few minutes later and fortunes have reversed again. Dr. Grof proposes that as the unconscious material is worked through and integrated it loses its affective charge but how disappointing to feel such infinite release and euphoria only to plunge back into the depths of suffering again. As long as the person is in a "holotropic state" powerful new unconscious dynamics can continue to emerge. Indeed in holotropic breathwork Grof advises participants to "breathe until something surprises you."

S19R5

"At one time I saw a bright white light stretching its rays to me. I started rising on one of these rays towards the light and received the thought that this was the big event and to go all the way to the light. Then becoming the light I saw that I was God and that I was the center of the Universe."

This subject was a 27 year-old immigrant labourer from rural Saskatchewan. He came from a very large family and did not complete high school.

Treatment Day

09:15 300 mcg. LSD – 150 mg mescaline

09:35 "I feel a heaviness in my legs – my throat feeling is of opening – it feels good"

09:40 "there are tensions in my face"; touches both cheeks 10:10 solar plexus agitation

10:17 pt. expressing pleasurable response

10:50 great depths of emotion; pt. goes through actions of singing mightily

11:15 sighs from the depths; many gestures – mouth opening wide

11:30 intermittent dry laughter – fear discharge

11:40 making various gestures – recognition acceptance rejection – one or more fingers placed in mouth occasionally, sometimes thumb, regression to babyhood

11:50 pt. appears highly amused

12:10 sits up swinging arms in time to music, laughing intermittently semi-hysterical

1:15 – posture of complete surrender, arms folded across breast, then in prayer

2:20 – "That experience was worth the full price."

Post-Treatment

I experienced no unpleasantness in taking the drug and didn't experience fear.

I was aware of various body areas that I had evidently targeted through repressed or unexpressed emotion. Physical somatic pains turned on that I recognized and discharged the tension. Particularly the solar plexus, throat and jaw. One experience had to do with when my face was frozen.

I had visual experiences of a time, which I considered the seventeenth century, seeing and hearing Russian people singing outdoors in a snowstorm. At another point I was experiencing something and I wondered what it was when I received the thought that I had just been born and the nurse was trying to start me breathing.

At one time I saw a bright white light stretching its rays to me. I started rising on one of these rays towards the light and received the thought that this was the big event and to go all the way to the light. Then becoming the light I saw that I was God and that I was the center of the Universe. From every direction the universe was flowing to me but there was no flow away from me. Here was my problem in life everything was flowing to me but I would shut it off as soon as it reached me. There was no outflow from me that I recognized must be expressed.

It seemed to me that I was receiving communication from the doctor. In several instances I heard his voice distinctly.

In visualizing myself as I desired to be I was enabled to see what was necessary to discard and the needed things to acquire. I feel extremely pleased with my enlightenment and re-evaluation through this experience.

Comments

This was an apparently well-adjusted young man. Age appears to be a critical factor in determining whether someone spends their day defending against or actually experiencing their "stuff" or "engrams" / repressed material. He describes tensions in his solar-plexus, throat and jaw, which are the locations of the "chakras" or "wheels of energy" in Yoga. His insight into the physiological processes occurring in his body was profound and once again the subject and sitter go into an apparent "mind-meld."

S32H0

"I have gone through very stormy and rough seas but I have made it and now reached port – I feel very, very battered but now after a rest I will be refitted to enter into beautiful clear waters."

Another apparently well-adjusted and healthy woman in her early fifties whose problems, once again stem from "men behaving badly," will be considered next. Her first Husband was an unemployable, angry and unfaithful brute who put her in the hospital for a week although she writes that she "doesn't know how much I had to do with it." She had two sons and had just separated from her second Husband.

Treatment Day

09:10 stroboscope – with your eyes shut a huge screen will open in your mind

09:17 300 mcg LSD – 150 mg mescaline

09:30 demonstration of kaleidoscope

09:37 feels nauseated, lying down, slight twitching of head perspiring freely

09:40 painful experience "no" crying, "I feel awfully ill. I don't like it. Please." spasmodic twitching – convulsive breathing

10:00 "it's not right … it's not … oh, no, no, don't do that"

10:06 "It tears you inside out … please … I must have rest. I'm tired.

10:10 I don't think I can stand anymore!

10:30 It has to stop sometime! My head always hurts on the right side from the blows."

11:05 slightly more relaxed though active movements

11:10 "I don't think I can stand another storm. "Yes you can. For those boys of yours you can stand anything."

11:12 period of intense tension – crying

11:55 "nothing matters" – crying, adjusting position "I'm so happy – beautiful people." Crying with hands over eyes 12:00 shown <u>rose</u> – gazing at it steadily

14:15 "Oh I feel an awful lot better. There wasn't anything I didn't get."

Post-Treatment

This could only be an attempt to haltingly describe an experience I don't feel there are words for. Some yes – but they would be rare and precious ones. The thoughts that come to me are that science enabled me to reach for, see and feel so very strongly and clearly the ultimate goal in religion that all of us search and long for. I don't know if I have put this properly, but to me there was a sense of blending with absolutely no question of the final victory. It was not shown but <u>said</u> so clearly and decisively, "there is only one way – God's way, lovingly and gentle." Not gently – but gentle. The beauty and depth of reaching for that plateau is so precious that even if I could use words, I wouldn't. I must say this – that I still feel – was it right for me to have been given so much, this way?

The whole experience was tense and many, many parts of it very painful and sad and hurting, so much so that you literally feel and express – sick in the stomach, but naturally it would have to be that way. When I came back into my room the first words that seemed to come into my mind were – "I have gone through very stormy and rough seas but I have made it and now reached port – I feel very, very battered but now after a rest I will be refitted to enter into beautiful clear waters."

One of the very clear and pronounced images, closer to the end was of a small gold-filigreed bucket heaped with softly creamy pearls. When reliving it over this morning, it was thrilling to recall the beautifully costumed men and some women – I recall pages bearing things on horses. Most of the colors I saw were very jangling and harsh, reds – they were very painful. The blending of, and with the music, was almost too perfect to describe, I was utterly transported. Only once or twice did the music intrude and hurt.

Not once, but many times was I borne along, as though on wings, with hands held out and such ecstatic eagerness toward that wonderful and dazzling plateau, through massive spiraling, softly lighted yet gleaming halls.

Even when I reached the depths, I knew, and the relief was great for I was able to say – so this is what it was.

Comments

This subject abreacted a tremendous amount of material and activated the positive dynamics as much as anyone. The constitution in Canada protects drugs that have medical use as determined by the courts, further, the principle of religious freedom generally clearly protects the breath-taking spiritual breakthroughs experienced regularly at Hollywood Hospital. This is where they were in 1957 when this clinic opened, now 55 years later imagine where we could be today?

S32X1

"The greatest thing about this experience is that I have no more fear. Something happened within that I cannot explain."

This subject was an Evangelical Christian from Saskatchewan who came to Hollywood Hospital to "have a more thorough understanding and to try and withstand constant obstacles in my life."

Treatment Day

09:26 300 mcg LSD – 200 mg mescaline

09:50 "I'm cold all over – I'm afraid"

10:10 pt. told to maintain silence after several complaints

12:45 "it's been marvelous"

1:15 – "I'm a bit nauseated"

1:45 – "It's been a wonderful experience, I've made my peace with Jesus."

2:05 – "The greatest thing about this experience is that I have no more fear. Something happened within that I cannot explain."

Subject's Report

I was given the LSD and it put me in a state of opening up my whole being and bringing out all the confusion, sorrows – pent-up tenseness and inner fears that have been dominating me for such a long, long time.

I feel that at that time I became in closer touch with God than ever before, although always having believed; I came face to face with all these mental difficulties that we think we can't withstand.

Today after having this marvelous experience I have no fear- no tenseness – but a loving feeling that was there and is now uppermost in my mind, that shall always be brought forth in my daily mode of living Praise God, He has lifted me up unto higher ground. Today I feel so happy.

S30E3

"Gradually and equally painfully I later began to feel as though I was being born or I was giving birth – this was very real and seemed to go on a long, long time."

This 40 year-old subject was a Scottish theater producer living in Vancouver and just finishing a divorce after eight years of marriage. A 7 year-old daughter lives with his ex-Wife. He was raised surrounded by women – his Mother, Sister and Aunts showered him with attention. The doctors expect sexual issues.

Treatment Day

09:50 700 mg mescaline – 350 mcg LSD

11:20 "fingers going numb"

Holst's *The Planets*

11:55 "remembering things – unpleasant – connected with my parents"

12:00 "My God he was teaching me to compete. Is the sun out? I can feel it." (drapes tightly closed)

13:05 "It's so simple. My Mother wanted a girl. I had a babysitter, an older girl, she put my hand under her clothes. She wasn't bad, she just liked me."

13:10 Pt. started singing suddenly; "Christ I've been afraid of being a fairy! My Mother had made me look pretty. Why should I resent her for that – perfectly natural."

13:15 pt. putting face down on pillow; "I've always had a fear of suffocation – why?" suddenly sitting up "That's it! I was afraid of my Mother suffocating me with affection."

13:20 "When I was little my Father took me to see my Grandfather. He was in an insane asylum. That always bothered me."; Pt. talked steadily for a half-hour coming-up with ego-shaking revelations every five minutes pt. felt guilty because he and a close boy friend learned about their bodies from one another; "Why should I feel guilty? It was just an awakening. An awakening and learning."

13:45 pt. continually sitting up suddenly and exclaiming "that's it!" – and throwing eye-cloth onto the couch with force. Immediately lying down and covering his eyes by himself.

13:55 "Why do I feel nauseous?"

14:15 Why do I have a heavy feeling around my heart?

14:20 "I want to sleep. I'm tired." Pt. pulse is high

14:25 "I feel like crying."

14:30 pt. quite excited and active for past two hours – now lying down quietly.

14:35 "I'm close to something Frank."

14:45 "I'm trying to be born again? Why am I trying to fight it?"

15:00 "Is what I'm feeling real?"

15:45 pt. spent last 45 min. pacing room – complained of strange feeling in his testicles.

18:10 pt. looking at picture of Christ. "Has a likeness to me." Pt. looking in mirror finds he looks favorably.

20:30 pt.'s girlfriend allowed visiting pt. for 20 minutes

21:25 pt. returned to D1. Chicken dinner provided.

Post-Treatment

The very first feeling I experienced shortly after taking the chemical was one of extreme tenderness that sent tears running silently down my cheeks. I heaved several sighs and shortly afterwards lay down on the chesterfield wrapped in a blanket. Next I noticed objects in the room began to move and blur. The very next emotion was a desire to seek truth and understanding – mainly understanding, and this emotion involved understanding of my parents over such points as – why was my Father insistent on taking me to various musical festivals each week to sing? The answer to this came easily and clearly and made me feel an intense feeling of love for him – he was teaching me to compete. Next came my Mother's insistence on dressing me prettily and keeping my hair long – she wanted a little girl and when my sister was born shortly after when I was six years old – I was dressed like a normal little boy. Concerning her over- protection of me, this was simply an exaggeration of her keen love and affection for me – a natural instinct for any Mother.

An important revelation that next made itself clear to me was the thought that my Mother had been unfaithful to my Father, when I was a child. I couldn't decide whether I was looking for the truth, when equally suddenly and with clarity I realized it didn't matter – I loved her.

I felt I was making tremendous progress and a great load had been removed by me. I recalled a childhood playmate – a boy my own age with whom I had indulged in the sexual game of rubbing ourselves against each other, and achieving a sexual satisfaction. In my subconscious I was convinced that this had been a homosexual act, but it clearly became understandable that since we were friends and healthy normal inquisitive children it was only natural that we experimented – and felt this new and deep emotion together.

It was shortly after this particular experience that I became agitated. I felt afraid and I did not understand why or of what – I insisted on talking to stall the impending disastrous awakening that must come before total realization bursts inside my whole being. I now know that this is my main adversary – the fear of a homosexual tendency. Oh how I fought and struggled – my breath came in short gasps and felt as though I was in the throes of death. I was horrified to see that Frank was a homosexual with designs on me. I began to protest and walk around still not willing to submit to the "showdown." My knees would buckle and suddenly I noticed blood on my hands – I continued to walk and suddenly realized in complete and utter despair I was emulating a feminine gait complete with hands on hips moving in time with the music. It was like a death dance and suddenly this is precisely what happened. Hearing the voice of God I collapsed in anguish and died. Immediately I tasted bile and staggered to my feet, reached the chesterfield and lay down. Gradually and equally painfully I later began to feel as though I was being born or I was giving birth – this was very real and seemed to go on a long, long time. Slowly and gradually this sensation flowed into a much more pleasurable and erotic sensation, which enveloped my whole being, and I felt on the verge of the most magnificent and perfect orgasm, which would have satisfied every creative fiber in my self.

Later my masculinity swept through me in an intense wave, which filled me with such joy, that I felt myself grin and flex my muscles with pure and selfish love and pride.

I felt greatly relieved but there were doubts that remained – not such that shouted at me, but rather sneaked at me, and these doubts manifested themselves when Dr. MacLean talked to me and I saw the devil's face in his face, but just briefly, then it changed to an expression of love and trust. It is then that I looked into the face of Jesus Christ and saw him look at me, opening his eyes then he too changed his face or rather I did.

I looked into a mirror and gazed deep into my eyes stripping every bit of flesh and then transforming my image again and again until I was back with me. I know who I am, I know what I am and I have a tremendous feeling of humility and a new found quiet strength.

Words will never fully do complete justice to the description of my experience – but I don't need words to tell me – I felt it.

Comments

His Mother had his hair long and dressed him "pretty" until his sister was born at six and he had a homosexual experience in his early teens and the obvious conclusion is this subject was homosexual and living in more repressive times, simply denied it.

Stan Grof links male homosexuality to unresolved material in BPM III and with identifying with the birthing Mother in terms of having a foreign object inside the body and the mixture of extreme pleasure and pain. By this logic integration of the perinatal unconscious might "cure" homosexuality but no such claim is ever made. The problem is one of "chicken and egg" as well because unconscious dynamics or activated governing systems may lead the psyche into homosexuality and the most frequent trigger for depression in one study was "failure to act, feel or think consistently with one's own gender." Another complication is the issue of the "ego death triumvirate" – of homosexuality, physical death and permanent insanity, even the purely heterosexual may need to accept being gay in order to complete the process.

S28D7

"It somehow makes me feel stronger to know that I suffered what I suffered and could not be destroyed. One thing that has puzzled me and is one of the reasons why I have not written before this – is how such a monstrously hideous experience could lead to such positive results."

This subject was in his mid-twenties and planning on attending graduate school. It would appear he was suffering from what might be called a minor adjustment disorder regarding his education and relationships and problems with stuttering.

08:50		325 mcg LSD – 325 mg mescaline
09:05	ther.	"Go with it – let the music take you with it"
	pt.	"I feel a slight queasy feeling" – points to throat – he has a moderate degree of congestion
09:08	ther.	place cloth over pt. eyes
09:22	pt.	"I just had an insight now – incredible – as if the whole world were an ether cone – incredible!"
09:37	ther.	"Why does the world seem like an ether cone?" Refer it to the tonsillectomy (at age 2 1/2) "Go back under it and see it for what it was."
09:40	pt.	"Is that all coming from myself?"; reliving the ether cone from tonsillectomy
09:45	ther.	"Let it come. Let it try and destroy you and you'll find out it can't"
09:50		pt. feels nauseous, music turned up louder
	ther.	"Let the ether cone press on you completely and perhaps you can come through it – not from under it."
10:05	pt.	"I'm trying to grasp the concept of what you're trying to do."
	ther.	"Work over this hostility to parents."
	pt.	"Where did they come into it?"
	ther.	"They left you to the horror of fear—but you are the one who reacted to it – you put it there."
10:15	ther.	"Go back under the ether cone."
	pt.	"No I want some human support."
	ther.	"Go back under it and die under it – are you afraid?"
	pt.	"Why do I have the feeling that I'm crazy?"
10:50	ther.	"You're afraid to put the cloth over your eyes?"
	pt.	"Yes, I'm afraid – but why? That's right. I'm not afraid anymore." "Cone and stutter, yeah," repeats it.
	ther	"Don't be afraid."
	pt.	"I'm afraid of you." (tries to leave room)
11:30-12:30		the next hour was replete with constant questioning by pt. – ending in overt hostility to both therapists. We finally had pt. sit down although there was a considerable struggling against us physically
12:35	pt.	"You miserable bastards – figments of imagination. Who is holding me back?"

	ther.	"Only ourselves."
12:56	pt.	"Macdonald you miserable sniping bastard, Macdonald you enema bag... Cassius M. Clay, Archie Moore, James Meredith – you son of a miserable bitch. You're the devil."
	ther.	"No more than you are."
1:30		there has been no evidence of stuttering in the past hour or more.
4:00		To room willingly. Has been silent for over an hour. Appears to be completely relaxed.

Post-Treatment

I started to feel the effects of the drug quickly. As I lay down I felt nauseous. Soon I had the feeling that I was under an ether cone. It was suffocating me and the nausea swelled and felt like a choking mass anchored in my throat. I knew that this was the experience I must have gone through as a child when I had my tonsils out at 2 1/2 years of age. I struggled with the ether but I could not let it completely devour me. I felt the whole world was an ether cone.

Then my frame of reference with the world began to recede. The room and the two therapists looked like shimmering figures of bright and frightening colors. I had the feeling I was in the world of a Salvador Dali painting.

The majority of the experience, as I remember it, was a desperate struggle to create a frame of reference in this weird and terrifying world. I pleaded with the therapists for aid, but after awhile they seemed like taunting figures, part of the conspiracy that I thought had put me into this situation.

I recalled existing in the real world and I began to try to re-establish connection with it. I put forth concepts like love, women and shouted the names of friends and other people whom I had known in my other life. All to no avail. I was in Hell 3/4. This was the ultimate suffering. Everything I had suffered in the real world or any thing I could suffer in the future was as heaven compared with this paranoid hell.

Finally exhausted from my efforts, both verbal and physical, I gave up the struggle. As I gave up the fight, things seemed to become more pleasant. The therapists now seemed like friendly figures, humorous and very solicitous of the poor subject. Now the room seemed clothed in a magnificence of color and detail. The air seemed infinitely fresh and cooling and I smelled wonderful food. Yes, I saw a platter of beautiful sandwiches on the table. I heard Godly music on incomparable speakers. The air around me seemed to reverberate with thousands of speakers. I shall never forget this quality of this heavenly music.

I remember being moved back into my room. Then I started to be aware of pleasant dreams. I thought I was sleeping and that when I awoke I would have command of the material world. I contemplated all the experiences of a sensual character that would be mine. I had a swelling feeling of pleasant anticipation and bliss. It was then that I regained complete consciousness with a start.

Even though I suffered through hell I am glad I went through the experience and would go through it again. I would like to explore other areas that perhaps my great fear and hostility blocked off this time. It somehow makes me feel stronger to know that I suffered what I suffered and could not be destroyed. I feel very calm now and I have experienced no fear of any kind since the session.

Follow-Up (six months later)

First of all let me say that I think the psychedelic treatment was tremendously beneficial to me. I might even go so far as saying that it was the turning point in my life and as such the key event in my short existence. The experience started a process of development in me that is still continuing. When I came to you I was a hopelessly static, enormously fearful person who was holding on to reality by my fingernails. I felt that my life as a functioning member of society would shortly be over.

Although I have not by a long shot overcome my feelings of alienation and fear, I progress every day by the experience of life itself rather than hopeless repetition of neurotic patterns.

One thing that has puzzled me and is one of the reasons why I have not written before this – is how such a monstrously hideous experience could lead to such positive results. This question has plagued me. This is why I always hesitated to write you that I had been helped.

Comments

Two primary goals of psychedelic therapy are the activation of the positive systems and the working through of the negative ones – this subject succeeded beautifully at both. His experience began with regression to an operation that led to the perinatal domain, becoming extremely aggressive and finally breaking through. In an apparent synchronicity the numbers ¾ were written into the text while the subject described being in the third perinatal matrix

Part III

Towards An Integral
Psychedelic Theory

Chapter Eighteen

The Eight-Brained Biped Migrates to the Stars

"A high percentage (perhaps half) of alienated humans are in trouble with their hives because their brains are operating in "neuro-realities" that will not be conventionally acceptable until the 21st century."
    –Timothy Leary, *Changing My Mind Among Others*

So far we've explored the notion of panspermia, the simple idea that DNA based bacteria and psilocybin mushroom spores, possibly from a common intelligence, landed here about 4 billion years ago. After several billion years of random mutation and natural selection the right neurological hardware emerged between 100,000 and 7,000 years ago when *homo sapiens* first consumed psilocybin, which would eventually trigger an international revolution in altered states of consciousness. From the drug experience many non-drug methods of trance induction were developed because, according to the theory of morphic fields, once a member of a species experiences a state of consciousness all members can access the new information.

A history of psychedelics was followed by a survey of the different constitutional types of people and the changes in brain activity that occur in each under increasing stress to the point of total collapse and how this knowledge was applied to treat battle trauma during WWII. A look at how developmental trauma (childhood) effects later life preceded the importance almost all therapists place on "metabolizing the trauma."

Psychiatrist Stan Grof's career with non-ordinary states of consciousness to work through the traumas of life after birth, during birth and even before conception was juxtaposed with social psychologist and "stand-up philosopher" Timothy Leary's life and work ending with his theory of *the serial imprinting of the eight- circuit brain.*

In this model each human's brain goes through four *critical windows* where *imprints* are taken that will determine the functioning and limitations on further learning of the nervous system. These imprints compose a "reality tunnel" through which each of us is condemned to experience the world. By about sixteen your mind has been made up for you and unless you activate the proposed higher four circuits, Leary's definition of adult – "stopped growing" – applies to you.

Each of the eight circuits is further divided into three phases – reception, integration and transmission, modeled after the neuron which receives chemical messages, processes the information and then communicates to the other neurons either with excitation (firing) or inhibition (not firing). Timothy Leary described energy being received by structure as producing consciousness and when a structure receives, integrates and *transmits* energy intelligence must also be present. Therefore each of the eight circuits receives, processes and transmits information according to the imprints.

In my opinion Leary's eight-circuit model integrates well with modern psychopharmacology and psychiatry. Just as a student completes four years of high school before four years of college, the chemical circuits recursively recapitulate their emergence through human history, evolving interdependently all the time. Ancient shamans were probably, in many ways, more skillful at operating the higher circuits than anyone is today. After all, the brain hasn't structurally evolved that much in the last 250,000 years. The next section will extrapolate further, based on new research.

Circuit I
"We are safe"
"I'm going to live forever or die trying"

The first circuit in Leary's model is the bio-survival circuit, programmed during the first six months of life; it began when life on earth began about 4 billion years ago, when, 10 billion years after the big bang, the next transformation began. Circuit I is composed of the basic one-dimensional simplicity of approach-avoid – the floating amoeba's unicellular consciousness. If a newborn infant does not receive enough love and contact during their first six months, this circuit takes a negative imprint and the child becomes isolated and withdrawn. Thus a schizophrenic or autistic person who's first circuit has been imprinted this way is given LSD and loved and held, re-imprinting/programming their first circuit with a positive imprint. A type of therapy called anaclictic therapy was utilized in Britain where clients who suffered vital neglect took LSD, then were regressed to infancy, wrapped in blankets and held for hours. The first circuit's "drugs of choice" are opiates and heavy doses of alcohol.

Adrenalin and/or glutamate may be the primary first circuit activators and each circuit's chemistry seems to operate in dialectic with an opposite compound – in the first circuit that seems to be the endorphin system.

One of the great contributors to the eight-circuit model was Robert Anton Wilson particularly his groundbreaking book *Prometheus Rising*, in which he described some circuits as taking a heavier imprint than others, which determines the dominant circuit and personality structure for life unless the higher circuits are activated. Someone who takes a heavy first circuit imprint is likely viscerotronic (social – comfort oriented), orally fixated, often round and if unhealthy – emotionally and materially dependent on others. The circuit a drug activates will determine the nature of the addiction that emerges and it is this first circuit that gives us our understanding of the word.

Addiction as we understand it today didn't emerge until a hundred years after the introduction to the west of the *smoking/vaporizing* of opium. The key elements of this new conception of drug addiction are withdrawal and tolerance whereas *psychological* addiction is closer to the original meaning of the word. Smoking breaks the compound down before introducing it to the brain and consequently works faster and stronger than even injecting or snorting – smoking opium for a person who has taken a heavy first circuit imprint is likely particularly dangerous.

Leary described heroin, which he tried in the early seventies, as "holding down the off button on your nervous system." It is likely only the most desperate among us that will choose the "vegetable serenity," as Bill Burroughs described it, of the first circuit.

Circuit II

"I'm free, you're free, we're all free – we can either join forces or go our separate ways"

About 500 million years ago the *mammalian-political* or *emotion-loco-motion* second circuit emerged when "the first vertebrates began to rise up against the pull of gravity."

The second circuit imprint is taken from six months to three years of life when issues of domination and submission, terror or predation forge the relationship with others and self. Up-down and over-under adds a second dimension to the binary approach-avoid dichotomy. The first circuit remains active even as the second circuit emerges, resulting in more complex two-dimensional brain activity. The second circuit's drug of choice is alcohol, but in pre-stuporous ego-lifting doses. Perhaps noradrenalin activates this circuit while gamma amino butyric Acid (GABA) inhibits it – GHB, the benzodiazepines like valium and alcohol all increase the activity of this neurotransmitter.

The second circuit began with the emergence of social (pack) animals and although it is primarily concerned with one's relationship to the other it is through these relationships that the second circuit produces a sense of self (ghost in the shell or ego) – a new level of sentient meta-consciousness. Someone who takes a heavy imprint on this circuit will likely be physically strong and aggressive. The typical male hunter-warrior fulfills the second circuit stereotype. My next-door neighbour's seven-year-old boy walks around on tiptoes to make himself bigger. The second circuit is concerned with territory and power. Leary said, "Politics should be discussed on all fours."

I studied under a meditation/spirituality teacher named Dyhan Vimal who developed an active meditation exercise where we tried to enhance our sense of self, first by looking at all of the objects around us and contemplating how that was *not* self, and then by considering the body, mind and feelings and how none of these were self either. "You *are* in the center of it," he would remind us. In the Hindu teaching eventually exploration of this elusive self will yield it's true identity – God.

Varieties of Psychedelic Experience by Jean Houston and Robert Masters is another classic in the field; in it they describe 5% of people as reaching the pinnacle of this kind of therapy – what they call the *integral level* of the unconscious. This would correspond to the transition from the third perinatal matrix to the fourth in Grof's system, which Grof may have achieved more often but no statistics are available. 5% working with pure pharmaceuticals and the best and brightest guides, sitters and doctors were able to get to the level I believe I did one wintery Ottawa night in 1995 – the death/rebirth experience in the introduction. A year earlier I had a panic reaction triggered by prozac, marijuana and a visit to an ex-girlfriend – but this time, triggered instead by mushrooms, the panic was even worse – but somehow it resolved in a way I could never even have imagined. How is this possible?

Perhaps the mushrooms pushed my psyche past the point of panic. Panic seemed preferable but wasn't an option – I was in a new world, where feelings of intense fear were building to increasingly unbearable proportions.

I was also taking desipramine.

In *Listening to Prozac* Peter Kramer notes this drug is "perhaps fifteen hundred more times as effective on noradrenalin as serotonin." In other words, when the mushrooms had dilated my brain to the holos of consciousness my sense of self was chemically augmented preventing my dissociation and allowing for perinatal integration and even a hint of transcendence. If the "ghost in the shell," or ego, has abandoned his post, retreating into the abyss to wait out the storm (dissociated), such results are impossible. This is reminiscent of the shaman calling the soul back to the body. Perhaps when noradrenalin levels are high the soul-self sits in the seat of the brain.

The bioamine hypothesis of depression states that the disease is caused by an under-activity of one or more of the bioamines – serotonin, noradrenalin and dopamine. Yet in over half of those hospitalized for depression noradrenalin levels are *higher* than average. As though the brain's "self" has been "called to arms" and is trying to resolve a crisis. There is a category of disease known as *dissociative disorders* such as Dissociative Identity Disorder (multiple personalities) and Fugue States all of which relate to problems surrounding sense of self and dissociation.

Stated differently, as what I like to call *the noradrenalin hypothesis of self-consciousness,* quantitative sense of self is correlated with noradrenalin levels in the hypothalamic – pituitary – adrenal axis (HPA axis) in the brain. In an attempt to test this hypothesis in 2008 I took desipramine again to see if I felt more "selfy" or as Eckhart Tolle has described it, more "fierce acceptance and intense presence." Unfortunately, the side effects were too awful to continue more than four days.

If there proves to be any merit to this hypothesis the effects of psychedelic drugs could be improved by treatments enhancing the functioning of noradrenaline or the second circuit.

Once again it is only when people are experiencing severe distress that they will choose to live down in the reality tunnels produced by activation of the first and lowest two circuits.

Circuit III
"We are right"
"I am smart enough to get smarter"

Roughly two million years ago the *mental-symbolic* circuit emerged when primates began using tools. It is imprinted beginning when a child first learns to speak until about age five and adds the dimension of left-right because at this time the left brain usually becomes unilaterally dominant. Circuit three's drugs of choice are any stimulant like cocaine or caffeine. Also the third circuit's development was likely related to the high-protein diet that emerged with hunting – prior to 2 million years ago our ancestors were foragers and scavengers, as far as we know.

Someone who takes a heavy imprint on this circuit will be hyper-rational and dismissive of intuition and subjectivity. Two such super-smart cocaine enthusiasts were the fictional Sherlock Holmes and the very real Sigmund Freud. All of these stimulant drugs no doubt helped with the alpha taxonomy whereby all living plants, minerals and animals were indexed from the 1500s on.

The third circuit may be mediated by dopamine – which is positively correlated (as one goes up the other goes up) with attention or concentration.

Schizophrenia and schizoid personality disorders are sometimes referred to as *thought disorders* and treatment involves drugs called *neuroleptics,* which reduce dopamine activity (dopamine antagonists). Conversely, attention deficit and hyperactivity are treated with dopamine agonists that increase dopamine activity. Many find it counterintuitive to give the hyperactive stimulants, but some researchers believe it is impulse control and planning that are being stimulated.

Conversely, schizophrenia is treated with dopamine antagonists that decrease dopamine activity. Physician and author Dr. Andrew Weil writes in his landmark book, *The Natural Mind,* dopamine antagonist antipsychotic drugs "make it harder to think."

The treatment of schizophrenia with dopamine-reducing drugs does not mean the disorder is *caused* by dopamine over-activity. It may be that the over activity is a reaction to a fundamental instability of space-time-self that seems to accompany this disease. If we view the brain as an instrument capable of receiving, integrating and transmitting consciousness/ intelligence, what Leary called contelligence, rather than as the *source* of contelligence, schizophrenia can be viewed differently. Whereas the dissociative disorders represent the retreat of the self from consciousness perhaps schizophrenia represents a kind of incontinence of consciousness that cannot keep the holos out long enough to sustain space-time-self.

Dopamine is also associated with reward and drugs that increase its action are known to be particularly addictive such as crystal methamphetamine and crack cocaine (although liquid alcohol and fibrous tobacco remain the most destructive substances for society). This reward property of the third circuit may have been necessary to sustain the mental effort required for its development.

It is towards the end of this circuit's developmental stage that humanity as we understand ourselves was born 30 – 100,000 years ago.

Circuit IV
"We are good"
"I will experience financial security and luxury"
"Love and do what thou wilt."

To synthesize Leary's ideas with McKenna the fourth circuit may have emerged as recently as 10,000 years ago when the orgiastic Goddess mushroom society was defeated by the further evolution of agriculture, city-states, moralistic religion and the discrete "skin-encapsulated ego" – whereby men could now own land and women. The move from Circuit III to IV was the move from hunter-gatherers to farmers. Your sexual style, your career, your family and your tribe are all critical. Those with a heavy imprint on this circuit will likely identify strongly with these elements of their lives. The fourth circuit takes its imprint at puberty and is pretty much programmed by sixteen and Dr. Leary even claimed he could tell when someone lost their virginity by what kind of music she listened to and hence when this circuit was imprinted.

Leary described "adolescent hormones" as the chemical activator of this circuit but MDMA (particularly as it relates to the "tribal ecstasy" of rave culture) and other serotonin drugs like prozac are also candidates. He also cited "just say no" as a fourth circuit stimulant indicating this moral social circuit or superego applies the brakes to the will or id (circuit I), ego (circuit II) and mind (circuit III) so that we can have some measure of civilization. Leary viewed World War II as the human evolutionary midpoint crescendo, where the tribal frenzies of the fourth circuit reached their culmination and a more evolved human began metamorphosing into being.

Aldous Huxley described the mind as being like a reducing valve – filtering the trillions of bits of data the brain processes each second into a usable quantity of information. But which data will the mind allow through to reach the conscious ego? This depends on the reality tunnels carved out of the nervous system's imprints. Leary in 1964 spoke at Cooper Union in New York City and described the loss of all the brain's activity outside the mind as the "greatest swindle in history." He offered as a motive for the crime DNA's need to keep the species going – cosmic consciousness must be postponed until basic survival needs are met.

What this means is that without the higher circuits being activated your four-circuit reality tunnel is imprinted permanently and only instrumental (reward and punishment), associative (classical) conditioning or learning (3rd circuit mapping) can modify the brain's networks. If during those critical windows a person experienced severe trauma this prognosis is devastating.

At the end of one of Leary's last books called *Chaos and Cyberculture* he showed a graph with time on the *x* or horizontal axis and "realities per minute" on the *y* or vertical axis. The point being that, as evolution unfolds, people process more and more realities than ever as more and more of the brain's better half lights up.

The first drug that ever taught me the multiple realities lesson was the fourth circuit libation prozac. My first bout of depression was at eleven and by eighteen it had infiltrated my being and become a permanent leaden weight filling my cells. The winter of '93 I drummed up the courage to call and make a doctor's appointment and our family physician prescribed the drug that has proven the only significant "revolution" in psychiatry since LSD, valium, thorazine and the antidepressant imipramine emerged in the 1950s.

Equally as important, I bought *Listening To Prozac* by Dr. Peter D. Kramer and realized that I was part of a worldwide experiment in intelligent brain change. My mind was not only transformed by the direct effect of the drug itself, but also by the *fact* that such changes were even possible. It wasn't merely my illness cured or symptoms managed, nor was it just a change in my sense of identity – it was *reality* as external as the sun in the sky that seemed new and different.

I was nineteen. The boomers *took* drugs while the subsequent generations have been *drugged*, given stimulants to pay attention and *selective serotonin reuptake inhibitors* (SSRIs) like prozac to feel better, and anti-psychotics and sedatives of an ever-increasing variety. *Trainspotting* author Irvine Welsh calls us the chemical generation, inundated with new drugs every day. This makes the war on drugs and the Partnership for a Drug Free America such anachronisms because *only* drugs can be experimentally tested – double-blinded with active placebos and thus scientifically evaluated and marketed through science-based medicine. Ironically among the three top funders of the Partnership for a Drug Free America are the pharmaceutical, tobacco and alcohol lobbies. But whatever the moral failings and hypocrisy of the pharmaceutical industry every once in a while they totally redeem themselves – MDMA, LSD, ketamine, Viagra, prozac.

On prozac I was transformed, confident, creative, sexually assertive, optimistic and happy. After two weeks on the drug I remember being at a party on New Year's Eve where I had retired early, anticipating a night of empty misery when suddenly the notion of sitting in a room by myself on New Year's Eve seemed utterly preposterous. I joined my friends and a new life.

After six months my doctor took me off the drug and within days I was right back where I started. Coupled with whatever chemical withdrawal I may have suffered was the bone-crushing realization that the transformation I had undergone over the past six months was a *drug experience.*

The general medical practice is that once the patient responds adequately the drug is discontinued after six months and in many cases the depression doesn't return. The length of time required to eliminate half the drug is called the half-life. Prozac has a very long half-life of five days, five times that of some other similar anti-depressants, but when those ten days were over I felt a deep angry burn seething from deep within my body.

It would be interesting to have a time machine and go back and take the drug again without reading *Listening to Prozac,* in light of the notion of set and setting. In the book Kramer describes the phenomena of patients becoming "better than well," usually these were higher functioning people to begin with, but they had troubling symptoms that motivated Dr. Kramer to medicate them, resulting in the transformation of many traits and even their sense of self.

I have always found the period of greatest transition coming off and on a serotonin antidepressant to be the most psychedelic. In December of 1992, a few days after starting prozac, I went to an all-you-can-drink bar with two strapping ladies-men who had the author badly outgunned. The feeling of utter desolation had a new spin compared to what I was used to, a dark and suicidal tone, but fascinating because it seemed such an obviously pharmacological interaction. Perhaps it was the change in brain chemistry that undermined the ego's defenses, allowing the perinatal unconscious to break through.

The role of SSRIs in suicide and even homicide is very controversial, but if in certain cases, the drug had a psychedelic effect, perhaps perinatal or transpersonal material is capable of emerging. Generally however the feeling of being on a SSRI is a sharp but calm positive affect. If 1 in 1000 LSD takers has a serious adverse reaction requiring at least 48 hours hospitalization, even a comparable risk for these drugs is well worth it.

Although this psychedelic effect when the serotonin changes in the course of SSRI treatment may produce dangerous or even lethal behaviour there is evidence that the use of these drugs prevents more suicides than it triggers. Given the frequency of suicide in adolescents and young adults with these types of antidepressants a "black box warning" was placed on these medicines when prescribed to those demographics. Prescriptions went down but suicides went *up*.

Once the brain has stabilized, prozac and similar drugs seem to operate as a kind of neurological bleach, chemically inhibiting the strongest anxious thoughts and feelings and leaving space for the ego to operate. How the ego operates in its new space depends on the imprints taken by about age sixteen.

Sometimes called the social neurotransmitter, serotonin is the primary activator of the fourth circuit. LSD has been called a conditioned response inhibitor; although the drug affects many other neurotransmitters as well it is known to interact with numerous subtypes of serotonin especially and its capacity to affect social behavior was evident even in early animal research, as is obvious from the reminisces of one scientist:

> One day Rothlin injected LSD into a lab chimp and then reintroduced the animal to its colony. Within minutes the place was in uproar. The chimp hadn't acted crazy or strange, per se; instead it had blithely ignored all the little social niceties and regulation that govern chimp colony life.

Serotonin is usually an inhibitory neurotransmitter whereas noradrenalin and dopamine are excitatory; it may be that higher levels of the compound or a more efficient serotonin system are able to quell the riots happening in those lower excitatory circuits. Perhaps this fourth circuit inhibits or allows the activity of the other neurotransmitter circuits according to how it has been sexually and culturally domesticated (programmed). The fourth circuit introduces religious cultural morality into behaviour, serotonin quells the riots of despair and anxiety and dampens the drives of the will or id (first circuit), the ego (second circuit) and the mind (third circuit) acting as a "superego" (fourth circuit), which Freud used to describe as the part of the mind usually referred to as the conscience.

Serotonin levels are also positively correlated (as one goes up so does the other) with social status in rhesus monkeys. If the alpha male (the one in charge) is removed from the tribe prozac-treated males are more likely to adopt his position. Interestingly, if the alpha male remains the prozac treated monkeys will not challenge him. It is only in the instance of a power vacuum where high serotonin levels lead to changes in hierarchy. The second circuit seems to be associated with a less cultivated form of aggression – frantic and desperate like a pit-bull while the fourth circuit is more controlled and effective like a cobra.

Kramer further speculates that the lower serotonin in the lower castes of the tribe may have evolved out of the need to keep them in their place – self-effacing and passive – a society where more and more people have higher and higher serotonin may be more and more competitive and chaotic.

Juxtaposed with the vignettes of his patients Kramer makes the case for the biological underpinnings of depression. In epilepsy less and less stimulation is required over time to induce seizures. He argues depression works analogously where less and less stress is needed to trigger an episode until the causality of stress disappears completely and symptoms become "functionally autonomous." The continuum model for affective or mood disorders is also presented in *Listening to Prozac* where a minor episode of depression sits at the mild end and the rapid-cycling form of bipolar or manic-depression sits at the severe end. According to the kindling model it takes less and less stress to move us along the spectrum as we deteriorate.

The stress/risk model proposes illness occurs when a necessary and sufficient amount of stress activates disease in people with a vulnerable constitution. Studies on primates show easy-going biological parents produce easy-going offspring even if raised by other parents specifically chosen for their fretful, anxious behaviour. But Kramer also argues that genetically less vulnerable people can catch up through repeated trauma to the same level of vulnerability to serious depression as their "born under a bad sign" counterparts.

When exposed to stress the body releases the activating hormone adrenaline (1st Circuit) as well as the hormone/neurotransmitter noradrenalin (2nd Circuit). A hormone is a less precise and elegant chemical than a neurotransmitter, which operates only on nerve cells. Noradrenalin is unique, however, and operates as both.

The body seeks a state of *homeostasis* or equilibrium, a stressor is called an *allostatic* load, meaning "outside of stasis" or equilibrium. If your car skids off the road you turn the wheel the other way but if you overcorrect you have to spin the wheel back again to stay on the road – this process may take a few pendulum swings before it stabilizes or you might end up in the ditch.

One of the most basic principles of biology is the negative feedback loop – if high levels of anything are detected, sensitivity to and production of the molecule are automatically reduced. In the case of stress when the brain receives a huge flood of noradrenalin it responds by reducing its sensitivity to this chemical by reducing its *receptors* for the compound. Early models of depression proposed the symptoms were caused by the under-activity of noradrenalin in the brain.

This model proved too simplistic but it is supported by the fact that unlike the less severe forms of the disease, *major* depression involving loss of appetite, changes in sleep patterns, loss of sex drive and psychomotor changes responds better to noradrenalin drugs than serotonin drugs.

Kramer describes older patients who never show depression at all until their late sixties, when they suffer with a severe form of the illness. "Maybe serotonin is like the police. On a normal day you don't have many riots and so the serotonin/police supply is adequate to quell them, but if there are too many riots at once, the system breaks down." In other words the impact of stress to the noradrenalin system is masked by serotonin until that system too is overwhelmed and the severe underlying damage becomes apparent.

Kramer also describes prozac's ability to quicken thought, improve self-esteem, transform social behaviour and of course protect the kindling or sensitizing of the brain from getting more and more damaged with more and more severe episodes of depression resulting. It should be noted that prozac and other antidepressants often do not sustain their effects. Antidepressants in my experience are like lovers: after the first two years, even if it's still good, it's not *as* good. Perhaps, however, had I not been taken off the drug in the summer of '93, the bone- crushing unfolding that led to my psychedelic breakthrough would have never happened, I'd be a contented yuppie time-bomb somewhere.

Also, a recent study showed that the placebo subjects in the antidepressant studies had lower relapse than those in the drug group, implying raising serotonin causes long-term destabilization and vulnerability – caveat emptor.

These circuits and the drugs that activate them could be described as *hydraulic* – a linear shift up or down, with a predictable linear reaction.

Psychedelic means mind manifesting, Grof used the term holotropic, Leary referred to re-imprinting, but, opiates, booze and stimulants just push and pull in a linear space-time path. Prozac, MDMA (ecstasy) and the fifth circuit's libation – cannabis, seem to straddle the categories – dilating the brain's reality tunnels, while delivering a simultaneous dose of euphoria.

MDMA obviously has a much more pronounced psychedelic effect than prozac due to its rate of action, set and setting and pharmacology. Prozac and its cousins block the re-uptake pump on the pre-synaptic (sending) serotonin neuron, which "bathes" the post synaptic neuron with the (usually) inhibitory brain messenger chemical, MDMA does the same thing but also contains methamphetamine as part of its molecule. Amphetamine, dextroamphetamine and methamphetamine are obviously similar but Methylene-Dioxy-MethAmphetamine is warmer, clearer, softer and more opening than its non-psychedelic cousins of the speed family.

Many writers have speculated that the introduction of MDMA in late eighties Britain resulted in a significant reduction in football hooliganism. Additionally Catholic and Protestant youth were known to rave together on the drug in Northern Ireland. MDMA use went up 4000% from 1988 – 1995, also in 1988 with the similar prozac emerging, followed by the other copycat antidepressants serotonin levels were cranked more and faster than any neurotransmitter in history. This may have been evolution's way of easing our transmission from the terrestrial to the digital cyberian dimension.

Psychedelic researcher Andrew Feldmar recalls asking the legendary psychiatrist Ronnie Laing what his favorite psychedelic drug was and he said, "MDMA because it opens the heart." The gentle opening of the mind that accompanies it make it a hydraulic heart opener and a holotropic mind opener.

The drugs associated with the lower circuits are the most addictive – the first circuit opiates, second – alcohol and benzodiazepines (valium) and third circuit stimulants definitely compose the vast majority of the addiction sufferers who seek treatment. Conversely, although 10% of the population is estimated to be taking antidepressants and every weekend a few million take MDMA, the fourth circuit's drugs are generally not as habit-forming.

The time between each surge in evolution shortens with each event as is illustrated on this timeline:

Big Bang	Life on earth begins Circuit I	Vertebrate Circuit II	Symbol Monkey Circuit III	Civ. C. IV
14 Billion years ago	4 billion years ago	500 million years ago	2 million years ago	10 000 BCE

Leisure begins – Yoga, cannabis Circuit V	Buddha (rebirth) Circuit VI	DNA structure discovered Circuit VII	John Lilly Ketamine C. IIX
5000 BCE	500 BCE	1959	1970s

Circuit V

"We are beautiful"
"My body is an infinite playground of pleasure and joy"
"I will experience perfect tantric fusion and community/tribal ecstasy"
"How good I feel depends on my neurological know how"

The second four circuits are even more speculative than the first because they have only emerged within the last 5,000 years or so and *really* only make sense to people living in space. According to the telescoping nature of evolution, time between transformational metamorphoses shortens with each one. After about 10 billion years from the big bang we have life on earth, 500 million years ago mammalian life begins, then only 2 million years ago the smart monkey emerged and about 10,000 years ago agriculture and cities started and when there was luxury enough for a class of leisure to survive about 5,000 years ago the fifth – *neurosomatic-hedonic* circuit emerged.

Leary believed the first four circuits were generally left-brain while the higher four were located in the right hemisphere, although he recognized this was just a metaphor. In *Neurologic* Leary wrote, "Activating the 'silent hemisphere' creates a hedonic boom that momentarily shatters all previously imprinted and learned values." Hatha Yoga is one way but Leary believed the drug that best activates this circuit is cannabis.

The endo-cannibinoid or internal cannabis system runs through every organ in the human body and contains at least 400 subtypes of compounds. It was of course for the crime of possessing very small amounts of cannabis that Timothy Leary served many years of hard time. In Los Angeles one of the hundreds of medical marijuana clinics is named after the late Shaman-Psychologist. Self- indulgence, compulsive hedonism and laziness might be associated with the infinite eroticism of this circuit.

"Medical cannabis is God's joke on marijuana prohibitionists," is how activist Rob Kampia puts it. Two things regarding cannabis medicine are particularly striking – the range of conditions it is useful for and it's total non-toxicity. In pharmacology every substance has what's called a *therapeutic ratio* that compares the average lethal dose with the lowest effective dose. Alcohol's therapeutic ratio is ten, which would involve consuming about twenty beers in five minutes. Heroin's is only five; the club drug GHB's is six.

Cannabis only has a theoretical therapeutic index or ratio because it hasn't caused an overdose, but some speculate it is around 1000 or 100 times less toxic than alcohol. In 1988 the Drug Enforcement Agency's own "Administrative Law Judge" Francis Young observed, "Cannabis is the safest therapeutically active substance known to man."

Neurologist Dr. Ethan Russo goes so far as to suggest that Fibromyalgia, Irritable Bowel Syndrome and Migraine headaches are all linked with deficiencies in the endo-cannibinoid system. Further, THC, the most psychoactive compound in cannabis, binds to cancerous cells and causes them to produce a fatty substance called ceramide, which results in the cancer cell's death while healthy cells are unaffected. Read that again.

The first reference to medical cannabis may date back to about 2800 BCE China and was widely available in patent medicines until WWI. Queen Victoria used an alcohol-based cannabis product or tincture for her menstrual cramps. Yet with the exception of the bohemian artistic fringe, which has always embraced taboo, people in the west generally weren't interested in the states of consciousness cannabis facilitates for their own sake.

Things have changed – from the 1930s to now cannabis use in the United States has increased 30 times or 3000%. It was in the 50s and 60s, when humankind first explored outer space that cannabis really became popular as a mainstream recreational pursuit.

In Leary's model the first four circuits are "gravity based" terrestrial brains and the top four circuits don't really "come into their own" until humans start living in space. Yoga and cannabis have a long history together but both are undergoing a renaissance right now. Leary was a diehard yogi and believed Hatha Yoga was able to turn on the fifth circuit all on its own. Of course the most practical solution remains the combination of Yoga and cannabis with sex.

Different from the mechanical instinctive thrusting sex of the animal kingdom, fifth circuit sex is *sensual* or even polymorphously perverse. "My body and brain are an infinite playground of pleasure and joy," the fifth circuit reminds us.

An especially compelling use of cannabis is the Rastafari religion of Jamaica. Although modern ibogaine and peyote religions began in the nineteenth century, as recently as the 1930s a dynamic convergence of factors synthesized the venerable spiritual system of Rastafari.

One was the ascension of Haile Sellasie to the throne of Ethiopia, combined with the firebrand Marcus Garvey's vision of a return from the slave plantations of Jamaica home to Africa (Exodus) and the rising popularity of cannabis. After the British abandoned slavery in the eighteenth century, they replaced the practice with indentured servants. European, Chinese and Indian labourers indebted to British companies were sent to Jamaica to pay off their debts, where they worked alongside Africans. The Indians may have introduced the Africans to ganja, named after the holy Ganges River in India.

African cannabis smoking may go back millennia but smoking in pipes, cigarettes and cigars only became widespread in the 16th century when tobacco was brought back from the New World. Although a hollowed bone dating to about 15,000 years ago with burnt plant material has been found in present day Thailand, if humans smoked back then they had forgotten the practice until Columbus found Cuba – opium and cannabis use was transformed.

The cultivation of hemp goes back 10,000 years in modern China. The medical, spiritual and recreational use of cannabis dates back at least five thousand years in India and to this day many if not most Sadhus or holy men use it there. While the Chinese labourers must have brought opium its use was marginal and certainly not a catalyst for a new religion. The long-oppressed, cannabis intoxicated Jamaicans, fired up by the self-determination rhetoric of Marcus Garvey, celebrated the ascension of Haile Sellasie as the second coming of Christ – a word that literally translates to messiah. Reggae is considered the "king's music" and it's major musician the late third-world superstar Bob Marley is a universal symbol of peace and equality.

Although obviously in reference to Africans living in Jamaica returning to Ethiopia, on another level perhaps the perennial Rastafari theme of Exodus may be a metaphor for space migration.

CIRCUIT VI

"We create our realities"
"My brain can reprogram and communicate with itself"
"I can transmodulate my reality by feeling a feeling through to completion."
"I make my own fate, coincidences, synchronicities, kismet, fate, luck and destiny"

The sixth circuit is called *neuro-electric*. Taking a psychedelic and activating circuit six suspends the imprints of the first four, which allows you to reprogram them. Leary claimed that, "before our era, the existence of circuit 6 was known to many educated epileptics and courageous yogis (certainly Lao Tse)" – who wrote the book *Psychedelic Prayers* was based on. The drugs that activate this sixth circuit are the full spectrum psychedelics – mescaline, psilocybin, and especially, LSD.

Psychedelics tend to increase (agonise) activity at some serotonin, noradrenalin, or dopamine receptor subtypes and to decrease (antagonize) activity at others. Perhaps the sixth circuit doesn't have a corresponding compound but instead scrambles and interrupts the first four circuits: the fifth circuit seems to elude programming.

Psychedelics at one time were believed to mimic madness and were called *psychotomimetic* (mimicking psychosis) – recently researchers have readdressed this model. One example of this is the "hollow mask experiment." Being hollow, one side of the mask is convex and protrudes outwards and the other side is concave and open. The subjects were divided into three groups – schizophrenics, LSD intoxicated healthy people and sober healthy people. All three were shown the same picture of a hollow mask, convex side up, in a complex setting first and then another picture of the hollow mask, concave or open side up, on its own.

The sober healthy people would consistently incorrectly assume that the mask was the same in both pictures; whereas both the schizophrenics and LSD-intoxicated normal people would get it right. In schizophrenic and psychedelic minds the conditioned perceptions are interrupted and what replaces it is the chaos of infinity itself – non-imprinted experience. Recall Huxley's metaphor of the mind as reducing valve and psychedelics as opening up consciousness beyond the mind's constraints. The ego must negotiate a totally new world, freed from the neural shaping of reality tunnels created by imprinting, and the conditioning and learning that has shaped them further. The Internet is to the global brain what Circuit VI is to the individual brain.

The shaman navigates this sixth circuit of infinite potentialities with technology but the schizophrenic may lack the skill and the battle to maintain space-time-self continuity proves unwinnable. When a brain is placed under this kind of ego- crushing stress perhaps the heightened dopamine (3rd circuit) activity is simply the frenzied efforts of the rational mind to sort it all out.

Grof's and Leary's theories don't merge easily, but the transition from the third perinatal matrix to the fourth or the moment of rebirth would certainly involve a fundamental reprogramming or resetting/bootstrapping for the brain. But not without its risks – even by Leary's figure of 1 in 1000 serious adverse reactions, involving hospitalizations for at least 48 hours, if 50 million people, 40,000 of them clinically, have taken LSD, 50,000 souls were subjected to "worst trips" not just bad trips.

In Connie Little's documentary *Hofmann's Potion* Grof said of Leary, "He didn't give people fair information, he didn't tell them that they may have to go to hell before they get to heaven and if they don't know what they are doing they may stay there."

Treatment for acid psychosis usually involves benzodiazepines like valium, although the dopamine antagonists (decreasing activity) like Thorazine or Seroquel are sometimes used as well. However, Grof believes valium freezes the energetic processes the drug has activated so that the horrible experiences they are trying to work through may become permanent.

In one lecture Leary acknowledged "there is nothing in life as bad as a bad acid trip." When asked directly about the risks of experimentation he challenged back with, "Of course there's risk! Have you forgotten that your ancestors sailed over here on leaky boats." A drug that reliably facilitates religious ecstasy with each dose is beyond current scientific knowledge. Most experts agree that when psychedelics trigger a psychotic illness, the illness would have been triggered anyway. But acid can definitely make you go crazy.

Our culture is fond of the expression "get over it" – the masterful use of the 6th circuit allows the brain to "work through it." It is not strictly the activation of different realities or dynamic transmodulation of governing systems but the ability to navigate or pilot – Leary's synonym for cyber – creating a designer reality.

Successfully integrating biographical or perinatal material represents the skillful use of this circuit. The shaman is a specialist in using his own nervous system to facilitate similar positive transformations in others.

Even while the brain undergoes the unbearable sufferings of the negative perinatal matrices a "six brained biped" is able to maintain "fierce acceptance and intense presence," as Eckhart Tolle describes an ideal state of being. The ego is therefore able to exist in the present instead of simply managing the residual pain that hasn't been integrated – "the infinite variety of responses to the infinite variety of life."

Leary was a chameleon. He was a party animal student, then a brilliant Psychologist, then a zealous psychedelic researcher, then chemical-messiah, then prison escapist and violent revolutionary, then fugitive philosopher/mystic, then a stool-pigeon, then a technology guru. Timothy Leary knew how to program new identities and new realities apparently at will.

Leary was already discussing the Internet in 1977 and comparison to the sixth circuit is obvious. The Internet allows no hierophants to create a hierarchy of information – it is all there, basically equal, different electrical energy ready to be programmed. In the 60s Leary described the human being and their brain as a baby with a computer, but now the babies have grown up *with* computers.

McLuhan theorized transportation extends the limbs, media the senses and computers the nervous system – the Internet is the next level linking all the brains together the way the sixth circuit links the brain's circuits to itself.

In the most "ham-fisted" analogy, psychedelics do for the brain what turning the computer off for thirty seconds and restarting it does for the silicone brain. The 6th circuit suspends the reality tunnels carved through the lower circuits allowing for neural plasticity and transmodulation.

The activation of this circuit is perhaps the most threatening because the ability to program consciousness through culture is undermined *neurologically* – Chomsky's "manufacturing of consent" becomes impossible. We each become our own hierophant or high priest/pagan-scientist.

The idea of psychedelics activating the sixth circuit and resetting the neural networks is further supported by the successful use of indole hallucinogens like LSD in the treatment of cluster headaches, but the most salient application of meta-programming is addiction, which will be discussed in detail later.

There are nondrug methods for activating the sixth circuit. Certainly starvation and life-threatening levels of stress would have been common prehistoric occurrences and are capable of producing the kinds of altered states of consciousness needed, but in my opinion drugs represent a more parsimonious gateway. It is by no means obvious that nondrug methods are safer – that fasting, chanting, trance dancing, and sometimes becoming dehydrated to the point of hemorrhage and nosebleeds – represent superior technology. If bioamine metabolism change (particularly serotonin) is a necessary feature of holotropic states non-bioamine or indirect methods are less specific and efficient, and produce more collateral damage.

Evidence of prehistoric drug use includes the cave-wall paintings (shamanic graffiti) of geometric shapes and "wounded or killed man," depictions of a man or woman with dozens of sticks piercing their body; this may illustrate the struggle of the perinatal unconscious and the pain that must be endured. But there are much more puzzling images common in ancient cave-art, such as therianthropes or animal human hybrids – their potential relationship with DNA will be reckoned with in the next circuit.

Circuit VII

"We are immortal"
"I can communicate with DNA"
"Future evolution depends on the decisions I make now"

The seventh circuit is called *neurogenetic* and while the previous circuit is located within the brain, circuit seven is, for the materialist Leary, "located within the neuron within the DNA" and therefore (at death) "consciousness retreats to the neuron itself." The seconds between the heart and lungs stopping but while there is still enough oxygen to prevent brain death were considered crucial.

Leary believed that as one died one's consciousness slowly retreated through the brain and when it moved into the neuron it was yet another ecstatic experience.

Before reaching the DNA within the neuron consciousness tunes in one more time to the brain itself (neuro-electric Circuit VI). Researchers have recently documented a final flush of energy immediately before brain-death that they believe may be responsible for the phenomena associated with Near Death Experience (NDEs). Rick Strassman has argued that the natural DMT in the body may be increased during high stress and create the "psychedelic" phenomena.

If consciousness is energy received by organized structure and processing- transmitting the energy (now information) is intelligence then DNA possess consciousness and intelligence (contelligence) in truly epic proportions. Each and every cell contains the instructions to make every single cell of every single organism past, present and future. Learning directly from DNA offers infinite opportunities for humanity.

Linguist George Kingsley Zipf's law states that in any language the ratio and rank of word frequency remains constant. So if the most common word appears 100,000 times the tenth most common word appears 10 000 times. The 3% of DNA that codes for protein synthesis does not obey this law of language structure but the other 97% does. In *Supernatural* Graham Hancock makes the case for the spirits, fairies and aliens in human culture as intelligences lurking in the jungle of the other 97% of DNA.

DNA co-discoverer Francis Crick was an early advocate for panspermia – the theory that the earth was *seeded* with DNA based bacteria. This threads the needle nicely between creationism and Darwinism. Crick was also using low doses of LSD based on the advice of Aldous Huxley when he made one of the greatest scientific achievements of all time. Further, Kerry Mullis, who won the Nobel Prize for his work on DNA replication, was also enthusiastic about LSD's contribution. Very high doses of psychedelics, especially DMT, are required to reach this level. Merging Grof and Leary – if the perinatal unconscious corresponds to the sixth circuit then the transpersonal unconscious corresponds to the seventh and eighth.

Thinking back to Frank's trip with its epic adventures, what were those images he was *"living"* – was that the transpersonal seventh circuit communicating the experiences of his ancestors? Materialism is the philosophy that the only thing that exists is matter. This was Leary's slant, at least from incarceration on – he did not believe in life after death and was described by friend and Grateful Dead lyricist John Perry Barlow as one of the "most anti-spiritual people the world has ever known…yet he turned more people on to spirituality than anyone who wasn't born in the desert."

Perhaps the first six circuits are more about the individual brain while the transpersonal seventh and eighth circuits transcend the neurons and represent a link to the higher intelligence necessary to program the startling amount of information DNA processes.

Or, it's like a computer hooked up to the Internet, only the uninitiated would think the information on the screen is coming exclusively from inside the box.

Many subjects report that on DMT you communicate with apparently discrete beings – intelligences that seem external – what the cynical would call projected hallucinations (as opposed to introjected which are recognized as coming from within).

"There squatting next to me are two magnificent insects...skin burnished, glowing metallic, with hammered jewels inlaid." Dr. Leary wrote this of DMT in 1966. Author Graham Hancock makes the case that the "magnificent insects" are intelligences within the 97% "function unknown" DNA and that they are evolving just like we are.

The spirits contacted by the shamans, the fairies and elves of the middle ages and the modern reports of alien abductions share common elements. They often feature flying or sinking into another world, contact with other beings, frequently animal-human hybrids or therianthropes, painful "shamanic surgery," attempts at or successful "mating," the women are often gently coerced to nurse or tend the hybrid offspring and important information is sometimes learned from the discarnate creatures.

This is all terrifying and has me longing for some good old scientific materialism, but the time I took ayahuasca I *felt* like I was contacting a being – although all I actually saw was a geometric light-show. I have seen some iconic imagery but never any therianthropes and there is no mention of animal-human hybrids in any of Frank's notes, but the phenomena of DMT and LSD are definitely very different.

In the middle ages the fairies were often accused of stealing children and sometimes replacing them with unhealthy "changelings." They would sometimes seduce people into their world and return them a hundred years later because of the time-change between the dimensions. Women often reported being forced to nurse or swaddle strange disfigured babies.

By the time the alien abductions emerged in the fifties children were no longer being kidnapped, there were no changelings left behind – they are returned to their normal world the next day and the offspring are described as less sickly – this is all attributed to evolution of the unknown 97% of our DNA much the same as the protein synthesizing other 3% has improved. To truly understand Hancock's argument in all it's 700-page glory you must read *Supernatural*.

If the perinatal unconscious does not resolve during the session the affective quality of the matrix evoked becomes a governing system. The brain has been re-imprinted so the sixth circuit has been activated, but the poor subject feels worse than ever. Such a nightmare would likely dissuade the hardiest of us from further exploration, but alas the perinatal sixth circuit consciousness usually must be transcended to activate the transpersonal seventh and eighth.

One long-time psychedelic researcher Psychologist Dr. Bill Richards discussed the many priests and ministers that came "seeking spiritual experiences but instead dealt almost exclusively with unresolved childhood sexual conflicts – but this is the wisdom of the psyche."

Leary advocated keeping the brain intact during death so one could fully appreciate the ecstasies it provides at the end. After the sixth circuit biographical-perinatal flush "my whole life passed before me in a flash," then, according to Leary... "as the dying experience continues, the neural network itself begins to cut out. The energy required to fire signals across synaptic barriers weakens. Consciousness retreats to the neuron. The final dialogue is between the memory synthesizing centers within the neuron itself and the DNA code in the cell nucleus. The last voice is the explanatory whisper of the genetic blueprint: "Here's where we came from, here's where going."

The seventh neurogenetic circuit emerges with Mendel's breeding discoveries in the 1850s and then again with Crick and Watson's visual masterpiece one hundred years later and now thrives with the DMT religions and healers.

CIRCUIT IIX

"In the province of the mind what you believe literally is true or becomes true within limits to be determined experientially and experimentally, those limits are beliefs themselves to be transcended."– Dr. John Lilly
"I can communicate with nuclei"

The eighth circuit is *neuro-atomic* or *quantum*. Here the smallest organized level of contelligence is communicated within the nucleus at the center of each atom. The experience of the "clear white light" in Leary's language or the "metacosmic void" in Grof's, reported by some trippers, may be examples of the final circuit's activation. Just as each DNA molecule contains all the same information universally, each nuclei is structured similarly so that tuning into this final level of human consciousness may allow for Out of Body Experiences (OBE)s.

In a lecture promoting his 2006 book *The Ultimate Journey: Consciousness and the Mystery of Death* Dr. Grof mentions congenitally (since-birth) blind subjects going out of their bodies during surgery and seeing (from the top of the hospital room) for the first time, but upon returning to their bodies they were once again blind. Along with Out of Body Experiences (OBE) the most far-out trip possible is the Near Death Experience (NDE).

Leary proposed in the sixties the future would provide a "g-pill" that would allow the total experience of death but without the unpleasant dying part. He became very enthusiastic about ketamine in the early eighties when it was still legal and claimed it provided him with such an experimental death. While the phenethylamines like MDMA and mescaline, the tryptamines like LSD and psilocybin and the Amanita Muscaria type "cholinergic" psychedelics like belladonna all scramble the noradrenalin, serotonin, dopamine, acetylcholine systems, ketamine is a more linear, NMDA (N-methyl d-aspartate) antagonist (decreaser). This causes a reduction in another neurotransmitter system called glutamate. Glutamate is the most common excitatory neurotransmitter in the vertebrate nervous system; lowering it to the extent ketamine does may inhibit ego function and brain function enough to allow access to the eighth and "final circuit."

This is how Russian Psychiatrist Dr. Igor Kungurtsev, who was one of the pioneers of using ketamine for alcoholism and heroin addiction, described his own ketamine experiences:

> "Three or four minutes after the first injection, I felt this world begin to disappear, and I experienced myself as a point of consciousness floating in strange worlds. The most unusual feeling was that I had no body, yet somehow "I" existed. The next development was indescribable. During the first stage, I seemed to exist only as a point of consciousness, but still, "I" existed. Then there was a stage where even this began to disappear, and I felt a real terror of dying. At that moment I managed to surrender and let go. All that remained was awareness; there was no "I" as *me*, as an individual consciousness. It was as if there existed only that which was aware of itself."

This was before the Soviet Union fell and they were quite secretive about their unpublished work, yet about a year into the project "three magicians" showed up who, in their own ketamine meditations had learned that the clinic had been "throwing people out onto the astral plane" and they wanted to see what was going on. The magicians inspected the operation and gave their approval, after which they supplied the fledgling psychedelic project with volumes of psychedelic literature at that time unavailable even to scientists in that country.

The Eighth neuro-atomic circuit emerged with quantum physics at the dawn of the 20th century, but it has a long way to go.

PCP is the "parent" chemical of ketamine and was actually researched for use in psychotherapy! But when PCP hit the street the negative publicity scared Parke Davis off researching the apparently much sleepier ketamine for this application. Dextromethorphan (DXM) the chief ingredient in many cough suppressants also fits into this category – NMDA (N-methyl d-aspartate) antagonist (decreaser), but adds serotonin and opiate agonist to its resumé, although if you take enough of any psychoactive it will bind to almost all receptors. Another interesting brain reset involves a debilitating rare pain disorder treated by the psychedelic anesthetic ketamine.

Occasionally during surgery or accident a nerve is damaged such that on a pain scale of one to ten sufferers are constantly at ten. Intravenous ketamine is administered intermittently over a month-long period in an attempt to "reset" the pain system and according to some the brain itself, as one doctor specializing in the treatment observed, "like a computer being shut off for a minute and then restarted." Hugh Laurie's character on the show *House* beat his vicodin addiction with this treatment. Also severe depression and pain from trauma when shock sets in are sometimes treated with this drug. In fact there are now twelve clinics in the United States offering Ketamine for treatment resistant depression and the therapy has been called the "greatest revolution in psychiatry since prozac."

In the eighth neuro-atomic circuit consciousness tunes into the nucleus, the densest intelligence of all for the personal *finale*. There was great controversy as psychedelics went mainstream in the mid 1960s regarding the experience of the "clear light" as the goal of psychedelic exploration. In the first of his two "psychedelic manuals," *The Psychedelic Experience*, Leary suggests the trip *begins* with "the primary clear light seen at the moment of ego-loss." Of course many dismiss any drug experience as merely toxic pharmacologic artifacts, but Leary's trip manual was based on *The Tibetan Book of The Dead*, which was used to guide the soul of the departed off "the wheel of incarnation and into enlightenment." In the second and in my opinion superior trip manual *Psychedelic Prayers*, in keeping with his evolving ideas on the brain – Leary again invoked first the "clear light" experience of the nuclei, then the DNA, then the external senses, the internal senses (chakras) and ended the trip with re- imprinting advising listeners to "flow like water."

Circuit	I	II	III	IV
Function	Biological – Survival	Mammalian – Political	Symbolic – Linguistic	Tribal – Domestic
Time	4 billion – 500 million years ago	500 million – 2 million years ago	2 million – 10 000 years ago	10 000 BCE – 1945
Age Imprinted	0 – 6 months	6 mos. – 3 yrs	3 – 5 years	12 – 14 years
Dimension	approach – avoid	up (dominant) – down (submissive)	left – right	time
Internal Chemistry	endorphins – adrenalin	noradrenalin-GABA	dopamine	serotonin
External Chemistry	opiates	alcohol	stimulants	prozac, mdma
"high" lights	opium eating emerges 4,000 BCE	Alcohol use popular by 3,000 BCE	Greek Homeric Hymns emerge 850 BCE	500 BCE Buddhism, 0 Christianity, 600 Islam
	opium smoking emerges 1500	Alcohol increases 1750	Coffee/ Tea 1850	prozac and MDMA in 80s

Circuit	V	VI	VII	VIII
Function	NeuroSomatic	NeuroElectric	NeuroGenetic	NeuroAtomic
Time	3 000 BCE – future	500 BCE – future	1959 – future	1980 – future
Internal Chemsitry	endocannibinoids	Combination of receptors	DMT	Glutamate
External Chemistry	exocannibinoids	psychedelics	DMT	Ketamine – Salvia
"high" lights	Sufism emerges 600	Psychedelic science emerges again 1950s	DNA structure discovered 1959	Ketamine emerges 1965
	Yoga/cannabis emerge in the west – 1960s	Consumer Electronics emerge 1970s	DMT tourism emerges 1990s	Ketamine used in psychiatry 2010

Chapter Nineteen

Addiction

"Impulsion by appetite alone is slavery."

– Jean-Jacques Rousseau

"What made a millionaire out of Mr. Frito-Lay made a fat motherfucker out of me."

– Adam Sandler

There are three areas where psychedelic therapy offers a safe and effective treatment solution that requires no more debate or research in my opinion – trauma, death anxiety and addiction. Of the thousand subjects at Hollywood Hospital over a third were alcoholic – of the 40,000 clinical psychedelic subjects worldwide thousands of addicts were treated. About two-thirds greatly benefited, and since that time hundreds of millions of people suffering with addiction have been deprived of something valuable.

Two particularly shocking losses caused by our society's conviction that only *patentable* chemistry is good for us are cannabis and cancer and ibogaine and addiction. Cannabis' anti-cancer properties have been documented since 1974 but it wasn't until the nineties that ibogaine's potential was scientifically validated.

In his classic *Lenson on Drugs,* literature professor David Lenson parses the meaning of the word addiction – "The word's etymology points to *addictus* – the past participle of the Latin word *addicere* (to say or pronounce – to decree or bind) – which suggests that the user has lost active control of language and thus of consciousness itself, that she or he is already "spoken for," bound and decreed. Instead of *saying* one *is said."*

Curiously the notion of addiction is a relatively recent addition to the collective imagination. Although references to "people suffering from 'drink madness', can be found in the civilizations of ancient Egypt and Greece," it apparently wasn't until opium smoking began in the sixteenth century that anything close to behaviour approaching the modern conception of the word occurred. Then when alcohol use tripled in The United States between 1790 and 1830 with the move from fermented grains and grapes to distilled spirits, added to growing opium smoking and then morphine injecting and the world was ready for a new archetype – the addict.

In the Victorian age (1837-1901) addiction was seen as a deficit of willpower but this changed in 1956 when the American Psychiatric Association officially labeled alcoholism as a disease and this conception persists to this day. Until the end of the nineteenth century addictions were not differentiated – the idea of an *addictive* drug was unknown, it was understood that addiction was something that happened only in a person. At that time with morphine and heroin added to raw opium, the notion of addiction occurring when *anyone* encounters drugs good enough that you cannot stop their use without treatment was born. "One hit and you're hooked for life." This is a very reductionist and deterministic position based on the phenomena of tolerance, withdrawal and the insatiable drug habits of caged animals. Social psychologist Dr. Stanton Peele has a radically different theory of addiction.

Dr. Peele sees addiction arising when a person fails to derive security and gratification, *reliably* from a *diverse* range of sources in their environment – so that when one does encounter a behaviour *predictable* enough in its effects on consciousness one engages in it too much, even to the detriment of their mental, physical, emotional and spiritual health. Many people will substitute addictions, possibly abstaining from all illegal drugs to use only legal ones or all drugs period and over-engaging in sex, exercise, work, shopping or gambling. The problem isn't what they're addicted to but the failure to develop an adequate portfolio of reward/gratification strategies to prevent "falling in love" with various and sundry psychoactive enterprises. Blaming the enterprises themselves no matter how foreign or sordid they seem to outsiders misses the point entirely. After all who is to decide which habits will be allowed?

"Consider the following description of drug addiction: 'the sufferer is tremulous and loses his self-command; he is subject to fits of agitation and depression. He has a haggard appearance... As with other such agents, a renewed dose of the poison gives temporary relief, but at the cost of future misery.' The drug in question is coffee (caffeine), as seen by the turn-of-the-century British pharmacologists Allbutt and Dixon. Here is their view of tea: 'An hour or two after breakfast in which tea has been taken... a grievous sinking... may seize upon a sufferer, so that to speak is an effort... By miseries such as these, the best years of life may be spoilt."

Dr. Bruce Alexander also challenged the dominant model of addiction and its supporting research involving self-administration of stimulants and opiates by laboratory animals simply by taking them out of their cages and putting them in "rat parks" where they had a more natural surrounding. If given a diverse and satisfying range of experiences they stop self-administering drugs, or they don't start in the first place.

Each society develops a hierarchy of values – a list of good and bad. From this list purification rituals emerge to purge the latter and encourage the former. The problem is the list is arbitrary and represents just another game with rules, rituals, roles, goals, language and values and God help you if you're not part of the caste or class or even team who controls the operation and designs the games.

Infamous critic and professor of psychiatry Dr. Thomas Szasz in his brilliant and devastating indictment of the drug war *Ceremonial Chemistry: The ritual persecution of drugs, addicts, and pushers,* compares our word pharmaco to the ancient Greek pharmakos or scapegoat which meant human medicine – a cruel pun for human sacrifice.

"The selection, naming, special treatment, and finally the ritualized destruction of the scapegoat was the most important and most potent "therapeutic" intervention known to primitive man." In the sixth century B.C.E. this practice was stopped and the meaning of the word pharmakos evolved into what it is today, drug, medicine or poison. But the human need for scapegoats continued.

The "trial" and burning of witches represents an obvious recursive (fractal) version of the practice of human sacrifice, but religious persecutions, book bans and burnings and the alienation of sexual misfits continues to this day. Two more unfortunate populations that face ritualized persecution are those deemed insane and those who use and particularly those who sell illegal drugs. In some countries the noble tradition of human sacrifice is perpetuated and "traffickers" of illicit drugs are still murdered by the state. Generally however, users are considered sick and only sellers criminals and each has rituals assigned accordingly. Szasz argued that our "understanding of drugs has as much to do with pharmacology as our understanding of holy water has to do with chemistry."

One modern purification ritual cited by Szasz is dieting. Traditionally because of menstruation and possibly due to male jealousy (misogyny) over the female capacity to give life, women have been seen as "polluted." Szasz speculated that this is the unconscious reason dieting is more popular among women.

In a society where over 80% of the population consume some form of caffeine *daily*, at least half of which are physiologically addicted – meaning they demonstrate withdrawal (usually headaches) and tolerance (needing more over time to achieve the same effect), the war on some drugs is pharmacological Calvinism at best and homicidal psychosis at worst. But what do you do with millions of desperate addicts?

Contemporary psychedelic researcher Dr. John Halpern of Harvard Medical School lays out the scientific evidence for psychedelic medicine with addiction in his paper – *The Use of Hallucinogens in the Treatment of Addiction. Addiction Research*, 4(2):177-189, 1996. Halpern's approach is essentially pharmacodynamic – rather than successful psychedelic treatment for addiction requiring the successful working through of trauma the drug simply alters the brain in a way that makes addiction unnecessary. As support he cites the capacity of ibogaine to reverse addiction in animals and the statistically significant frequency of alcoholics who remained sober for one to two months after LSD therapy.

> A significant decrease in cocaine self administration by Wistar rats was found after receiving ibogaine (40 mg/kg IV) (Cappendijk and Dzoljic, 1993). This effect lasted for more than 48 hours, and the researchers found that a longer positive response would occur after three daily doses were given. Moreover, cocaine self-administration diminished in a consistent trend in those rats infused with one 40 mg/kg dose each week for three weeks. In another study (Sershen, Hashim, and Lajtha 1993), cocaine intake diminished 38% for five days after.
>
> Similar findings have been obtained with opiate dependence. One research group (Glick et al., 1991) reported that Sprague-Dawley rats significantly decreased their self-administration of morphine after a single dose of ibogaine (2.5-80 mg/kg) lasting up to two weeks. Other rats showed a similar response only after two to three weekly injections. In another study with Sprague-Dawley rats (Maisonneuve, Keller, and Glick, 1991), ibogaine was noted to cause a decrease in dopamine levels in the striatum to near baseline (pre-opiate) levels. Numerous studies (Heikkila, Orlansky, and Cohen, 1975; Wise and Bozarth, 1982; Mathems and German, 1984; Mereu, Gadda, and Gessa, 1984; Clarke et al., 1985; Parker and Cubeddu, 1986; Di Chiara and Imperato, 1988; Moghaddam and Bunney, 1989), as noted by Maisonneuve, Keller, and Glick (1991), have shown addictive drugs (opiates, stimulants, nicotine, and alcohol) to cause an increase in dopamine levels in certain discrete regions of the brain.

These authors further suggest that this effect of ibogaine "may decrease the reinforcing efficacy of morphine" (1991).

Animal studies with ibogaine have also shown a decrease in some physical withdrawal signs from morphine (Dzoljic, Kaplan, and Dzoljic, 1988; Aceto et al., 1989; Glick et al.,1991; Glick et al., 1992; Maisonneuve et al., 1992; Sershen et al., 1992), cocaine (Cappendijk and Dzoljic 1993), and amphetamines (Maisonneuve, Keller, and Glick, 1992)." Pg. 11-13

Ibogaine is an extraordinary drug that psychedelic chemist, the late Sasha Shulgin, described as being in a "class by itself." It works on virtually every major neurotransmitter system and seems to operate almost as a "master key" filling up the abnormal receptor cells and allowing the brain to work through the pathologies in its chemical and electrical circuitry. The content of the session remains critical though as one Psychologist who analyzed the data from the Saskatchewan LSD and alcoholism program noted. "The people who got better either had a really good time or a really bad time." Ibogaine is also known as excellent for the working through of childhood trauma and is probably the best drug for addiction out there but its poor therapeutic index (small difference between lethal and effective doses) makes ketamine more likely to corner the market in "resetting" addicted brains, certainly as a first line before the heavy artillery of Iboga.

In 1935 Alcoholics Anonymous founder Bill Wilson was treated with belladonna for his alcoholism and he "saw a white light," had a full blown mystical experience, stopped drinking and formed the legendary self-help group. Twenty-five years later after having a few LSD sessions with Al Hubbard he believed the drug could facilitate the spiritual experience needed to begin the twelve steps to recovery. AA and Hollywood Hospital referred many patients to each other. Unfortunately by the early sixties Wilson was just another member of AA's board of directors, most of whom were horrified by their colleague's new paradigm shift.

In the same paper on addiction cited above Halpern argued that the key to psychedelic therapy for addiction is the "afterglow" following a peak experience – proposing an essentially materialist "brain-state" argument that for some reason this chemical afterglow lasts about six to eight weeks.

After an initial wave of positive psychedelic therapy research from '50-'63, very- high success rates in patients considered next to impossible along with the drug's escape from clinical supervision prompted a violent reaction by the scientific community at large. It was also in 1963 that

Leary and Alpert were fired from Harvard and the psychedelic drug story became part of mainstream culture.

When LSD was in the hands of medicine they loved it but when people started making it themselves or finding people who could – they disowned their Frankenstein chemical and turned viciously against it.

The claims of psychedelic therapy with alcoholism received the most attention. All the modern methodological systems were enforced and the results were often not promising. But even so a short–term positive effect was noted even in the most devastatingly negative studies. Halpern writes,

> When one weighs this literature, including the few double-blind, controlled studies, it can be seen that there could be anti-addictive benefits lasting one or two months. One of the better designed studies (Hollister, Shelton, and Krieger, 1969) had subjects (N =72) randomly assigned to two groups in which one was given a single dose of 600 μg of LSD and the other 60 mg of dextroamphetamine. No psychotherapy was provided to either group, and LSD or amphetamine was administered double blind. Both groups were independently rated for levels of alcoholism on two and six month follow-up. At two months the investigators reported a statistically significant improvement with the LSD treated group over the amphetamine group when comparing scores on a "Drinking Behavior Scale" ... It is quite possible, then, that this hallucinogen had up to a two-month anti-addictive property with these alcoholics.

In the Native American Church peyote meetings are usually held once a week or whenever anyone needs help. It may be that this repeated dosing of the peyote maintains a chemical equilibrium that prevents the self-destructive behaviour of addiction. However, what has hopefully been established by now is that this is no form of chemotherapy – but "a controlled reaction of the mind" where set and setting are vital. The alcoholics seem to sail through the unconscious to the positive perinatal matrices with little resistance. Perhaps every few weeks, whether you see it as taking place in the brain exclusively or not, "turning-on" those deepest "feel good" circuits is a natural treatment for addictions of all types.

Seeing psychedelic therapy as comparable to "methadone maintenance" where, instead of a daily dose you instead dose every couple of months, once again tries to rid us of that annoying ghost in the shell. However it vividly demonstrates the importance of chemistry in addiction. The chemical and electrical patterns create habits of behaviour that grow stronger with repetition. A conversation, even with the most persuasive of agents, isn't going to cut the mustard.

Dr. Eugene Kruptisky of Russia did some groundbreaking research with ketamine and addiction before this drug too escaped into the masses and subsequent legislation made continuing his widely published work impossible. Ketamine and ibogaine appear to be the most efficient means of "resetting" the brain.

> Banzie (the members of the Bwiti, properly, "those of the chapel") also say that eboga enables a man or woman to return to infancy and to birth – to the life in the womb...by returning initiates to the uterine condition, a condition in any case very close to life in the land of the dead [and so] restores them to their own integrity – their pristine conditions.
> –From *Bwiti: an Ethnography of the Religious Imagination in Africa.* James W. Fernandez, Princeton University Press, 1982, 491

The above quote is how Harvard neuroscientist Dr. Carl Anderson starts one of my favorite papers – "Ibogaine Therapy in Chemical Dependency and Posttraumatic Stress Disorder: A Hypothesis Involving the Fractal Nature of Fetal REM Sleep and Interhemispheric Reintegration." From the *Bulletin of the Multidisciplinary Association for Psychedelic Studies MAPS – Volume 8 Number 1 Spring 1998* – pp. 5-14 – In it Anderson compares ibogaine with Rapid Eye Movement (R.E.M.) sleep in terms of the mathematical relationship of the electrical output of the left and right hemispheres of the brain. He noted that in people suffering from PTSD and/or substance abuse they showed higher levels of "functional asymmetry" between the left and right sides of the brain.

"In effect, ibogaine pharmacodynamically destabilizes the functional connectivity of the brainstem and its habitual interactions with bihemispheric temporal lobe structures such as the amygdala, creating a functional state of plasticity in these areas which facilitates the reintegration of traumatic memories by altering psychopathological interhemispheric dynamics, ultimately dissipating addiction- related behavioral patterns. They all share the signature of the self-organized critical state, $1/f$ (one-over-f) patterns of activity involving many levels of the nervous system from the sub-cellular to the behavioral." In other words, dreaming and oneiric or dream-inducing drugs re-open the relationship between the executive cortex and the perinatal limbic system. Then the system is driven into such a frenzy of heightening complexity – a self-organizing critical

(SOC) state occurs or a "transmarginal inhibition and terminal exhaustion supervenes" or the integral or perinatal unconscious moves from the third to the fourth matrix, the only metaphor experiencers use is rebirth.

Terrence McKenna, always a great fan of chaos, described the self-organizing critical state with the metaphor of a hydrofoil or foil, which is a tiny metal craft that lifts a boat or plane to reduce drag. The vibration (q) increases with the vehicle's speed up to a certain point (self-organizing critical state) after which the vibration almost stops.

Although the shamans themselves describe travelling to different worlds where they do their work, this model perceives the function of shamans differently.

Here their role in healing is encouraging the increase in their client's brain activity without defensiveness, dissociation or violence until it becomes strong enough that a self-organizing critical state emerges and the customer is reborn. In the ibogaine initiation ritual of the Bwiti religion in Africa and in most modern psychedelic therapy a male and female therapist team sits for the neuronaut – a Mother and Father present for the rebirth.

A Modest Proposal

The psychedelic treatment of addiction could begin with one to three ibogaine or ketamine sessions to reset the brain's chemical and electrical patterns to a pre- addicted state. This could be followed by one to three MDMA sessions, followed by one to six full spectrum (LSD, mescaline, psilocybin) psychedelic sessions to abreact negative biographical and perinatal dynamics and activate their positive counterparts. Finally, to maintain their progress subjects could, if they wished, join a psychedelic religion of their choice.

Leary's organization, the League for Spiritual Discovery (LSD), has recently re- emerged as has a new Czech group advocating the religious use of ibogaine. The Native American Church, the Iboga church of Gabon and the ayahuasca groups spreading throughout the world are more established alternatives.

Such an approach would seem to require the unconditional surrender of the drug war and The Partnership for a Drug-Free America is financed largely by merchants of drugs (alcohol, tobacco, pharmaceuticals) so this is not likely to happen any time soon. However, with addiction to sex, food, shopping, work and gambling becoming more widely recognized the logical leap to treating all addicts with compassion instead of vengeance becomes more palatable.

Chapter Twenty

Drug War

"The darkest places in hell are reserved for those who maintain their neutrality in times of moral crisis."

–Dante Alighieri

"Down here at the pawn shop, it's a nifty way to shop... but what they sell; not strictly made of stone, please remember that's flesh and bone"

–Sublime

The brain and the natural and synthetic drugs that operate it are evolving synergistically. More recently an ideological war has raged between puritans and individualists with everyone else caught somewhere in the middle. In 2,000 B.C.E. we find possibly the first recorded drug prohibition by an Egyptian priest who writes, "I, thy superior forbid thee to go to the taverns. Though art degraded like beasts."

But apparently much of the rest of the world, including Rome and Greece, had a liberal approach to drugs. Opium, cannabis, alcohol and a few harsh psychedelics like henbane and belladonna were widely used. The Christian bible is loaded with effusive praise of alcohol reminiscent of Soma and Haoma a millennium before. Islam's emergence in the seventh century however brings the first widespread official drug prohibition with the same drug the Christians had made sacred – alcohol.

The Qur'an specifically bans alcohol and gambling – 'In Surah Al-Baqarah: 219, it states, "They ask Thee concerning Wine and Gambling, Say: In them is great sin, and some profit, for men; but the sin is greater than the profit." Finally, "intoxicants and games of chance" were called "abominations of Satan's handiwork," intended to turn people away from God and forget about prayer, and Muslims were ordered to abstain (5:90-91).

Although cannabis is not specifically mentioned in the Qur'an since it is an intoxicant it is implicitly forbidden, use has been tolerated, especially among the poor throughout the Islamic world. It is interesting to note the

gender segregation and sex-phobia that emerges from a culture favour-
ing cannabis while forbidding alcohol – not what Leary's model would
predict, but perhaps the fifth circuit wasn't evolved enough yet. Although
campaigns against cannabis emerged in Islam in the middle ages, medical
use was always exempt.

In the year 350 we find the first mention of tea in China but it is opium that dominates the psychopharmacological culture of the time – but
eaten in its raw "crude" form, no mention can be found of our concept of
addiction. The introduction of smoking would change this.

Until Europeans traveled to the new world the practice of smoking was
apparently unknown to them although some people in the Middle East
and Europe did burn cannabis in "braziers" and breathed in the smoke.
Combusting, breaking down and inhaling psychoactives is the fastest and
strongest means of introducing them into the bloodstream, apart from directly injecting into the fluid filled sacs (ventricles) located in either side
of the brain. The Indians of the Americas apparently also invented snorting (insufflation) as well as smoking.

It was about 1,000 B.C.E. that smoking tobacco, a stimulant drug that
seems to work on the third (symbolic-intelligence) circuit, began in the
western hemisphere, but it didn't reach Europeans until 1492 when a
Spanish explorer named Jerez took up the habit while visiting present day
Cuba. "On his return to Spain, Jerez frightened the local people who were
amazed to see smoke coming from his mouth and nose. The holy inquis-
itors, who were influential in Spain at the time, are understood to have
thought that Jerez was possessed by the devil and imprisoned him for sev-
en years. Ironically, by the time he was released, smoking had become a
custom in Spain."

Coffee emerged with tobacco in the fifteenth century and both drugs
gained popularity fast, along with fanatical opposition. In the 17th century the Russian Czar Michael Federovitch ordered anyone caught with
tobacco executed, after being "tortured until he gave up the name of the
supplier." In the 16th century coffee was banned throughout the Ottoman
Empire of modern-day Turkey.

Another third circuit stimulant called the printing press was invented
in 1440 and the suppression of translations of the Bible were just as ve-
hement as any medieval drug crusade, "the men are beheaded, the wom-
en buried alive." Prohibitions on sex, especially masturbation, followed a
similar path of violent condemnation, slowly waning as history advances
– can more enlightened drug policies be far behind?

Prohibitions on tobacco, caffeine, cannabis, opium and alcohol waxed and waned over the middle ages falling under one of four categories, totally legal, legal but you have to buy it from us, legal for only medical use or the rare puritanical total prohibition. Which category the rulers applied depended on the state of their treasuries, although the explanations were politically correct and usually moralistic – a trend that continues to the present day.

Two revolutions in opium economics have occurred contemporaneously with industrial revolutions. The first was the emergence of smoking as a way of using the drug through the 16th and 17th century, particularly in Asia and the Middle East, and the second came in the decisive period of the 1830s with the invention of faster cargo ships and where America's current imperial aristocracy finds its origins.

The relationship between opium and Europeans has always been deeply conflicted. Dutch colonialists in their efforts to enslave the people of present day Indonesia found the introduction of opium smoking indispensible. The British had developed their own drug problem with Chinese and Indian tea and had run out of things to trade for it so they started to encourage opium smoking through the East India Tea Company. Opium became the world's biggest business in the 1830s aided by the newly invented clipper ships capable of making the opium runs six times faster and resulting in a proportional increase in sales. The East India Tea Company started to get flack from Chinese officials plagued with an epidemic of drug addiction and, in a brilliantly equivocal move – the company stopped shipping but continued to mass-produce the narcotic.

At about the same time, secular Harvard was suppressing a rebellion from religious fundamentalists who ultimately broke off and started Yale University. Opium smuggling heir and Yale exchange student William Huntington Russell studied in Germany where he joined a secret society and upon returning home in 1832 began what would become "Skull and Bones." After the East India Tea Company stopped shipping opium the entrepreneurial smugglers who filled in the vacuum became filthy rich at the dawn of the second industrial revolution – timing is everything.

Raising huge amounts of capital in the 1830s was necessary for the creation of the modern world – alcohol drinking Americans and opium smoking Chinese would have kept their money for themselves were it not for their drug habits. A recent study of Ottawa crack users revealed the average consumer spent $450 a day. Maybe drug addicts are the financial martyrs of progress.

If you control the trade in a substance – if it's made illegal – the price is higher and proportion for smugglers even greater. In 1909 Skull n' Bones member and American President William Howard Taft convened the Shanghai Convention with the goal of "controlling morphine and cocaine." In 1925 an updated treaty was ratified and Egypt, China and the United States tried to have cannabis added but India cited social and religious use and this extension of prohibition would have to wait a decade.

Since its inception to this September each year Skull and Bones hand-picks 15 – until recently – exclusively male, students from the first year class, yielding about 2,700 souls – most of whom are paragons of the American Elite. Having a lot of money to invest, whether generated through opium/alcohol sales or not, in the 1830s was a stroke of luck. Industrialization, railroads, shipping, manufacturing, finance and newspapers could leverage money exponentially – but when a financial crisis hit in 1837 people got desperate. Two years later 2,000 chests of opium were seized by China's Emperor Manchu. Queen Victoria was not amused. Two opium wars would rage, the second ending in 1852, when the British forced opium upon China's ports and occupied Hong Kong.

In 1898 United States Ship U.S.S. Maine inexplicably exploded starting the Spanish American War that resulted in the American invasion of the Philippines whose capital, Manila, was a key opium port. Places with lots of drugs and lots of oil have hosted wars ever since.

Morphine and codeine were extracted from the opium plant at the beginning of the 19th century but it was when heroin emerged that the plot really thickened. A form of morphine three times more quickly absorbed than its predecessor Heroin was marketed by Bayer, a German pharmaceutical company, from 1898 – 1910 as a cough suppressant and "non-addicting alternative to morphine."

At the same time as heroin was being given to children for coughs local governments began cracking down on opium dens. After completion of the railroads Chinese workers were competing with whites for scarce jobs – making opium smoking illegal (while still allowing it in patent medicines) eliminated some of the labour market competition. This was also a contributing factor to cannabis prohibition that targeted Mexican migrant workers who enjoyed the drug.

Cocaine became associated with African-American violence shortly after being sold as a panacea by Freud and the Pope. Asians, Latinos and Africans were made scapegoats and victimized by alcoholic Europeans and one hundred years and one hundred million arrests later drugs are everywhere.

The wave of prohibition would eventually reach alcohol as well in 1919 with the passage of the Volstead Act by the United States Congress. The years leading up to Volstead saw a fierce propaganda war waged by puritans where a technique was perfected that is still a staple of the drug war to this day – taking the worst example and presenting it as the normal inevitable consequence of trying the drug even once. Thus the heroin menace of the seventies becomes the crack menace of the eighties and the meth menace of the nineties and violent expensive campaigns are justified and popular.

Another tactic employed by the drug warriors is blaming every negative aspect of drug user's lives on the drugs they use. Correlation is not causation, however, and most heavy drug users have severely disturbed nervous systems that make them desperate for any kind of change to their internal landscape. The drugs aren't the only cause of their distress, trauma to a vulnerable brain is the primary source of the problem and the drugs are an attempt at survival. Society fails its most vulnerable three ways – first in preventing the abuse and neglect, second in persecuting survivors for using drugs to cope with the pain, and third virtually outlawing psychedelic research in the sixties.

Prohibition encourages concentrating the desired compounds to the smallest possible form to transport undetected and then the high price encourages injecting so the entire dose is introduced into the body. The invention of the hypodermic syringe allowed the opium smoker to graduate to the morphine addict – in the early years of the 20th century the average addict was a middle-aged, middle-classed housewife. Expensive kits could be purchased to house the needle and other tools for evenings out.

Needless to say the use of opium and her stronger sisters rose dramatically during the first half of the 20th century. Corsica, birthplace of Napoleon, a small island of 300,000 off the coast of France, and its port city Marseilles were critical to narcotics trafficking. Addicts, throughout Asia and the United States were sold junk made from opium grown in Iran and Turkey that was then processed into heroin in Marseilles factories, all controlled by the Mafia.

British, French and Dutch Imperialists actively encouraged opium addiction throughout South East Asia but local governments forbade growing the drug. This changed during World War II when France could no longer access Turkish and Iranian opium and had to start producing it on the land in Asia they had colonized, using primarily ethnic Chinese farmers living in present day Vietnam, Thailand and Laos – the golden triangle of opium was born. From there production moved to Columbia and then to Afghanistan where 90% of the opium used to produce heroin is now grown.

James Kent, author of *Psychedelic Information Theory,* observed recently that American heroin epidemics immediately follow military involvement in heroin producing regions. In Vietnam in the late sixties, Afghanistan in the early nineties and then in again in the early aughts Americans got involved militarily in those countries and then sent cheap and pure heroin home, he alleged.

Making a commodity illegal allows the greatest return on investment possible. *The Economist* estimates a gram of cocaine in Columbia to cost about two dollars, in Vancouver a gram costs $80, in far-flung New Zealand a gram costs $714. The multiplier from Columbia to Vancouver is forty times or 4,000%. A gram of heroin in Kabul, Afghanistan sells for about five dollars and earns $100 – $300 in Vancouver – a price increase of up to 6,000%. The profit margins for the illegal drug cartels are exponentially higher than the next most profitable business – legal drugs (pharmaceuticals).

All of that *cash,* about $320 billion a year, has to be laundered through banks and corporations in order to be used. How big a role drug money plays in the economy and how much drug money exists is really only a matter of speculation because governments estimate intercepting about a third of the illegal drugs, so however much they recover, they triple it and that's the end of it.

American tobacco continues to expand because of governments subsidizing tobacco farmers and companies dumping excess supply in the third world with the familiar "first one's free" approach. The use of advertising by tobacco and alcohol distributors is yet another example of the hypocrisy, mendacity and delusion of drug policy.

"The Partnership for a Drug-Free America is an organization funded by people who sell drugs," California Judge Mike Gray observes, "alcohol, tobacco and pharmaceutical companies are its major financers." But the drug war gravy train has many more cars attached to its engine – drug testers, bureaucrats, police, prosecutors, prison guards, treatment centers and the military hardware business all join with merchants of legal drugs that compete with illicit ones in a brutal war that has lasted a century. Taking it one step further is the organization Keep Arizona Drug Free – does that mean you can't get an aspirin in the entire state?

The philosophy that the addiction is in the drug rather than in the person has resulted in one hundred years of terror. The notion that some drugs are addictive and some are not is a misleading one – even *water* is sometimes associated with addiction. The hunt for the demon molecules has proved a humanitarian calamity. Combining the real costs of enforcement with the opportunity cost of lost tax revenue, each year the United States loses $77 billion! But that's everybody's money – the "illegal" drug seller's and "legal" money launderer's money is at least

$320 billion but for a very select few. Financing covert military operations without paper trails, providing governments with an excuse to arrest dissidents, the ritualized persecution of scapegoats, racism and of course keeping the drug war gravy train rolling are five important reasons why some drugs became and remain illegal. But the most important one is providing low-interest investment capital in the form of perfectly liquid cash into an artificially expanding economy.

> *"No one tells the truth before 5 pm."*
> Hunter S. Thompson

Our economy can be said to have three levels, there is the direct basic capital itself, the investments (stocks and bonds) behind that basic capital and then something called derivatives. It was in the 1600s that Europeans started forming corporations and selling shares to raise the enormous capital required to finance their expeditions into the new world. But it was only in the Richard Gecko "greed is good" 1980s that the third economic level arose and derivatives became common.

"A derivative is a financial instrument that is derived from some other asset, index, event, value or condition (known as the underlying asset). Rather than trade or exchange in the underlying asset itself, derivative traders enter into an agreement to exchange cash or assets over time based on the underlying asset. The practical meaning in financial terms is a promise to pay." – Wikipedia

Some of these elaborate bets are so complex that even companies performing the transactions don't really understand what's being sold.

To some extent the initiation of opium laws in the early twentieth century started an endless tap of money along with a new brand of hardcore addict whose habit instantly became exponentially more expensive, often to be liquidated (disposable income then possessions then body then death) and the proceeds used to finance the economy. It may be that the investment class hasn't found a way to replace this fountain of progress. Of course 99% of the people in favour of the war against some drugs are doing it because they think it's the right thing to do, not because it keeps the weird new economy afloat.

This is the sordid milieu psychedelic drugs must operate in, making them as psychedelic chemist Sasha Shulgin observed, "The dolphin caught in the tuna net of the drug war."

Chapter Twenty-One

Risks, Contemporary Psychedelic Research and Practical Applications

"The revolution is in the ditch until we get our chemistry right."
– Terrence McKenna

C hemist Sasha Shulgin and his Wife Anne have written two books
on psychedelic chemistry – *Tihkal: Tryptamines I have known and
loved* and *Pihkal: Phenethylamines I have known and loved*, doc-
umenting his research inventing new drugs, Timothy Leary called him
one of the most important scientists of the 20th century. He considered
himself an inventor of tools to study and improve the mind; most of the
drugs he invented are psychedelic.

There are both clinical and non-clinical applications for psychedelic/
holotropic therapy to apply Dr. Shulgin's research. Psychedelics show
promise with rites of passage, creative problem solving, spiritual experience and death and dying, which are all outside the general field of psychiatry and include psychology, theology, philosophy and gerontology.
The primary psychiatric indications are trauma, fixated or reactive depression, addiction and the entire range of dissociative, psychosomatic,
sexual and personality disorders. The three primary contraindications for
psychedelic therapy are serious heart or liver problems, severe epilepsy
and paranoid psychosis.

Hollywood Hospital also included many subjects with heart disease
and histories of psychosis – people applying electrical shocks and grams
of chemicals to the brain are not terribly risk averse. The worst reaction
I studied involved a subject who had a terrible session and when she was
presented with the mirror she was horrified by what she saw and for several hours after could see an image of her own face, even with eyes opened.
Some subjects will have activated and not resolved negative material but
refuse to take the drug again for obvious reasons. This is why non-drug
techniques like SRT, primal scream, holotropic breathwork and Kundali-

ni Yoga are so important and should always be considered before bringing in the hallucinogenic heavy artillery.

The three serious negative outcomes to psychedelic use most common outside of a clinical setting, but not exclusively, are prolonged reactions, flashbacks and Hallucinogen Persisting Perceptual Disorder (HPPD). The most extreme form of prolonged reaction is the manifestation of a mental illness, most often schizophrenia. Stimulants, cannabis, spousal infidelity, marathon encounter groups, meditation retreats and Yoga intensives are all also guilty of triggering psychotic illness so a specific chemical link is unlikely, rather the stress of the experience causes the psychological and possibly biological decompensation.

"Flashbacks" or "re-emergent phenomena" can involve any element of a trip being re-experienced and some have suggested this is due to chemical residues being metabolized later but according to some researches only 0.1% of the drug enters the brain and it only remains there for twenty minutes, making this explanation unlikely.

A better explanation for flashbacks is unresolved/integrated material re-emerging during states of low ego defenses – falling asleep/ waking up, using alcohol and other drugs or under extreme stress. Flashbacks are never mentioned once in any of the files but Frank had a couple himself and there are many reports in the literature of re-emergent phenomena.

Another negative effect of psychedelic drug use beyond flashbacks and prolonged reactions (over 48 hours) is what has been labeled Hallucinogen Persisting Perceptual Disorder (HPPD), a rare reaction to psychedelics, particularly LSD, occurring in between 1-5% of users, with 0.1% of cases severe enough to require medical attention. However, nothing like this appears in *any* of the early research, and some people suffer the same symptoms without ever having ingested any drug and most symptoms are minor and disappear within a few months.

The explanation of poorly integrated material seems reasonable for re-emergent phenomena and prolonged reactions but Hallucinogen Persisting Perceptual Disorder (HPPD) is sometimes explained in purely physiological terms. Some scientists believe visual perception is organized according to several layers – horizontal lines processed by one layer, vertical another, colour another etc. The speculation is that LSD and to a lesser extent other psychedelics increases or decreases the signal intensity of one or more of these layers and can cause visual distortions indefinitely. Dr. Leo Zeff treated an estimated 3,000 people and doesn't mention it –

and in surveys of therapists who used psychedelics clinically with 40,000 subjects treated nothing resembling HPPD is even mentioned.

Thoroughly integrating the experiences but mostly delivering pure substances will certainly reduce the risk, for as Terrence McKenna wryly observed, "The revolution is in the ditch until we get our chemistry right."

One practical application for psychedelics is in *rites of passage.* In Huxley's *The Island,* when children turn 14 or 15 they are given a challenging physical and mental test, and upon succeeding take a psychedelic drug called moksha as part of achieving a new identity as an adult. Possibly psychedelics could act as preventive medicine if people integrate negative dynamics and release them from their unconscious during these ceremonies before illness manifests.

Pioneering psychedelic psychologist Dr. James Fadiman did some research with psychedelics and creativity where, "each of the subjects had some kind of, he felt, major creative breakthrough." The focus here is less on personal development and unconscious dynamics but instead on problem solving – however people who have worked through their negative unconscious dynamics and are consistently governed by the positive are generally going to be better thinkers.

Death and dying is another interesting domain where psychedelics are currently being applied constructively. As he lay near death stricken with terminal cancer Aldous Huxley requested that he be injected with LSD just as his characters had taken moksha during their passing in his final novel *The Island.* In this utopian opposite to *Brave New World* written thirty years later Huxley describes a paradise where the intelligent use of moksha (from the Sanskrit word for liberation) medicine creates a heaven on earth of fully conscious citizens.

Haoma, Soma, Kykeon and peyote have all played slightly less ambitious roles in history. Huxley asked his wife to read from Leary's then not yet published *The Psychedelic Experience: Based on the Tibetan Book of the Dead* as he tripped off into the afterlife.

One of the first researchers to explore this avenue was Dr. Eric Kast. In 1964 he published a study comparing standard opioid painkillers dyhydromorphinone (Dilaudid) and meperidine (Demerol) compared to LSD in 50 patients suffering severe physical pain usually from cancer. Not only did the soon-to-be-notorious psychedelic beat the other drugs for pain relief, Kast noticed, "These individuals showed a striking disregard for the gravity of their personal situations. They frequently talked about their impending death with an emotional attitude that would be considered atypical in our culture."

243

Later Kast experimented on 128 sufferers of metastatic cancer, this time broadening his focus to include more than pain but sleep, emotion and attitude towards death. No psychotherapy was used – the patients weren't told about the experiment – Kast simply injected the LSD. "A precipitous drop in pain occurred in many individuals about two to three hours after 100 mcg LSD was given and lasted for an average of twelve hours." But even three weeks later their pain and attitude remained greatly improved.

In another 1966 study with 80 subjects, if the person became agitated or upset Dr. Kast gave them the anti-psychotic Thorazine. This study looked specifically at "religious or philosophical experiences and ideas of the patients," and produced more encouraging results.

Between 1967 and 1974 another hundred dying patients were given LSD or other psychedelics while a control group was given a placebo and later offered the real drug if they wished at Maryland Psychiatric Research Center. While in Grof's seventeen-bed locked ward in Prague he treated the psychotic and/or suicidal these subjects were excluded from this study. One exception was a woman with a very traumatic childhood that would normally exclude her from this type of experiment, but because she had enjoyed a quick and uncomplicated birth she was given the golden ticket.

All subjects were prepared with several weeks of interviews and developed an intimate connection with the team. As always music was carefully used to optimize the psychedelic reaction – as Grof remembers in his recent book on death and dying, *The Final Voyage,* music was even more critical with these subjects. "At the beginning we played flowing and comforting music that gradually became more intense. Later in the session we shifted to powerful, dynamic and evocative instrumental and orchestral music. Between the third and fourth hour of LSD sessions – a period that in many sessions brought an important turning point – we introduced what we called 'breakthrough' music.

These were powerful pieces, usually with strong spiritual emphasis, in which a full orchestra was combined with human voices."

After the session the subject was reunited with family for a "reunion" where communication often reached new levels of intimacy. *General Archives of Psychiatry* published a very successful similar psilocybin study with death anxiety in January of 2011.

A recent MSNBC news report claimed one in five Americans suffer from a mental illness – that's sixty million souls, and if prevalence around the world is less than that at one in seven, that still yields over one billion globally. And this psycho- spiritual-emotional vacuum is filled with psychiatric medicines, booze and other drugs, gambling, sex, shopping and every entertainment imaginable.

Psychedelics work best where imprinting and learning are etiologically instrumental in the development of the disease, whether by the direct trauma of a COEX system or the activation of a perinatal or transpersonal matrix through some stressor internal or external. It seems some disorders are more purely genetic (hardware) while towards the less severe end of the spectrum imprinting (operating system) is implicated and at the least severe end learning (software) plays a more pivotal role. Cognitive – Behavioural Therapy, where a client's beliefs, values and attitudes are analyzed and improved has proven effective with minor depression. This might be seen as a more superficial software upgrade while psychedelics involve the installation of a new operating system and medication and Electro Convulsive Therapy are aimed at the brain's hardware.

Epigenetics is the new field investigating the fact that while the genetic code is basically fixed the *expression* of that code depends on a wide variety of factors. One study revealed that victims of sexual and physical abuse showed changes in their DNA. In other words, experience can alter the expression of the genes and possibly even the genes themselves.

Schizophrenia, bipolar disorder, major melancholic depression, obsessive- compulsive disorder and autism, at their most extreme are likely fundamentally biological hardware problems and psychedelics aren't able to reverse the disease. Stan Grof believed obsessive-compulsive disorder a particularly outstanding failure for psychedelic therapy – some patients in this category required milligrams of LSD to show any effect at all and significant therapeutic progress was still rare. (1 mg = 1000 mcg, ten times the average dose)

However, a recent University of Arizona study concluded psilocybin reduced or eliminated the symptoms of obsessive-compulsive disorder much better than placebo. This use would be *hydraulic*, chronic use of the drug versus the *holotropic* use of the drug for a non-ordinary state that allows *reimprinting*.

The position of the dividing line between illnesses that operate completely independently of the stressors that caused them or "functionally autonomous" of any stress at all, on the severe side and illnesses that can be reversed completely simply with the abreaction or re-living of one causative trauma, as in PTSD, on the other, is a scientific question requiring a quantity of research impossible during an inquisition. Surgically implanting electrodes, "shock" therapy and lifelong daily drug use are all considered sound medical practice but doing one to ten holotropic drug sessions is considered too dangerous. Why?

Part of the resistance to psychedelics may stems from the perinatal unconscious provoking highly defensive reactions among scientists. From conception on the brain's electrical wiring is slowly coated with fat (myelin), a process called myelinization, which is not complete until the third year of life, therefore, according to conventional wisdom, no memories can be recorded until then. But take acid. Even in Grof himself, eventually the perinatal unconscious manifested in all it's terrible glory! But if the defenses remain adequate to prevent the release of this kind of elemental affect it is only a vague memory of a dream that repression, denial and projection can dispense with easily. But, like trying to direct molten lava, controlling the unconscious always proves a dangerous illusion in the end.

In medicine the initial treatment is known as "first line," for all minor conditions, even with most physical disorders nutrition, exercise and counseling should be where doctors start. But it isn't – when they say first line, they mean first drug. With this hydraulic approach you often take it every day indefinitely. A more rational approach in my opinion would be nutrition, exercise and counseling as the first line and psychedelic therapy as the second line. Hydraulic drugs would be among the last and most invasive interventions, followed by electrical convulsive therapy and surgical brain implants.

In addition to sexual disorders, reactive (life-events caused) but not major depression, anxiety disorders, PTSD and the full range of psychosomatic illnesses and even some pain disorders fall under the spell of these agents. Grof observed that all negative dynamics have physical pains associated with them. During the termination phase of one session a subject felt depressed and complained of a sore shoulder. He asked Stan to help him so the doctor pushed on his shoulder as hard as he could. "He started shaking and twitching and releasing and then the session integrated well." Another way of expressing the underlying concept popular in Yoga circles is, "tissues have issues."

In *Healing Back Pain* Dr. John Sarnos makes the case that a lot of pain is what he calls *tension myositis syndrome (tms)*, he proposes that the brain deprives nerves of oxygen in order to distract from experiences perceived as being too painful to endure. At first he offered psychotherapy and physiotherapy but later cancelled the latter as a distraction from the real emotional issues that were the heart and root of the problem. Czech neurosurgeons used to use LSD to determine the nature of back pain, discerning through the drug whether pain originated in the brain or elsewhere. Psychedelian author Robert Anton Wilson used to quote Nietzsche regarding human reality perception who said, "We are better artists than we realize."

Another field amenable to psychedelic therapy is the treatment of dysfunctional social behaviour. How we behave is determined by our personality – composed primarily of defenses against negative affect and in about 13% of Americans at some point in their lives, this personality will be diagnosable as disordered.

Problems with sense of self and relation with others characterize these types of people.

Critics of psychiatry point out that this class of diagnosis is particularly suspect because it is based on traits we all share – the difference is quantitative or dimensional. In any case all of these categories and systems exist entirely as maps, while the territory underneath them is *always* completely different – but you have to start somewhere. The frequent role of trauma in causing personality disorders is established; however, as with all disorders, *traumatic* stress is not always necessary; if the genetic vulnerability is strong enough any level of stress might be sufficient.

There are three clusters of personality disorders – the first related to thought, the second to self and the third to fear. One of the distinguishing features of the first two clusters of personality disorders is that sufferers often find it inconceivable that anything could possibly be wrong with them. Generally the people in their lives suffer as much or more than they do.

The thought group consists of paranoid, schizotypal, which relates to a lack of emotional attachments, and schizoid, which involves primarily disordered thought itself. As with schizophrenia the value of psychedelics in treating these disorders is questionable because there seems a permanent dilation of the sixth circuit and a consequent incontinent self – incapable of screening the logos to allow space- time-ego continuity. Certainly the affective dynamics can be improved but the risks are substantial and the process is longer and more complex.

In the case of the third cluster involving fear or anxiety like obsessive-compulsive, dependent (on others) and avoidant (socially anxious) personality disorders psychedelics may prove more useful, but it is with the second cluster involving *self* where psychedelics offer a complete breakthrough. In the case of borderline personality disorder 90% report childhood abuse or neglect but two other disorders in this cluster, narcissistic and histrionic (overly flirtatious), will likely respond favorably to psychedelic therapy as well.

Perhaps the third (fear) cluster involves the first bio-survival circuit, the second cluster the second mammalian (self-other) circuit and the third (thought) cluster the third symbolic intellectual circuit. Currently medication and psychotherapy have performed much worse with personality disorders compared to other forms of mental illness. The ability to see ourselves as others see us is a particularly useful aspect of psychedelic experience with these subjects.

Also in the second cluster is possibly the most *expensive* personality disorder in human and material costs – antisocial personality disorder (ASPD) especially when psychopathy is added to the mix. One way to distinguish them in my opinion is antisocial people are indifferent to the suffering of others, like a thief, while the psychopath enjoys seeing others suffer, like a serial killer, and it is these most cruel and passionate criminals that commit the vast majority of crime in our society. Prohibition naturally selects the most ruthless and effective among these social mercenaries and makes them millionaires and billionaires.

One characteristic of all of these is a lack of empathy. In addition to the likely causative traumas and perinatal material evoked and resolved, psychedelics tend to confer a strong sense of empathy with everyone, especially those close to you. Maybe Charles Dickens' *A Christmas Carol* is a metaphor for psychedelic shamanism.

When Leary wanted to definitively prove the value of psychedelic drugs he chose prison recidivism as his quanta – a fully objective measure being returning to prison versus staying out. He misrepresented the results, proving again that he was an excellent theoretician but poor researcher. But the value of a psychedelic experience where a prisoner sees his crimes from a cosmic perspective, given the context of this book, seems obvious. In 2014 a study showed that prisoners who used "hallucinogens" had lower recidivism than users of other drugs.

The mental disorders that tend to afflict boys more commonly may be associated with physical abuse while girls tend towards illnesses with sexual abuse as their cause. Psychiatric illness among boys is actually much higher because of the frequency of attention, conduct, autism and tic disorders. Conversely, girls are more prone to depression, anxiety, dissociative and eating disorders and by adolescence take over as the gender with more mental illness.

Conduct disorders in children can evolve into an antisocial personality and even psychopathic behavior. In prison, 50-80% have antisocial personality disorder (ASPD) and 15-30% are psychopaths, the general population has about 1% of people with ASPD and much fewer psychopaths. In other words there are fifty to eighty times and fifteen to thirty times more ASPD sufferers and psychopaths in prison that out. Obviously a highly specialized form of psychedelic therapy is called for when dealing with these particularly dangerous subjects. Psychedelic therapist Bill Richards once quipped, "If we can put a man on the moon we can treat psychopathy."

In the mid-sixties it became standard to deny almost all grant requests and licensing for any psychedelic research, but by the nineties the generation of government medical bureaucrats responsible had passed the torch. Since then momentum has slowly been building towards another psychedelic renaissance and at the center is Dr. Rick Doblin the president of MAPS, the Multidisciplinary Association for Psychedelic Studies.

Doblin has been committed to psychedelics since the early seventies when he longed to travel to Vancouver and Hollywood Hospital – unfortunately the $500 fee was too expensive. A Vietnam draft-dodger pardoned by President Jimmy Carter he emerged from the psychedelic underground and formed MAPS in 1986. Through this new advocacy group he tried to stop the emergency scheduling of MDMA by the Drug Enforcement Agency and would eventually receive a PhD in Public Policy from Harvard – his dissertation was on research with psychedelics and marijuana.

Dr. Peter Gasser, a Swiss physician, is working with LSD and anxiety associated with dying – the Swiss seem more comfortable with the controversial drug, having invented it. The failure to fully investigate ibogaine while its successful use continues in many clinics around the world is baffling but psilocybin, an active component in magic mushrooms, is being researched for addiction therapy at Johns Hopkins.

MAPS lists twelve different substances, each followed by a list of studies underway, under development or completed, with over three hundred studies catalogued. Most of the research is in the United States but Israel, Jordan, Switzerland, Spain and Vancouver all have studies approved or underway with MDMA and PTSD. In the completed pilot study by Charles Mithoefer the MDMA population improved at a rate three times (300%) the placebo. The two first-line treatments for PTSD are Paxil for men and Zoloft for women and these drugs only marginally beat placebo (< 50%).

By the mid-sixties over a half dozen teams were doing full time psychedelic therapy around the world and had they continued I believe they would have structured their work in the following way – "triple axis psychedelic therapy."

If ibogaine fills the abnormal receptors of addicts allowing the brain's resetting and ketamine changes the electrical activity in the brain to take the mind/ego off- line they represent a similar model and sufficiently strong medicine for highly abnormal behaviour patterns like addiction, child-abuse, criminal sociopaths and psychopaths. Ketamine is safer and so one to three sessions will initially be ideal and if unsuccessful the heavy artillery of ibogaine for one to three sessions is deployed. If even six psychedelic therapy sessions cannot move the addict this type of therapy can be deemed unsuccessful.

However if the addiction has improved the next phase of one to three MDMA sessions continues the process or starts it for trauma, death anxiety, some depressions, personality disorders, psychosomatic conditions, paraphilias, creative problem solving and spiritual experiences, then the third and final axis delivers the full spectrum of psychedelic experience and healing through psilocybin, LSD, mescaline and similar compounds.

The whole process involves up to fifteen sessions over as many as 18 months each with a male and female therapeutic dyad.

Phase	Phase One	Phase Two	Phase Three
Diagnosis	Addiction, Anti-Social Personality Disorder with or without psychopathy, coercive paraphilia.	Death anxiety, PTSD, certain forms of depression and personality disorder, psychosomatic conditions and paraphilias, creative problem solving, spiritual experiences and those who successfully complete phase one.	Those who have completed at least phase two.
Treatment	One to three ketamine sessions and if not successful followed by one to three ibogaine sessions with a male and female therapy team.	One to three MDMA sessions with a male and female therapy treatment team.	One to six sessions with psilocybin, LSD, mescaline or combination with a male and female therapy team.

Operation Resilient Dawn

On January 1, 1966 John Lilly estimated there were 210 independent investigative teams working with LSD in the United States alone; by the end of that year only six had survived. What would those thousands of scientists and clinicians have accomplished in the fifty years since had the field not been crushed almost to total oblivion?

Operation Resilient Dawn seeks to open 150 dedicated psychedelic clinics worldwide with at least two-thirds at hospitals or universities by 2030 with a budget of $30 million, applying the methods of psychedelic therapy described above as a possible starting point.

Chapter Twenty-Two

The Future

"Okay what's the future going to bring? It depends on smart people, mostly eight year olds, that are thinking in a different way than most people are here." Dr. Tomorrow – Frank Ogden

Emerging from the furor of the cultural revolution of '66-'73 was a radical movement known as *anti-psychiatry*. One of its champions was psychiatrist R.D. Laing who believed psychosis was an attempt at self-healing. He believed if it could be encouraged, explored and supported the psychosis would resolve and the person would be better for it. Most often, anti-psychiatry claimed, the problem stemmed from some form of abuse and then later denial and mystification surrounding it. This happens on an individual scale and a global scale by the perpetrators of war and environmental destruction.

> "We all repeatedly die partial deaths in order that the others, for whom we are the sacrificial offerings, may live. The archetypal Christ, in so far as he has any reality at all, is in each of us."
>
> – David Cooper, *Anti-Psychiatry*

The cost to society of developmental trauma is incalculable, and all efforts to reduce the incidence and damage will figure prominently in future psychology. As we become more familiar with transformation we will find new ways to integrate it into community. An excellent example from a lost future was the living experiment Number Nine, as described by Dennis and Yvonne Jaffe in their paper "Sarah's Odyssey – Acid and the Youth Culture."

The authors were running an alternative community (Number Nine) in New Haven, Connecticut where members were expected to work, pay rent and do chores but beyond that were free to create their own culture.

Sara was a Hispanic fifteen year-old runaway who, after encountering the meat hook, bone-crushing realities of life on the streets of New Haven

Connecticut, moved into Number Nine. A few years previously she had a serious bout of depression that prompted her to jump out of a second story window and visit a psychiatrist. A few weeks after moving in she took acid.

"She began to cry, moan and act afraid; her friends responded by taking her to trip intervention...Sara's acting out of strong feelings with her whole body was instantly recognized as tripping rather than craziness.

"At this stage Yvonne facilitated Sara's working through this conflict by creating a group fantasy with her, embracing her and finally asking all present to take off their clothes so as to increase Sara's regression. That maneuver led her into a second stage, a *death-and-rebirth experience.*

"It is easy to build rapport with someone who is tripping, even when people have not met before, because the tripper relates to people as fantasy versions of people important to him, particularly his parents...Once contact is made, the guide can tune in to the conflict the tripper is experiencing. There are only a small number of themes which make up the human condition, with infinite variations.

"In the supportive environment of Number Nine, Sara's conflicts were soon resolved in favor of the expression of the positive feelings, as her own words show. 'I remember Billy, he was my Father and Yvonne, she was my Mother and they were welcoming me, from all the hardships I had gone through.

"When I was born it was like paradise, it was so beautiful! It's like I came through this light, but they expected it and I expected it. I could hear an ambulance, and it was like they were bringing me. It was my Mother, and I'm coming out to her, and I did. Everybody was there to see it, and everybody's eyes were tearful, with the joy. It was like utopia. I felt feelings that were indescribable. There was happiness and joy, and I was crying. I was born with everything, all this knowledge."

The future will see expanded spiritual and medical psychedelic use, which will evolve into new kinds of societies where our concepts of the family, the tribe and the corporation may merge into a new creative political force. Critics will no doubt point out the demise of Number Nine and many similar sixties experiments – but some comparable projects like Stephen Gaskin's The Farm survive to this day.

Several groups have been doing psychedelic therapy in California since the 50s. The group setting is much less expensive and the sense of community-shared ecstasy facilitates is profound. With the introduction and U.S. Supreme Court approval of DMT churches into North America many such organizations will be available in the future.

When asked if enlightenment could be achieved through drugs, the Dali Lama answered, "I hope so." Joking of course, but the fusion of psychedelics with traditional spirituality seems an inevitable evolution for a future sexier, healthier and more fun.

Often called the Bard of Psychedelia Terrence McKenna often used to end his talks, lectures or workshops with an ancient Irish toast – "May you be alive at the end of the world" – followed by:

"Take it easy, keep the old faith and stay high."

Well there you have it –

That's what I see in the shamanic graffiti.

What to do you see?

Futurist Frank Ogden/Dr. Tomorrow

Alvin Toffler coined the phrase "electronic cottage" in the 80's. Futurist Frank Ogden carried the concept further. From his high-tech houseboat in Vancouver harbour, he was wired to the world by computer, phone, cable and phone modems, satellite, infrared transmissions and CD-ROMs. The *Financial Post* described Frank as a "20th Century visionary" and calls his ideas "outrageous," an ideal combination of qualities for a life of profitable nonconformity. From Papua New Guinea to the high-tech jungles of silicon, satellites and photons, Frank had a reputation for innovation and originality.

In 1979, he began monitoring 200 satellites and 2,000 data banks, to provide a video clipping service for forward thinkers wanting information on new and relevant business developments. Ogden circled the globe as consultant to companies and countries, preparing people to trek along the fast track. "A bulldozer of change is charging over the planet," he says. "And if you're not part of the bulldozer, you'll become part of the road."

Born in 1920, Ogden was educated in Canada and the United States and served as a flight engineer during World War II. Unflaggingly energetic and curious, he graduated to a dizzying array of jobs flying airplanes and helicopters and selling aircraft (He was checked out as Pilot-In-Command in 55 different flying machines), real estate and house wares.

During the 1960s, he joined a medical team researching LSD at Hollywood Hospital, and he crossed Canada by helicopter to celebrate the country's centennial. He also helped found Canada's first think-tank, taught at the Ontario College of Art and the New England School of Art in Boston, and managed a Montreal radio station, leading it boldly into progressive rock. He was also a founding member of the World Future Society in Canada.

While studying voodoo in Haiti and establishing a think-tank for the Prime Minister of the Bahamas, Ogden recognized the link that exists between primitive thinking and high tech. "Everything in life is information. So-called primitive cultures have known this for thousands of years," he explains. "Voodoo Priests get their information through a hierarchy of

Gods; we get ours through a hierarchy of technology." Concepts like these made Frank a celebrity speaker on the conference circuit, where he outlined the electronic and information revolutions of the current and coming decades. Frank suggested a future of teleports, limited labour unions, as more people become self- employed, and body implants to make cyborgs of us all. Audiences praised him because "he shakes people up and gets us thinking about the future!"

In1989, Frank was elected a Fellow of the Explorers Club; an elite group of adventurers including mountaineer Sir Edmund Hillary and astronaut John Glenn. Frank traveled continuously -- to present seminars and to research the latest in technological, educational, business, communications, political, social and environmental developments. He was at home on the untamed equatorial plains of East Africa and in the high-tech toy stores of Tokyo. From his Vancouver houseboat, Frank conducted the first two international seminars via satellite and fiber-optic technology, for Australia's Telstra Communications Network in Sydney and Melbourne. His CD-ROM, Dr. Tomorrow's Cyberspace University, received top ratings in the United States. Long before the World Wide Web became popular, Ogden opened a "page" there for global access, containing over 5,000 pages – www.drtomorrow.com was among the first 200 in the world.

Frank has been profiled on numerous television and radio stations and in newspapers and magazines around the globe, including, CNN's *Futurewatch*; PBS Television's *New Tech Times in the U.S.A.*; CBC's National TV show *Profiles*, with host Peter Gzowski; the Christian Science Monitor TV show *World Monitor*; Australia's TV 7 show *Eleven AM*; and CTV's *Canada AM*. As well, interview articles have appeared in Forbes ASAP, Leaders; Cryptych; *Maclean's*; Easy Living; Influence; *LA Times*; *Ottawa Citizen*; *Globe & Mail*; *Washington Post*; *U.S. News & World Report*; *Toronto Sun*; *WINGSPAN* (Nippon Airways in Flight); *Nairobi Nation* (Kenya, East Africa); *Financial Post*; *Travel Writer*; *Electronic Entertainment*; *Vancouver Sun* and *BC Discovery*. Dr. Tomorrow is a registered trademark in Canada and is also a registered trademark in the United States of America, Brazil and Argentina.

Ogden broadcasted a live one-hour weekly video-streaming future show each Saturday morning at Internet Beat 708 (PST 8 a.m. 20th Century time) directly from his floating Cyberden via the Internet narrowcast network: www.mediaontap.com. He also produced seven other Web-TV shows under the Cyberspace University Tomorrow Channels., appearing via the mediaontap Network.

Frank passed 2012 at age 91 from prostate cancer. The last time I saw him he was about fifty pounds and holding a promotional copy of *Shamanic Graffiti* – working until the last breath and the next adventure.

Marcus Rummery

Marcus has been an artist all of his life. Born to a journalist and scientist and raised in a community adjacent to a nuclear research facility in rural Manitoba called Pinawa – a community so extraordinary that some have suggested it was an early prototype for a future space colony – Marcus' upbringing was one of dynamic creativity and radioactive inspiration.

A member of numerous bands and comedy troops throughout high school, Marcus began performing stand-up comedy in 1996 in Ottawa. Less than a year later he came in third in Canada's Funniest New Comic contest and has been working ever since. He has performed all across Canada and L.A., headlining in Montreal, Vancouver, Ottawa, toured the country twice and been featured on CBC Radio's *Definitely Not the Opera* and more recently on XM radio where his material still circulates. In 2001 Marcus joined the comedy syndicate *Ménage et Trois* with Jon Steinberg and Ben Miner, but the pull of the west coast dissolved the promising enterprise when Marcus moved to East Vancouver with his eclectic tribal rock-band *Evoke*. Even Rummery's songs like the notorious *I Smoke Prozac* couldn't save the six-member ensemble and sadly the band folded shortly after moving west – the next band, *All Possible Humans*, yielded to *In Defense of Tim Leary*.

In 2002 Marcus became certified to teach Bikram's Method Hot Yoga – sometimes referred to as the punk rock or drill instructor Yoga led by notorious Yoga villain Bikram Choudhury, the heat is cranked to 40.6 degrees Celsius and the humidity to 40%. For almost eleven years, ten times a week you could here is sardonic ranting all around Lotus Land until 2014 when he premiered *Hot Prana* a new series that he calls the Crossfit of Yoga. He is also certified in yin Yoga and a subtype of the ancient Chinese subtle-energy exercise system qi gong.

In 1998 Marcus started his first screenplay with a biographical film about Timothy Leary that he finished in 2005. He is also working on a nine-chapter science fiction series that begins in 2012, with the subsequent chapters occurring every fifty years, based on the myths of Camelot, called *Arthur 2412* – four chapters have been written so far. In 2006 he traveled to the Banff television Festival promoting a Yoga sitcom called *Namaste* that featured a unique three-layered narrative – with a reality show, another sitcom written and produced on the show, and then the show itself.

After completing his BA in Psychology in 2005 in 2007 Marcus completed the Langara College digital documentary program and in 2008 finished Big Medicine – the techno-shamanism of Frank Ogden. In February 1995 (Mushroom Armageddon) Marcus began the research that would lead to his interest in Frank's work when he started investigating psychoactive drugs.

He is currently working on his second book, *Shamanic Enneagram: Change your life with the number nine,* the second in his three part *Shamanic Future* series before *Shamanic Revolution,* where he will travel the globe sampling the shamanic cultures of the world.

Index

A

Aetiogoly of Hysteria, The 39, 125
Alexander, Bruce 227
Alpert, Richard 54, 60, 63, 65-68, 86, 160, 230
Amanita Muscaria mushrooms 13-14, 19, 21, 29, 59, 222
Amphetamine 211
Anderson, Carl 38, 231
Anderson, Paul Thomas xiv
Annual Review of Psychology 60
Armstrong, Louis 32
Ava Maria 165
Avesta 24
ayahuasca 19, 21, 31, 149, 220, 232

B

Baba, Neem Karoli 60
Baba Ram Das 68
Barlow, John Perry 76, 219
Barron, Frank 63
Basic Perinatal Matrices (BPM) xiv, 50-54, 56, 128, 135, 152, 184, 192
Battle for the Mind 33, 35-36, 38
Beatles 70
Beringer, Kurt 31
Big Medicine ix, 258
Bini, Lucio 166
Bolero 127-128, 130, 138, 171
Book of the Dead 22, 54, 119
Brotherhood of Eternal Love 71
Brown, J.E. 92
Bucke, Richard 81, 84
Bulletin of the Multidisciplinary Association for Psychedelic Studies 231
Burroughs, William S. 45, 66, 201
Bwiti: an Ethnography of the Religious Imagination in Africa 231
Byron, George Gordon (Lord) 30

C

Calder, Jake 81
Cameron, Ewan 36
cannabis 17, 21, 23, 30-31, 71, 211-214, 224-225, 233-236, 242
Carter, Jimmy 249
Celetti, Ugo 166
Central Intelligence Agency (CIA) 32, 35-36, 55, 67, 76, 90-92, 106
Ceremonial Chemistry: The ritual persecution of drugs, addicts, and pushers 227
Chaos and Cyberculture 206
Chomsky, Noam 217
Chopin, Frederick 97
Chwelos, Nick 86
Cicero 25
Cleaver, Eldridge 72
Clotte, Jean 6
Cohen, Sydney 113, 163, 228
Coleridge, Samuel Taylor 28, 30
Come Together 68
Cosmic Consciousness 81, 84
Crick, Francis 4, 219, 221
Cromie, Dom 93

D

Dali Lama 253
Davy, Humphrey 28
de Gamma, Vasco 101
Der Meskalin-Rausch (The Mescaline Inebriation) 31
Design for Dying 78
Dianetics 9, 44-46
Dianetics: The Science of Mental Health 45
DMT xi, xvi, 7, 18-19, 29, 68, 85, 218-221, 224, 253
DNA xvi, 4, 9, 11, 40, 199, 206, 212, 218-221, 223-224, 245
Doblin, Rick 249
Doors of Perception 86, 119
Douglas, Tommy 81-82
Dr. Tomorrow iii, vii, 252, 255-256

E

Economist, The 238
Electric Convulsive Therapy (ECT) 36,

47, 120, 121, 123, 166
Eliade, Mircea viii, 7, 15
Ellis, Dock 76
Emerson, Ralph Waldo 67
Existential Transaction, The 61, 62

F

Fadiman, Jim 83, 243
Feldmar, Andrew 211
Fernandez, James W. 231
Final Voyage, The 244
Financial Post 255, 256
Fisher, Gary 52, 65, 126
Flashbacks 62, 69, 70, 73
Frederking, W. 93
Freud, Sigmund xiii, xiv, 36, 39-41, 43, 49, 52, 125, 167, 176, 204, 208, 236

G

Garvey, Marcus 214
Gasser, Peter 249
Gates, Bill 5
General Archives of Psychiatry 244
Ginsberg, Allen 73-74, 87, 160
Glass Bead Game, The 69
Grant, Cary 65, 93, 136
Graves, Robert 27
Gray, Mike 238
Greenfield, Robert 69, 73
Griffiths, Roland 8, 64, 107, 112
Grinker, Roy 37
Grob, Charles 31
Grof, Stanislav xii-xv, xvii, xix, 9, 11, 44, 47-50, 52-59, 65, 72, 76-77, 83, 108, 133, 184, 192, 199, 202, 211, 216, 219, 221, 244-246

H

Halpern, John 228, 229, 230
Hancock, Graham 97, 219, 220
Handbook for the Therapeutic Use of Lysergic Acid Diethylamide-25 86
Haoma 21, 23-25, 27, 233, 243
Happy Days 88
Harcourt-Smith, Joanna 72, 73

Harvard Psilocybin Project (HPP) 62, 63
Healing Back Pain 246
Heaven and Hell 86, 111
Heffter, Arthur 29
Heilkunst homeopathy 44, 46
Heilkunst Homeopathy 44
Henighan, Tom 13
Herman, Judith 31, 39-40, 69, 70
Hesse, Herman 31, 69, 70
Hoffer, Abram 82-83, 85-86, 89, 92, 107, 123
Hoffman, Abbie 71
Hofmann, Albert vii, x, 47-48, 76, 216
Hofmann's Potion 76
Holloway, John 103
Hollywood Hospital ix, xiv, xvi-xvii, xix, 3, 43- 44, 48, 55, 59, 71, 79, 86-87, 92-93, 95, 107, 109, 112-113, 117, 120, 130, 136, 149, 152, 159, 188, 225, 229, 241, 249, 255
Hollywood Sanitarium ix, 44, 92, 95
House 223
Houston, Jean 202
Hubbard, Al vii, 5, 45, 53, 85-86, 89-95, 107, 113, 117, 121, 134, 229
Hubbard, L. Ron 9, 45
Huxley, Aldous 38, 62, 70, 84, 86-87, 91, 119, 205, 215, 219, 243

I

ibogaine 17-19, 21, 29, 38, 109, 112, 214, 225, 228-229, 231-232, 249-250
International Foundation for Internal Freedom (IFIF) 66, 67
Interpersonal Diagnosis of Personality, The 60
Invisible Landscape, The 11
Island, The 243

J

Jaffe, Dennis and Yvonne 252
James, William 28, 64
Janet, Pierre 39, 40
Janiger, Oscar 118
Jaynes, Julian 8
Jobs, Steve 5

Jost, F. 47
Journal of Psychopharmacology xiii, 89
Jung, Carl 39, 45, 53, 176

K

Kampia, Rob 213
Kast, Eric 243, 244
Katz, Sydney 85
Kennedy, John F. 65, 67, 71
Kennedy, Bobby 71
Kent, James 238
King, Martin Luther 71
Kleps, Art 60
Kramer, Peter vi, 120-121, 203, 206-207, 209-210
Krebs, Teri S. 89
Kruptisky, Eugene 231
Kubla Khan 28
Kungurtsev, Igor 222
Kykeon 21, 25-27, 243

L

Laing, R. D. 158-159, 211, 252
Lao Tse 215
Lashley, Karl 9
Laurie, Hugh 223
Leary (book) 69
Leary, Timothy vii, xii, xv-xvi, xix, 3-5, 8, 11, 28, 31, 54, 59-78, 86-87, 91, 93, 108-109, 199-202, 204-206, 211-213, 215-223, 230, 232, 234, 241, 243, 248, 257
Lennon, John 68, 69
Lenson, David 225
Lenson on Drugs 225
Levine, Peter xii, 14, 41
Lewis-Williams, David 6
Liddy, G. Gordon 69
Lilly, John 212, 221, 251
Listening to Prozac x, 120, 203, 207, 209
Lord Buckley 32
L.S.D. 117, 163, 182-183
LSD ii, vii, ix-x, xiii, xv, 5-6, 18, 29, 36, 38, 41, 43-44, 47-49, 51-52, 54-55, 57-58, 60, 64-67, 70, 72, 74, 76-77, 81-83, 85-89, 91-94, 96, 101, 106-107, 109, 113, 117, 120-121, 124, 126-127, 129-131, 133-137, 141, 144, 148, 150, 153, 160-161, 164, 166-170, 173-174, 176-181, 184, 186, 188-189, 193, 200-201, 206-208, 215-217, 219-220, 222, 228-230, 232, 242-245, 247, 249-251, 255
LSD, Man and Society 64

M

MacDonald, Linda 99, 106
MacLean, Ross xix, 92, 93, 94, 95, 96, 103, 106, 107, 113, 117, 123, 132, 135, 136, 137, 139, 140, 154, 158, 163, 166, 173, 192
Maclean's 85, 256
Magnolia xiv
Mahler 1st Symphony 150, 160, 165, 171
Manson, Charles 72, 73
Marley, Bob 214
Martin, Dean 137
Maslow, Abraham 60, 84
Masters, Robert 202
McKenna, Dennis 11
McKenna, Terrence xvi-xvii, 3-5, 7-8, 11, 13, 21, 38, 205, 232, 241, 243, 254
McLuhan, Marshall 70, 217
MDMA xiii, 29, 36, 52, 88, 112, 117, 205, 207, 211, 222, 224, 232, 249, 250
Meduna's Mixture 121
mescaline ix, 6, 15, 18, 29-32, 70, 85-86, 91-93, 96, 117, 124, 127, 129-131, 133-134, 136-137, 141, 144, 150, 153-154, 158, 160, 164, 167-170, 173, 176, 179, 181, 184, 186, 188-189, 193, 215, 222, 232, 250
Metcalfe, Ben 93
methamphetamine 36, 133, 136, 204, 211
methylphenidate (Ritalin) 88, 112, 133
Metzner, Ralph 54, 65, 68
Meyer, Mary Pinchot 65
Millgram, Stanley 76
MK-ULTRA 91
Monroe, Marilyn 65
Mullis, Kerry 219

Multidisciplinary Association for Psyche-
    delic Studies (MAPS) 231, 249

N

Napoleon 30, 237
National Institute on Drug Abuse xii
Native American Church 15, 17, 230, 232
Natural Mind, The 204
Near My God to Thee 142
Neurologic 75, 212

O

Ogden, Frank i, iii, vi-vii, ix, xix, 94-95,
    106, 135, 148, 154, 157, 252, 255,
    256, 258
Olson, Frank 92
Omni (magazine) x
*Origin of Consciousness in the Breakdown of
    the Bicameral Mind, The* 8
Orwell, George xii
Osmond, Humphrey 76, 82-86, 92, 123
Ott, Jonathan 14, 15

P

Pahnke, Walter 63, 64, 107, 112
Partnership for a Drug-Free America, The
    232, 238
Pavlov, Ivan 33, 34, 40, 41
PCP 222
Peele, Stanton 226
Penfield, Wilder 9, 45
peyote 15-19, 21, 29-31, 176, 214, 230,
    243
*Pihkal: Phenethylamines I have known and
    loved* 241
Playboy 72, 76
Post-Traumatic Stress Disorder (PTSD)
    xiii, 33, 36, 88, 52, 112, 231, 245-
    246, 249, 250
Potoroka, William 81
Prometheus Rising 201
prozac vi, x, 9, 43- 44, 120-121, 167, 202-
    203, 205-211, 223-224, 257
psilocybin x, xvii, 3-9, 11, 18, 21, 29-30,
    61-64, 66, 70, 91, 112, 199, 215,

222, 232, 244-245, 249, 250
*Psychedelic Experience: A Manual Based on
    The Tibetan Book of the Dead, The*
    54, 68, 223, 243
Psychedelic Information Theory 238
Psychedelic Prayers 70, 215, 223

Q

Queen Victoria 213, 236

R

Reagan, Ronald 71
Reich, Wilhelm 76-77
Religion, Values and Peak Experiences 85
Richards, Bill 220, 249
Rig Veda 21-23, 27
RNA 11
Ruck, Carl 29
Russell, William Huntington 235
Russo, Ethan 213

S

Sandison, Ron 91
Sandoz Pharmaceuticals 47, 60, 85
Sargant, William 33, 35-38
Sarnos, John 246
Scientology 44-45
Seattle Post Intelligencer 90
Secret Chief Revealed, The 117
Self-Regulation Therapy (SRT) xii, 14,
    44-46, 51, 241
Sellasie, Haile 214
Sergeant Pepper's Lonely Hearts Club Band
    70
Serra, Raimundo Irineu 18
Shakespeare, William 30
*Shamans of Prehistory: Trance and Magic in
    the Painted Caves, The* 6
Sheldrake, Rupert 6, 7
Shelley, Percy 30
Shulgin, Sasha 117, 229, 240, 241
Sinatra, Frank 137
SMILE – Space Migration Intelligence In-
    crease Life Extension. 77
Smith, Colin 85, 86

Smythies, John 82
Soma 21-25, 27, 84, 233, 243
Spiegel, John Paul 37
Sports Illustrated 76
Stalin, Joseph 14
Steppenwolf 31-32, 70
Stolaroff, Myron 117
Strassman, Rick xi, 93, 218
Supernatural 219-220
Szasz, Thomas 227

T

Taft, William Howard 236
Taylor, Thomas 26
Thompson, Hunter S. 71, 239
Thurman, Robert 68
Thurman, Uma 68
Tibetan Book of The Dead, The 223
Tihkal: Tryptamines I have known and loved 241
Toffler, Alvin 255
Tolle, Eckhart 203, 217
Trauma and Recovery 39
Tricycle xi
True Hallucinations 3
Truman, Harry 90

U

Ultimate Journey: Consciousness and the Mystery of Death, The 221
Use of Hallucinogens in the Treatment of Addiction. Addiction Research, The 228
Use of LSD in Psychotherapy and Alcoholism, The 120

V

Vancouver Magazine 93
Vancouver Sun 93, 256
Varieties of Psychedelic Experience 202
Vicari, R. 47
von Schlebrugge, Nena 68

W

Waking The Tiger 14

Watts, Alan vi, xii, 123
Weil, Andrew 204
Wilson, Bill 65, 76, 81, 91, 201, 229, 247
Wilson, Robert Anton 65, 76, 201, 247
Woodruffe, Rosemary 69, 72, 74, 77

Y

Young, Francis 213

Z

Zeff, Leo xiii, 117, 118, 242
Zipf, George Kingsley 219
Zoroaster 24